The Young Earth

The Real History of the Earth – Past, Present, and Future

John Morris

Original Edition
First printing: June 1994
Fourteenth printing: July 2006

Revised and Expanded
First printing: November 2007
Second printing: May 2008

For information write Master Books, P.O. Box 726, Green Forest, AR 72638.

ISBN-13: 978-0-89051-498-6
ISBN-10: 0-89051-498-4
Library of Congress Catalog Number: 2007925406

Cover and interior design by Bryan Miller
Unless otherwise noted, all Scripture is from the King James Version of the Bible.

Printed in the United States of America

Please visit our website for other great titles: www.masterbooks.net

Also visit www.creationeducationstation.com
The above is a homeschool division of Master Books

For information regarding author interviews, please contact the publicity department at (870) 438-5288.

Contents

Foreword....4

Introduction....6

1. What Do the Rocks Say? 10
2. What Does the Bible Say? 26
3. The Two Views Contrasted 34
4. Dating Methods 42
5. Radioisotope Dating....48
6. Human History and the Young Earth 72
7. Worldwide Physical Processes 78
8. Geologic Evidence for a Young Earth....96
9. What Do the Rocks Mean? 120

Index 141

Foreword

Foreword to the First Edition

I believe this book is destined to meet a great need "for such a time as this" (Esther 4:14). The issue of origins is crucial to our understanding of the future, and there has been a significant revival of belief in creation as men and women have realized this fact in recent decades. The frightening glimpses of imminent world catastrophe and crises of all kinds should drive every person to a serious confrontation with the meaning of his or her life and destiny.

After all, there are only two basic world views: the God-centered world view or the man-centered world view, creation or evolution. If there is really a great personal Creator God behind the origin and meaning of all things, then we urgently need to know Him and to order our lives according to His will, as revealed in His inspired Word. If human beings, on the other hand, are simply the end-products of a long process of evolution from the primordial nothingness (as taught today in most secular schools and information media), then "let us eat and drink; for tomorrow we die" (1 Cor. 15:32).

The decision obviously is one of urgent importance. Our personal lives (and possibly the present world itself) are ephemeral. The worldwide revival of true creationism in recent decades has occurred as more and more people have awakened to the urgency of this decision.

As one who has been directly involved with the creation movement for over 50 years, I can testify to this remarkable growth of intelligent belief in divine creation. There are now many thousands of scientists who have become creationists, and this includes scientists in every field and every nation. Polls show that half of the people in the United States now believe in special creation.

Even though most scientists and other intellectuals still continue to believe in evolution, the facts of science oppose evolutionism, and most people see this, once these facts are shown to them. There is no evidence whatsoever — past, present, or possible — that *vertical* evolution of one kind of organism into a more complex kind or organism has ever occurred, or ever can occur.

All the changes ever really observed in nature (e.g., different varieties of dogs and cats, different tribes of people) are *horizontal* changes, within fixed limits. Many kinds of creatures have deteriorated and become extinct in human history, but none has ever evolved into a higher kind. Similarly, in the fossil record of the past, there are many examples of deterioration and extinction, but no real transitional fossils from lower kinds to higher, more complex kinds. As far as *possible* evolutionary changes are concerned, the two basic laws of change in nature have been expressed scientifically as the law of conservation of *quantity* and the law of decay of *quality* — that is, the first and second laws of thermodynamics, which seem to indicate that "vertically upward" evolution is impossible.

While such scientific data do not seem to impress the doctrinaire evolutionists who control our scientific and educational establishments, they have convinced great numbers of people — scientists and laymen — that creation is a much better scientific "model" of origins and history than evolution.

As a result, in recent years, organizations studying and promoting scientific biblical creationism have been established in at least 25 countries around the world. In this country alone, there are probably 100 national, regional, or local creationist organizations. Perhaps the most influential of these (at least judging from the outcries of the evolutionists) is the Institute for Creation Research and its Graduate School of Science. Dr. John Morris, the author of this book, serves as ICR's president, and has established a solid reputation as speaker and writer in the field of geology, a vitally important field of biblical and scientific creationism.

In addition to the scientific case for creation (which is essentially the same as the scientific case against evolution), there is an overwhelming biblical case for creation, as well as a moral and social case against evolution, as documented in the many publications of the Institute for Creation Research.

However, there still remains one serious problem, and that is the question of the age of the earth. Evolutionists, realizing that evolution requires immense periods of time to be even marginally feasible, have repeatedly fallen back on the supposed multi-billion-year history of the world as their main defense. Using their assumption of "continuity" or uniformitarianism ("the present is the key to the past"), it is relatively easy for them to find numerous natural processes whose present-day rates of action might suggest long ages of operation to produce the present structure of the world.

The fallacy in this approach, however, at least to a Bible-believing Christian, is that it rejects the divine revelation from the Creator of the world that He did it all in six days several thousand years ago (Gen. 1:1–2:3; Exod. 20:8–11). Further, God defined the word "day" (Hebrew *yom*) the very first time the word was used, as the "light" period in the cyclical succession of light and darkness (Gen. 1:3–5) that has continued regularly ever since that first day.

Some, however, consider the Old Testament as conveying only theological concepts instead of historical facts. But the Lord Jesus Christ, who is actually the Creator of all things (John 1: 1–3; Col. 1:16) and who therefore knows how it was, completely rejected the long-age notion of the ancient evolutionary philosophers (Stoics and Epicureans). He reminded us that "from the beginning of the creation [not several billion years after the beginning] God made them [i.e., Adam and Eve, citing Genesis 1:27] male and female" (Mark 10:6; NKJV).

But what about the supposedly scientific indicators of great age for the earth and the universe? Must we choose between science and Scripture? No, of course not! The same God who created the world has given us His Word, and He does not contradict himself. If there seems to be a problem, either the world or His Word must have been misunderstood. At this point, most scientists and even many Christian leaders opt for the uniformitarian-age estimates of the evolutionists, and either reject the biblical testimony altogether or else "wrest . . . the scriptures" (2 Pet. 3:16) to try to make them accommodate the billions of years demanded by evolutionism.

Since John Morris is my son, I am both pleased and thankful that he has chosen a "more excellent way" in this book, knowing that God has magnified above all His Word and His Name (Ps. 138:2). John himself is both a scientist and a Christian leader. With a Ph.D. in geological engineering and many years of personal Bible study, he is eminently qualified to write this book. He believes, as I do, that God is able to speak plainly, especially on such vital issues as origins, meanings, and destinies. Therefore, the infallible biblical record of the recent, literal creation of all things and then the subsequent cataclysmic destruction of the world in the great Flood must be taken as established fact, with all the real data of science (as distinct from the uniformitarian interpretations of these data by fallible scientists) reinterpreted within a creationist context.

The home of ICR's scientific laboratories in the San Diego, California area.

That this is the God-honoring (rather than man-honoring) approach is confirmed in the climactic words of the apostle Peter shortly before he died. "In the last days," he wrote, "scoffers" will be saying that "all things continue as they were from the beginning of creation" (2 Pet. 3:3–4;NKJV). This is an explicit prophecy of the latter-day prominence of the doctrine of continuity, or uniformity, which undergirds evolutionism. But then Peter says that they "willingly forget" two great facts of history. First, there is the special creation of all things "by the word of God," not by continuing natural processes. Second, "The world that then was, being overflowed with water, perished" (2 Pet. 3:5–6; ASV).

Thus, the key to resolving the modern conflict between the Bible and evolutionary uniformitarianism, prophetically revealed two thousand years ago by the Holy Spirit through the apostle Peter, is to recognize and apply to the study of earth's processes and systems the two great facts of God's primeval, complete creation and the subsequent global deluge.

When this is done, as Dr. Morris has shown in this book with scientific insight, biblical conviction, and clarity of explanation, these processes and systems provide compellingly strong support for the biblical revelation of the recent creation and worldwide flood. There are no proven scientific evidences that the earth is old, but there are scores of circumstantial evidences that the earth is young. The only way we can know for certain the age of the earth is for God (who was there) to tell us. And this He has done! We should believe what He says.

— Henry M. Morris
President Emeritus, Institute for Creation Research
Passed into glory as this second edition was being completed

The Institute for Creation Research stresses the creation foundation for the Christian world view. Headquarters are in Dallas, Texas.

Introduction

This is, without a doubt, a fascinating time to be a Bible-believing Christian. On the one hand, the forces of evil are running rampant, with the earth seemingly on a collision course with its ultimate destiny. But on the other hand, there has never been a time when more support for the biblical world view was available. You might not have heard it in the media, but discovery after discovery confirms the truth of God's Word and the benefits of living according to God's guidelines.

Today we can watch as the concept of evolution self-destructs. It has never been well supported by the evidence, and now many scientists are coming forward to point out its weaknesses. Many have recognized the total inability of chance and random processes to produce the incredible complexity we see around us, especially in living systems. Students of earth history have abandoned the creed of former decades, that "the present is the key to the past," and are proposing instead secular theories of past events that sound almost biblical in their proportions. The problem for Christians is gaining access to this revealing information, for many educators, politicians, and media outlets have joined forces to continue promoting the evolutionary, humanistic, naturalistic world view.

The American educational system has particularly done a great disservice to many Americans. Not only is its social agenda a disaster, but its academic training has also failed. The achievements of American students are lagging behind those of other developed countries. Many important facts and ideas are censored out of the classroom, and students are seldom taught how to *think* about the material they are allowed to see. Instead, they are taught certain facts and theories (expected to remember them and repeat them on a test), but skills in gathering and interpreting data are neglected.

Day 1

This is especially true when dealing with ideas about the past. The idea of evolution has come to be so firmly entrenched in our educational system that most people assume it is true. Scientific facts are placed within this interpretive scheme. End of discussion! Remember and repeat. Never mind the fact that no one has ever seen evolution take place, neither have the fossils documented evolutionary trends in the past, scientific law refutes the whole idea of evolution, and evolution is contrary to logic. Many people intuitively suspect evolution is not true, but still "believe" it anyway, because it is all they've been taught. "All educated people believe in evolution," they're told. "Only ignorant, bigoted Christian fundamentalists still deny it."

If people were taught to think, taught to recognize the difference between scientific facts, which can be observed in the present, and taught ideas about the past which can be used to interpret the facts, then the issue would clear up, for the intellectually honest, anyway. SAT scores would climb once again as *science* classes spent more time on *science* and less on ideas about evolutionary history.

Day 2

Even many Christians are ensnared in the trap of not thinking critically. In the Bible they read that God created all things in six days. They have come to know the Lord and love and trust His Word, but they have heard that all educated people know that evolution has been proven. And so, they find themselves in a dilemma: creation or evolution, the Bible or science? Since science is true, and since it disagrees with the Bible, then Scripture must be untrue, they think.

Several options present themselves. A frequent response is to believe in creation at the appropriate times, but to believe evolution at other times, and try not to think about the inconsistency.

Or maybe the two are somehow compatible. Maybe God used evolution to create. Maybe the days of Genesis were long periods of time. Maybe evolution occurred in a "gap," then that original world was destroyed, and God re-created in six days. Maybe, maybe . . . "Well I'm just not going to think about it. I'll stay in the New Testament."

But those doubts! Where do the dinosaurs fit in with Scripture? Where did Cain get his wife? Where did the races

Day 3

come from? What about the Ice Age? How did all those animals fit in Noah's ark? Where did all the water come from to cover the mountains? And where did it go? Reasoning from an evolutionary mindset, there are no good answers to these questions. And so, many think, maybe Scripture has errors. Maybe it can't be trusted. Maybe even the New Testament can't be trusted.

The result: a weak church, with weak, doubting Christians. Young people from Christian homes and good churches go off to college and come back doubting and defeated or worse. Pastors don't teach the whole Scripture. Denominations go liberal. Seminaries teach a smorgasbord of ideas — choose whichever compromise you like; we can't know the truth.

The Institute for Creation Research (ICR) exists to address these issues. Its purpose is to study the evidence and give better interpretations, consistent with Scripture, and to discover new scientific truth where it can. But perhaps most of all, ICR's desire is to teach people how to think about the past, and how to interpret scientific and historical data from a scriptural perspective and to get it right! We have seen how evolution has been used as an excuse to doubt the gospel, and this roadblock needs to be removed.

In recent years, we have noticed an incredible resurgence of interest in creation thinking. Individual Christians and families have become desperate for good teaching on the subject of origins and science. Evolutionism and humanism have become so pervasive and so distasteful that more and more Christians no longer feel comfortable with the compromised message they've been taught.

Day 4

ICR's most popular seminar series is called "Back-to-Genesis," and that is the theme of much that we do here at ICR. We're all scientists, but we're also Christians. We love science, but we also love the Lord, our Savior Jesus Christ, and His Word. We encourage Christians to go "back to Genesis," to see the *true* history recorded there and then interpret the scientific data relating to the unobserved past in submission to Scripture.

We do not spend the majority of the time in our seminars presenting new and different data. Instead, we take the same data used by our evolutionary colleagues (i.e., dinosaur fossils, racial differences, geologic deposits, etc.) and show how the data can be better interpreted from a biblical perspective. We have found that the Ph.D. scientist needs exactly the same teaching as the high school youngster. All of us need encouragement to think correctly — to think in terms of biblical fundamentals!

Day 5

The scientist already knows the data and will immediately see how it should be reinterpreted. The layperson will recount evolution lectures and TV specials and recognize the error. Committed Christians rejoice to get their questions answered and doubts removed, to get the monkey of evolution off their backs. God's Word is true! It can be trusted, even in these difficult areas of science and history.

This book represents an outgrowth of my Back to Genesis lecture, "The Age of the Earth." At the end of each lecture, folks always rush up and ask where my material is in print. Numerous ICR books deal with this vital question (among others), but there seemed to be a need for a book that focused on both the data supporting a young earth and the way data are interpreted.

Presenting the age of the earth lecture always frustrates me. As a geology professor, I want to say so much, use so many examples. But in a 45-minute lecture, I just can't do it. Here in this book, much more information and much more support has been included, although much more could still be added.

This book does not pretend to be a complete technical treatment on the age of the earth. It hopefully provides a good lay understanding of the general subject, in such a way as to be of use to both lay and technical readers. It does, however, cover numerous important subjects, even technical subjects treated in a non-technical manner. My desire is that all readers will not only learn new information, presented in a non-threatening format, but a new and helpful way to think about the information as well.

This is not to say that the material is presented in a less-than-correct manner. We serve the God of truth, and *must* be both truthful and careful in all our study.

You will note that some of the references I've cited will be other creationist books where more complete

Day 6

discussions of pertinent points are made, and where original sources are given. I would very much like to see each reader introduced to the wealth of good creationist books and articles, including my own. On other occasions, I have included references to particular technical sources, to aid in deeper understanding. On still other occasions, I will merely report on my own field work and observations, and thus *no* references may be given, if not published elsewhere.

Another question many people often ask after a lecture is where they can get copies of my illustrations. And so, I have endeavored to make the book "user-friendly," to provide the photos and sketches in a format that can be directly used in teaching. Additionally, I would encourage each teacher and creation speaker to acquire his own photos and examples from personal observation and investigation whenever possible, supplementing the material herein. The evidence for creation, the Flood, and the young earth, once rightly interpreted, is everywhere. Hopefully, this book will inspire many to take new notice of the evidence all around us. And hopefully this book will inspire many students to take up geology as a vocation and also inspire Christian geologists to join the work and solve some of the remaining problems for the young-earth concept. I do not claim, by any stretch of the imagination, that we have all the answers. What I do claim is to have access to the Book giving the framework for solving the problems. Let us proclaim what we do know, propose a model based on the biblical framework, continue to solve the remaining problems, and correct any flaws in our understanding as we go.

Before we start into the discussion, it probably would be helpful to give some definitions, so questions in the reader's mind can be avoided. You will notice that even these definitions and graphics are user-friendly, designed less for completeness than for ease of teaching.

Biblical Creationism: Supernatural creation of all things in six literal days by the God of the Bible.

Scientific Creationism: Each basic category of life appeared abruptly, without descending from an ancestor of a different sort. Much variation within a category is expected, but each possesses genetic limits to its variability, and thus exhibits stasis.

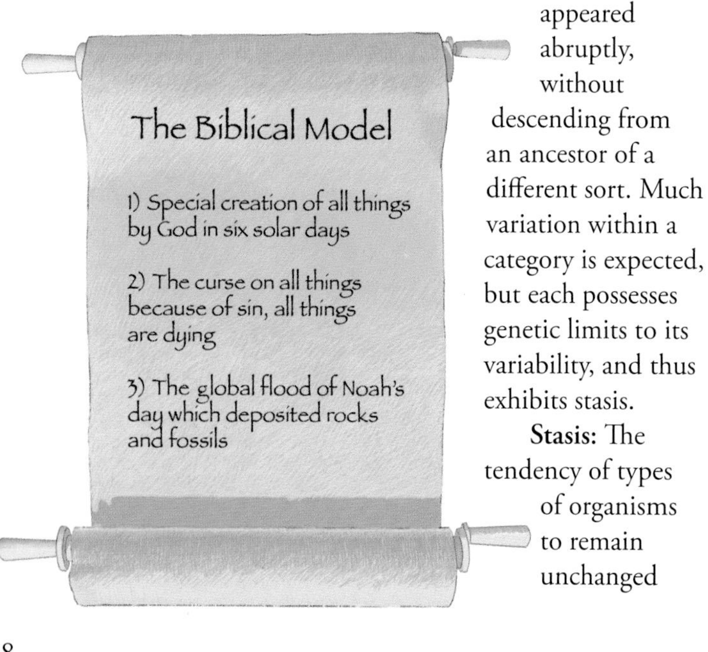

Stasis: The tendency of types of organisms to remain unchanged over time; static or stationary with respect to evolutionary progress.

Catastrophism: There have been episodes in the past that occurred at rates, scales, and intensities far greater than those possible today, or which were of an entirely different nature than those of today. This certainly includes special creation and the great flood of Noah's day, which would have restructured the entire planet and been the source of the rock and fossil records.

The Creation Model

1) Supernatural origins of all things with design, purpose, and interdependence of parts

2) Net basic decrease in complexity over time and limited horizontal change

3) Earth history dominated by catastophic events

Evolution: The idea that all of life has come from a common ancestor through a process of modification over time. Thus, man and the apes are thought to have descended from an ape-like common ancestor. All vertebrates came from fish, which in turn came from an invertebrate. All life descended from a single-celled organism that arose spontaneously from non-living chemicals. Changes occurred through natural processes, including mutation, natural selection, and genetic recombination.

Micro-evolution: Small adaptations within a population of organisms which allow a certain trait to be expressed to a greater or lesser degree than before; variation within a given category. This is regularly observed to occur within living populations.

Macro-evolution: Large hypothetical changes which are thought to occur in an individual or in a population of organisms that produce an entirely new category or novel trait. These changes have never been observed to occur within living populations.

Mutations: Changes in the genetic material of an organism, potentially expressed in offspring. Many times a single mutation affects more than one trait. While some are neutral, many are lethal. No beneficial mutations that add information to the genome have been observed.

Natural Selection: The process observed within populations of organisms that select those traits best suited for a given environment. This conservative process tends to maintain the status quo and never produces new genetic material.

Punctuated Equilibrium: Macro-evolution on a rapid pace in brief periods during otherwise long ages of no change. Invoked to explain and allow for evolution in the absence of fossil transitional forms.

Uniformitarianism: "The present is the key to the past." Episodes of dramatically different rates or character than processes possible today have never occurred. Present processes are extrapolated into the past under the assumption that things have remained "uniform."

Geologic Column: The column of fossils, with ancient ones on the bottom and more recent ones on the top, within the observed local sequences of the rock layers which have been systematized by correlation on a global scale. Does not exist in complete form in any one location, but as a trend on a global scale. Index fossils are thought to be unique to individual eras, periods, and systems. The time interpretation superimposed on the rock layer sequences is called the geological time scale and is linked to evolutionary dogma.

Index Fossils: While almost every stratum of rock contains many of the same basic fossil types (i.e., clams, coral, etc.), certain individual organisms or variations are thought to have existed in only a brief period of supposed geologic time, and thus can be used to determine the layer's age.

Neo-catastrophism: Natural catastrophes occurred in the past, which, while perhaps of great intensity and scale, were no different in character from processes possible today. These catastrophes were episodic, separated by long periods of uniformity. Popular theory among geologic thinkers today.

Theistic Evolution: Essentially the same as atheistic evolution in its relation to scientific data. God may have either started the evolution process, and then left it to natural processes, or may have guided the evolution process.

Progressive Creation: Sometimes called the day-age theory. The days of Genesis were long periods of time, roughly equivalent to the supposed geologic ages. Each basic category of life was created by supernatural intervention at various times throughout the ages.

Framework Hypothesis: The idea that the Bible, when it speaks of things historic or scientific, is to be understood in a theological sense only, assuming that God was involved but not as actually recorded. Genesis is not to be taken as factual history. This view is very popular in many modern evangelical seminaries, and allows theologians to fully accept evolution and/or long ages.

Local Flood Theory: The teaching that the flood of Noah's day covered only the Mesopotamian Valley — a major flood, but not global. This view (or its counterpart, the tranquil flood theory, which says that the Flood was global but had no discernible effect, i.e., no erosion, no rocks, no fossils) is a necessary part of any compromise with evolution or old-earth ideas, since the world's rock and fossil record is usually misinterpreted as evidence for evolution and an old earth.

Evolutionism: The application of evolutionary ideas in the public arena. Includes concepts such as social Darwinism, man is an animal, animal rights equivalent to human rights, low view of human life, etc.

New Age Thinking: The modern equivalent of ancient pantheism, melding evolution science with Eastern mysticism, espousing a one-world government, a combination of all religions, and evolutionism in society.

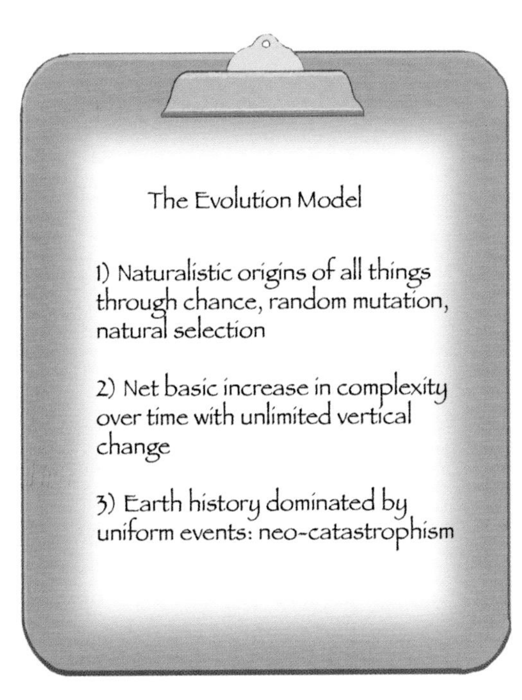

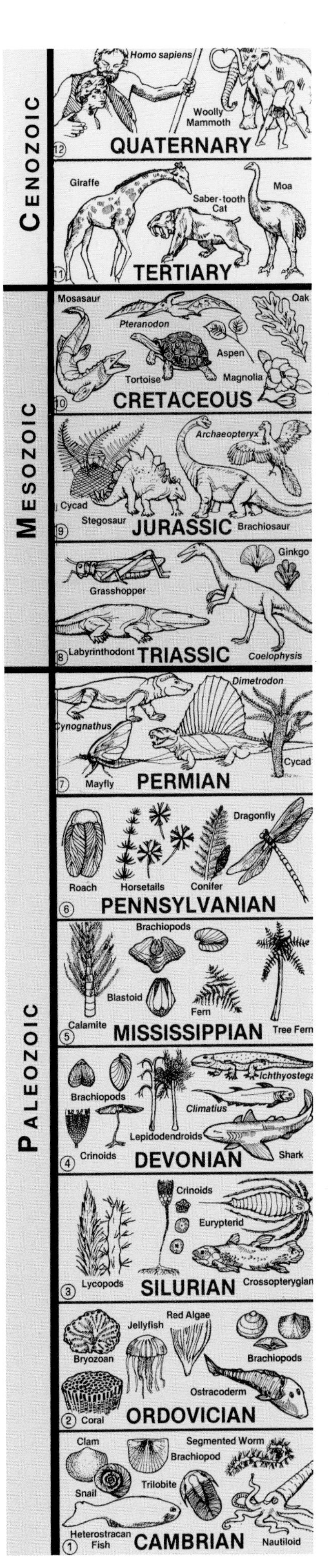

Chapter One

WHAT DO THE ROCKS SAY?

How many times have you opened a newspaper and read an article describing the discovery of a new fossil, archaeological find, or underground fault? After describing the nature of the discovery, the article explains how scientists are so thrilled with its confirmation of evolutionary theory. An age is reported, perhaps millions or even billions of years. No questions are raised concerning the accuracy of the date, and readers are led to feel they have no reason to question it either.

Did you ever wonder how scientists got that date? How do they know with certainty something that happened so long ago? It is almost as if rocks and fossils talk, or come with labels on them explaining how old they are and how they were fossilized.

As an earth scientist, one who studies rocks and fossils, I will let you in on a little secret. My geologic colleagues may not like me to admit this, but rocks don't talk! Nor do they come with explanatory labels.

I have lots of rocks in my own personal collection, and there are many more in the ICR museum. These rocks are well cared for and much appreciated. I never did have a "pet rock," but I do have some favorites. I have spent many hours collecting, cataloging, and cleaning them. Some I have even polished and displayed.

But what would happen if I asked my favorite rock, "Rock, how old are you?" "Fossil, how did you get that way?" You know what would happen? Nothing! Rocks do not talk! They do not talk to me, and I strongly suspect they do not talk to my evolutionary colleagues either! So where then do the dates and histories come from?

The answer may surprise you with its simplicity, but the concept forms the key thrust of this book, which I have designed to explain how rocks and fossils are studied and how conclusions are drawn as to their histories. But more than that, I have tried to explain not only how this endeavor usually proceeds, but also how it *should* proceed.

Inclined rock strata

Before I continue, let me clearly state that evolutionists are, in most cases, good scientists, and men and women of integrity. Their theories are often precise and elegant, and we can learn much from their endeavors. It is not my intention to ridicule or confuse. It is my desire to expose the mind trap they have built for themselves and show a better way. Let me do this through a hypothetical dating effort, purely fictional but fairly typical in concept.

How It Is Usually Done

Suppose you find a limestone rock containing a beautifully preserved fossil. You want to know the age of the rock, so you take it to the geology department at the nearby university and ask the professor. Fortunately, the professor takes an interest in your specimen and promises to spare no effort in its dating.

Much to your surprise, the professor does not perform carbon-14 dating on the fossil. He explains that carbon dating can only be used on organic materials, once-living things that consist mostly of carbon, not on rocks or even on the fossils, since they, too, are rock. Furthermore, in theory, carbon dating is only useful for the last few thousand years, and he suspects your fossil is millions of years old. Nor does this expert measure the concentrations of radioactive isotopes to calculate the age of the rock. "Sedimentary rock, the kind which contains fossils," he explains, "ordinarily cannot be accurately dated by radioisotope methods. Such methods are only applicable to igneous rocks, like lava flows and granite." Instead, he studies only the *fossil's* shape and characteristics, not the rock. "By dating the fossil, the rock which contains it can be dated," he declares.

For purposes of this discussion, let us say your fossil is a clam. Many species of clams live today, of course, and this one looks only a little different from those you have seen. The professor informs you that many different clams have lived in the past. These were the ancestors of modern clams, but most have now become extinct.

Next, the professor removes a large book from his shelf entitled *Invertebrate Paleontology* and opens to the chapter on clams. Sketches of many clams are shown. At first glance many seem similar, but when you look closely, they are all slightly different. Your clam is compared to each one, until finally a clam nearly identical to yours appears. The caption under the sketch identifies your clam as an *index fossil*, and explains that this type of clam evolved some 320 million years ago. With a look of satisfaction and an air of certainty, the professor explains, "Your rock is approximately 320 million years old!"

Notice that the rock itself was not examined. The fossils in it dated it, and the fossil type was dated by the assumption of evolutionary progression over time. The limestone itself might be essentially identical to limestones of any age, so the rock cannot be used to date the rock. The fossils date the rock, and evolution dates the fossils. Evolutionists determined the order of evolution and estimated the ages involved even before the discovery of radioisotope decay and long before the formulation of radioisotope dating methods, but these were used to calibrate the fossil succession. The many problems with these methods are discussed in chapter 5, but today they give fossil dating an air of credibility.

You get to thinking. You know that limestones frequently contain fossils, but some seem to be a fine-grained matrix with no visible fossils. In many other limestones, the fossils that appear seem to be ground to pieces, and other sedimentary rocks, like sandstone and shale, might contain no visible fossils at all. "What do you do then?" you ask. "How can you date those rocks?"

The professor responds with a brief lecture on stratigraphy, information on how geologic layers are found one on top of the other, with the "older" ones (i.e., containing the oldest fossils) beneath the "younger" ones. This makes sense, for obviously the bottom layer had to be deposited before the upper layers. "But how are the *dates* obtained?" you ask. "By the fossils they contain!" he says.

It turns out that many sedimentary rocks cannot be dated all by themselves. If they have no fossils which can be dated within the evolutionary framework, then "We must look for other fossil-bearing layers, above and below, which can help us find the range of possible ages within which the true age must lie," the professor says. Such layers may not even be in the same location, but by tracing the layer laterally, perhaps for great distances, some evidence can be found.

"Fortunately, your rock had a good fossil in it, an *index* fossil, defined as an organism which lived at only one time in evolutionary history. It is not that it looks substantially more or less advanced than other clams, but it has a distinctive feature somewhat different from other clams. When we see *that* kind of clam, we know that the rock in which it is found is about 320 million years old, since *that* kind of clam lived 320 million years ago," he says. "Most fossils are *not* index fossils. Many organisms, including many kinds of clams, snails, insects, even single-celled organisms, did not change at all over hundreds of millions of years, and are found in many different layers. Since they did not live at any one particular time, we can't use *them* to date the rocks. Only *index* fossils are useful, since they are only found in one zone of rock, indicating they lived during a relatively brief period of geologic history. We know that because we only find them in one time period. Whenever we find them, we date the rock as of that age."

Let us pause in our story to identify this thinking process as circular reasoning. It obviously should have no place in science. In circular reasoning, instead of proceeding from observation to conclusion, the conclusion interprets the observation, which "proves" the conclusion. The fossils should contain the main evidence for evolution. But instead, we see that the age of rocks is determined by the stage of evolution of the index fossils found therein, which are themselves dated and organized by the age of the rocks. Thus, the rocks date the fossils, and the fossils date the rocks. The unquestioned assumption of evolution provides the context for the entire process.

Back to our story. On another occasion, you find an interesting piece of hardened lava, the kind extruded during a volcanic eruption as red hot, liquid lava. Obviously, it contains no fossils, since almost any remains would have been incinerated or severely altered. You want to know the age of this rock, too. But your professor friend in the geology department directs you to the geophysics department. "They can date this rock," you are told.

Your rock fascinates the geophysics professor. He explains that this is the kind of rock that can be dated by using *radioisotope-dating techniques,* based on precise measurements of the ratios of radioactive isotopes in

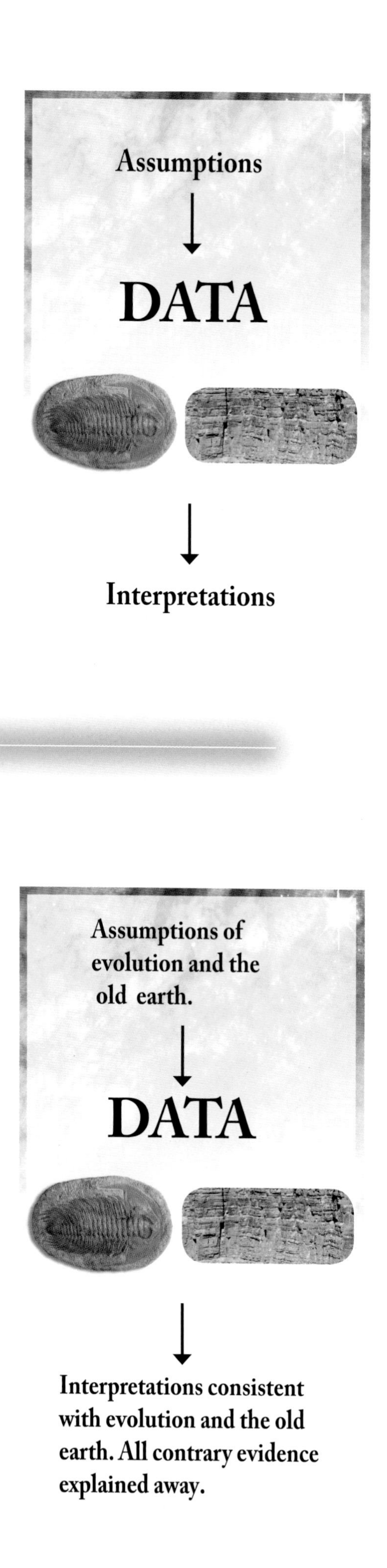

the rock. Once known, these ratios can be plugged into a set of mathematical equations that will give the *absolute* age of the rock.

Unfortunately, the tests take time. The rock must be ground into powder, which then must be sent to a laboratory where they determine the isotope ratios and report back. A computer will then be asked to analyze the ratios, solve the equations, and give the age.

The geophysicist informs you that these tests are very expensive, but since your rock is so interesting, and since he has a government grant to pay the bill, and a graduate student to do the work, it will cost you nothing. He may even be able to publish the results in a scientific journal, thus advancing his career. Furthermore, he will request that several different tests be performed on your rock. There is the *uranium-lead* method, the *potassium-argon* method, *rubidium-strontium* method, and a few others. The tests can be done on the whole rock or individual minerals within the rock and then can be analyzed by the "model" or the "isochron" techniques (to be discussed later). All these tests can be done on the same rock. "We are sure to get good results that way," you are told. The results will come back with the rock's *absolute* age, plus or minus a figure for experimental error.

After several weeks the professor calls you in and shows you the results. Finally you will know the true age of your rock. Unfortunately, the results of the different tests do not agree. Each method produced a different age! "How can that happen on a single rock?" you ask.

The uranium-lead model method gave 500 ± 20 million years for the rock's age.

The potassium-argon model age test gave 100 ± 2 million years.

The rubidium-strontium model test gave 325 ± 25 million years.

The rubidium-strontium mineral isochron test gave 375 ± 35 million years.

Then the professor asks the all-important question. "Where did you find this rock? Were there any fossils nearby, above or below the outcrop containing this lava rock?" When you report that it was just below the limestone layer containing your 320 million year old fossil, it all becomes clear. "The rubidium-strontium dates are correct; they prove your rock is somewhere between 325 and 375 million years old. The other tests were inaccurate. There must have been some leaching or contamination." Once again, the fossils date the rocks, and the fossils are dated by evolution.

Our little story may be fictional, but it is not at all far-fetched. This is the way it is usually done. An interpretation scheme (evolution) has already been accepted as truth. Each dating result must be evaluated — accepted or rejected — by the assumption of evolution and the billions of years it needs. The whole dating process then proceeds within the backdrop of the old-earth scenario. No evidence contrary to the accepted framework is allowed to remain. Evolution stands, old-earth ideas stand, no matter what the true evidence reveals. An individual fact is accepted or rejected as valid evidence according to its fit with evolution.

Let me illustrate this dilemma with a few quotes from evolutionists. The first is by paleontologist Dr. David Kitts, a valued acquaintance of mine when we were both on the faculty at the University of Oklahoma. While a committed evolutionist, Dr. Kitts is an honest man, a good scientist, and an excellent thinker. He and many others express disapproval with the typical thinking of evolutionists.

> The record of evolution, like any other historical record, must be construed within a complex of particular and general preconceptions, not the least of which is the hypothesis that evolution has occurred.[1]

And this poses something of a problem: If we date the rocks by their fossils, how can we then turn around and talk about patterns of evolutionary change through time in the fossil record?[2]

A circular argument arises: interpret the fossil record in the terms of a particular theory of evolution, inspect the interpretation, and note that it confirms the theory. Well, it would, wouldn't it?[3]

In God's Image

Is circular reasoning the best science has to offer? Are better decisions possible? Are scientists doomed forever to run in this circle? Is the human mind capable of more?

The Bible reveals that hope exists. In fact, even "the invisible things of him from the creation of the world are clearly seen, being understood by the things that are made, even his eternal power and Godhead; so that they are without excuse" (Rom. 1:20). Thus, by studying the creation, the things that are made, we ought to be able to accurately determine certain things, especially the fact that things were made by something or someone separate from the creation, an entity that was *not* made in the same fashion as everything else. The exquisite design of living things far exceeds the potential of natural processes, like natural selection. The character of the creation reveals (among other things) the character of its Maker.

Surely this verse means that the natural man, using his own senses and reasoning ability, is capable of correct observations and interpretations, perhaps within certain limits, but indeed an observer is "without excuse" in concluding that the creation has no maker, or that the maker is part of

1. David B. Kitts, "Search for the Holy Transformation," review of *Evolution of Living Organisms* by Pierre P. Grasse, *Paleobiology* 5 (summer 1979): p. 353.
2. Niles Eldridge, *Time Frames: The Rethinking of Darwinian Evolution and the Theory of Punctuated Equilibria* (New York: Simon & Schuster, 1985), p. 52.
3. Tom S. Kemp, "A Fresh Look at the Fossil Record," *New Scientist* 108 (December 5, 1985): p. 67.

the creation. At least some understanding of the character of the Creator, "even His eternal power and godhead," must result. But the tenor of the passage indicates that people do not always come to the right conclusion. Sometimes they suppress what they see, and choose not to perceive. What is wrong? What has happened?

The Bible teaches that humankind is created "in the image of God" (Gen. 1:27). Man is not God, nor is man omnipotent, omniscient, or omnipresent; but being God's image brings certain abilities and characteristics. What does God's image entail?

The image of God does not refer to God's physical body. On occasion, God took on human flesh in order to reveal himself to man in the Old Testament (Gen. 18:24), but God in man's flesh was most powerfully revealed when Jesus Christ "took upon him the form of a servant, and was made in the likeness of men" (Phil. 2:7). On other occasions, Scripture talks of His arm or face or hand in communicating God's attributes or actions, discussing them in terms understandable by humans, but not implying that God has a physical body, for "God is a Spirit" (John 4:24).

Rather, the "image of God" refers chiefly to the fact that man possesses personal, rational, and moral qualities and has a God-consciousness, making him totally distinct from the animals. Much of man's physical and emotional make-up is shared (to a lesser degree) with the animals. Animals were created "after their kind," but man was created "in God's image," somehow adequately reflecting His glory and attributes. This image was in the beginning "very good" (Gen. 1:31). Notice that man was not and is not God, but a representation of His image.

God's image carries great potential for the study of God's creation and the accurate understanding of it, and Adam and Eve were told to do just that (Gen. 1:26, 28). It is hard to imagine what they and their descendants would have been capable of had they been obedient to God's command.

But we know they were not obedient. They chose to rebel against their Creator and incurred His wrath (Gen. 3). They were placed under the penalty of death and along with all of creation began to deteriorate and ultimately to die. The image of God was marred so that even man's spiritual and rational abilities were shackled. Beginning with Eve, every man's natural desire has been to avoid the consequences of sin and to elevate himself to a position of power, refusing to acknowledge God as Creator. Little wonder that today Adam's descendants so often make false conclusions. "Because that, when they knew God, they glorified him not as God, neither were thankful; but became vain in their imaginations, and their foolish heart was darkened. Professing themselves to be wise, they became fools" (Rom. 1:21–22). "The fool hath said in his heart, There is no God" (Ps. 14:1), for "the god of this world hath blinded the minds of them which believe not" (2 Cor. 4:4). They walk "in the vanity of their mind, having the understanding darkened, being alienated from the life of God through the ignorance that is in them, because of the blindness of their heart" (Eph. 4:17–18).

This incomplete reasoning ability and lack of a complete desire for truth, coupled with lack of access or unwillingness to discover and discern all the relevant data, as well as imperfect logical tools, lead to "science falsely so called" (1 Tim. 6:20).

In principle, the marred image of God is capable of discovering limited truth, but in practice man seldom, if ever, accomplishes this in an ultimate sense. God exists, creation occurred, but can we truly understand it as it needs to be understood? Dim approximations are about the best we usually achieve.

One must recognize that determining the age of a rock delves into the long-ago past, before human observers were present or cared to make observations. A good rule of thumb to follow when evaluating pronouncements about earth history is to separate valid observations from interpretations of those observations, especially if the interpretation process involves an anti-God component.

Man, in the image of God, can make valid observations, although necessarily incomplete in most cases. A scientist can measure the precise abundance of elements in a rock, and can discern its stratigraphic position among other rock strata. The scientist can describe and catalog the fossils present and compare them to other fossils. But since the deposition and timing of the rocks and fossils were not observed, interpreting the ages and origins is much more difficult, if possible at all, and many times interpreters resort to circular reasoning.

Is There an Alternative?

How should a creationist react to circular reasoning? In fact, how should a scientist of any persuasion react to circular reasoning? Obviously, with skepticism and even rejection. Circular reasoning has no place in science. We *can* do better.

The key is understanding our assumptions held at the start. Is the assumption of evolution necessary to do science? Despite the pronouncements of some modern-day evolutionists, obviously not! Are other assumptions possible? Yes! Can good science be done without an exclusive commitment to naturalism? Certainly! How can we determine which assumption set is correct?

Before discussing this, let me clarify something that too few people recognize, and evolutionists seldom admit. Science operates in the *present*, and in a very real sense is limited to the present. Scientific theories must involve, among other things, the *observation* of data and processes that exist and occur in the present. But who has ever seen the long-ago *past*? Rocks and fossils exist in the *present*. We collect them, catalog them, study them, and perform experiments on them, all in the present! The scientific method is an enterprise of the *present*.

Of course, observations and records dating from within human history are usable, to the extent that the observers are deemed reliable.

Theories must also be *testable* and potentially *falsifiable* (i.e., there must be some conceivable test which could prove them wrong). But who could disprove an idea about the past? What test could be run to conclude that evolution (or creation) is impossible?

Another requirement for good science is *reproducibility*. This means that observations made today of a particular event or object will be the same as observations of an equivalent event or object tomorrow. Similar events will yield similar results and similar observations.

Events that occurred only once might have been observed, and their results studied, but they cannot be repeated. But some events that occurred only once (such as the origin of the earth) may not have been observed at all. When scientists have only the *results* of an event or its after-effects to study, a full reconstruction of the one-time event (sometimes called a singularity) is lacking.

Even if someone did observe an event in the past (or claimed to), can we really know his observations were accurate? And is the written record complete and trustworthy?

Let me further expand on this difficult concept. I am not trying to discredit science; I am only trying to show its limitations. For example, geology is science. Studying the nature of existing rocks and fossils and the processes that act on them — that is science. Predictions about the future of the rock are another matter. Likewise, historical geology — the reconstruction of the unobserved past of rocks and fossils — is also another story. The same difficulty exists in biology, ecology, astronomy, archaeology, etc.

Note that evolution, if it ever occurred, did so in the unobserved *past*, and each supposed stage only occurred *once*. No one ever saw the origin of life from non-living chemicals. No one has ever seen any type of organism give rise to a completely different type (macro-evolution). No one has ever even *claimed* to see meaningful evolutionary changes take place. The minor variations (micro-evolution) in plant and animal groups (e.g., DDT resistance in insects, shift in

There are two different views on the formation of canyons like the Grand Canyon. Evolutionists believe it was carved over millions of years; creationists believe it was formed by the Genesis flood.

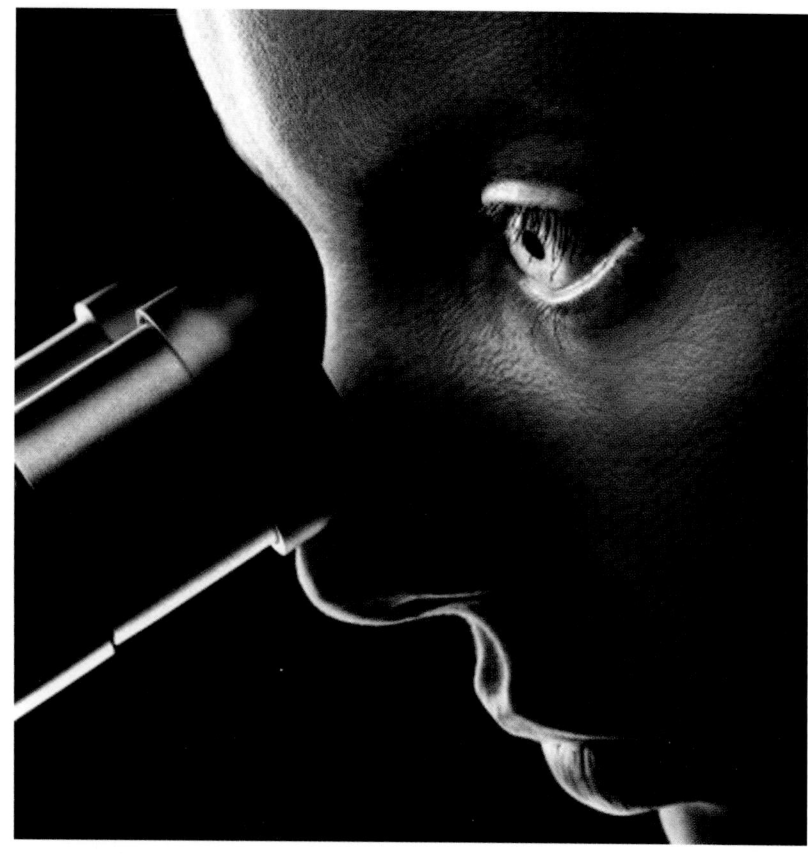

Scientific proof requires observation and repeatability.

dominant color of peppered moths, etc.), which do occur in the present, are not evolutionary changes. In fact, since creation allows for adaptation and variation *within* created kinds, small changes are perfectly compatible with creation theory as well, and are certainly not proof of evolution. Major changes (macro-evolution) have *never* been scientifically observed, and thus the theory of evolutionary descent from a common ancestor has not been and could never be proven scientifically. How could you ever run a test to see if it happened in the past? Or how could you ever prove that it did not happen in the past? Evolution is a belief system some scientists hold about the past, and they use this view of *history* to interpret the evidence in the present.

Likewise, creation, if it ever occurred, did so in the unobserved past. It is not going on today. No human observer saw the creation of the world take place. Thus, creation has not been, nor could it ever be, scientifically proven. It, too, is a belief some scientists have about the past.

Appealing to scriptural authority for proof, while appropriate for Bible-believing Christians, does not constitute *scientific* proof, in a modern sense, which requires observation and repeatability. But if Scripture is truly God's Word, and He is reliable, then we *can* have confidence in it. But how do we come to the notion that Scripture is authoritative and its Author reliable? Many books have been written on this subject, each one taking a slightly different approach, and I don't pretend to have the final word. For our purposes, suffice it to say that our confidence in Scripture does not spring from nowhere, nor is it a blind leap of faith. We all live in a real world and deal with realities that do not always fall into any neat philosophical framework. We can and do observe which ideas make sense to us — which ones seem to work. If an idea repeatedly fails, or lacks common sense, we reject it.

Scripture makes many statements that are testable and potentially falsifiable. And each time we investigate, we find Scripture to be true or at least possibly true if we had all the data and perfect reasoning skills. Even though many detractors have claimed otherwise, never has a charge against Scripture stood up under close and objective scrutiny. We see scriptural teachings work in medicine and economics, and in science and history. We see prophecies come true long after they were made. We see societies and families thrive if guided by biblical principles, as do legal, governmental, and educational institutions. Scriptural values such as love, honesty, and truth witness in our spirits that they are correct.

In short, Scripture works! We see it provide useful results and good fruits in every realm. Other systems and teachings don't work nearly as well. This does not prove Scripture; we must still believe it by faith. And we must always be willing to fine-tune our interpretation of it as our understanding grows, but we have every reason to accept it as God's true and authoritative Word. So, while we cannot scientifically *prove* Scripture, it is, at least, valid for us to hold the position, by faith, that Scripture is true and applicable in all areas. And since Scripture speaks of a recent creation, it provides us with a basic scientific model that can guide our research and understanding, a model that warrants consideration in the marketplace of ideas. But, because it involves one-time events in the past unobserved by humans, supernatural creation cannot be scientifically proven.

Thus, both evolution and creation are outside the realm of empirical science, inaccessible to the scientific method. Neither is observable or repeatable. They are in the category of singularities, one-time events. It is not illegitimate for a scientist, who exists in the present and conducts his or her science in the present, to wonder, "What happened in the unobserved past to make the present, which is observed, this way?" Scientists can then try to reconstruct history in the most logical way possible, but no historical reconstruction can be proven (or disproved). Any view of origins must be held ultimately by faith.

Having said that, let me also say that as a scientist, I am totally convinced that the creation view of history is correct. I am a Christian, a child of God, a fact which I know to be true beyond a shadow of a doubt, but which likewise

I cannot prove scientifically. I know the Creator personally and trust His account of past events. After all, He was there, and in fact, He was doing it all! His record, the Bible, does not give me all the scientific details, but it does provide the general framework that guides my own scientific study. I am convinced it is an accurate record of real events.

A Christian's Resource

All other factors being equal, a Christian, reasoning from a scriptural position, has greater potential for understanding these things than the non-Christian, who starts the process with a non-biblical (i.e., false) world view. This is due to the fact that the Christian has input from a source not available to the non-Christian — the Holy Spirit. Jesus taught that when "the Spirit of truth, is come, he will guide you into all truth. . . . He shall glorify me" (John 16:13–14).

The presence of the Spirit does not guarantee a right conclusion, for even a Christian is subject to practical limitations. All of us live in a world whose education system and popular media has been taken over by those who often emit false knowledge. And Christians still live in a sin-dominated world, and bear the *marred* image of God. Getting saved does not change that. Furthermore, we all live in a society that brainwashes its citizens with a secular viewpoint, and we experience difficulty in ridding our minds of ingrained error. And how about personal sin? While we can be forgiven and victory gained over wrong habits, sin still clouds our thinking processes and inhibits the Holy Spirit from complete control.

But a Christian can start from the right perspective, and many times he receives enlightenment from the Spirit in varying degrees. Through the work of the Spirit, the recognition of truth can be realized by inner conviction and Spirit-directed thinking processes. We must always be willing to grow in understanding and change our opinion as more information comes in and our maturity in Christ deepens, but Christians at least have greater potential to arrive at truth than the non-Christian.

By adopting the view of ancient history given in Scripture, a Christian is then able to study the results of creation, the plant and animal types that were created. We can study the *results* of the flood of Noah's day, which certainly laid down the majority of the earth's sedimentary rocks that contain fossils. Although we did not witness creation or the Flood, we are convinced they really happened in history, and can attempt to interpret the *present* evidence, the results of

past events, within a true historical framework. In this way, we can fill in the gaps in our knowledge, more fully understand the past, and make sense of the present.

On the other hand, if the Bible is correct and creation, the Curse, the Flood, and the dispersion at Babel really happened, what occurs when someone assumes an evolutionary history instead? Obviously, if one *denies* true history, and accepts a false view by assumption, any attempt to reconstruct history is doomed to failure. It will not only be wrong, it will be inferior to a reconstruction based on *real* events, and it will neither be internally consistent nor scientifically satisfying. The data will not fit very well, yet it cannot be absolutely disproved. There will always be a story that can be told about the evidence.

In recent decades, a grave change has taken place that limits the parameters in which scientific study is allowed. The change has not so much happened as it has been foisted upon us. Previously, science was defined as "the search for truth," but now it is nearly always equated with naturalism, the search for a naturalistic answer to all questions, even those ultimate questions of the long-ago past that defy normal explanations. The very possibility of supernatural involvement is denied, excluded by definition. Thus, naturalistic evolution is science and creation is religion, which does not belong in scientific discussions.

My former faculty colleague, Dr. David Kitts, quoted previously, often engaged in spirited discussions with me on this issue. He claimed to be a religious man, who believed in God, yet he scrupulously kept his beliefs out of his reasoning about earth history. He insisted that even if creation is true, even if God created all things in six literal days, just like it says in the Bible, even if Noah's flood deposited the rock strata and the fossils, even if it happened just that way, even if that is absolute truth, it is still not science and its study has no place in science. Science is the attempt to find the best naturalistic explanation for things, even if the supernatural explanation is true and fits the data better!

My contention is that evolution is the religion of naturalism — that it is at least as religious as creation and that creation is at least as scientific as evolution.

Keep in mind that facts are facts, evidence is evidence. All too often, Christians who believe in creation only by faith are afraid to look at the facts. Many are afraid they might find something that will contradict their faith, so they choose not to look.

But we should never be concerned that facts, which exist in the present, will be incompatible with our assumptions about the past. Facts are like rocks: they don't talk; they must be interpreted by one's assumptions. When I was in graduate school, the professors frequently admitted, "There is no such thing as a value-free fact," especially when it comes to unobserved history. Facts must be interpreted: they must be placed within an existing world view before they have much meaning at all. Christians must try to discover *God's* interpretation of the facts. We must also be willing to fine-tune our presuppositions as our understanding grows in both science and Scripture. Truth does exist; and we must strive, with God's help, to overcome our limitations and discern it with diligent study.

To make matters worse, raw facts or data relating to the unobserved past can usually be interpreted in more than one way, within more than one world view, although both interpretations cannot be true. That fossil clam, mentioned at the start of the chapter, *can be* interpreted by an evolutionary historical reconstruction as a clam type that supposedly evolved from other animal types and ultimately single-celled organisms. In this view, it lived 320 million years ago, and its descendants either became extinct or they descended into modern clams.

Or, it can be interpreted by the creation historical reconstruction as an animal deposited in sedimentary material during Noah's flood, but which was a descendant of the original clams in the clam kind created on day five of creation week. Other clams survived the Flood, and their descendants survive to this day.

In this scheme, the Christian/creationist accepts by faith God's record of creation. Contrary to what some might think, the scientific research that stems from a creation view is anything but trivial and sterile. The details of the view are yet to be fully worked out, and much is to be learned. But, if the events in Scripture really happened, we have a chance to reconstruct the specifics of a particular fossil deposit correctly, while those who deny history have no chance at all. They are forever doomed to tell and retell an inferior reconstruction that offends our logic and makes a farce of the present.

The Christian should stand in submission to Scripture in every area of life, including science and reconstructions of the past. We must interpret scientific data within the framework given there.

Can the Matter Be Resolved?

Since neither view of history can be scientifically proved or disproved, what hope is there? Will the creation/evolution debate go on forever, or can it be resolved? Can it even be resolved in the mind of a particular individual?

I was lecturing at a seminar one time when a representative of the local atheist group showed up. He had brought a young man, a university graduate student. They sat in the front row, right below where I stood, and whispered and gestured at my comments, calling attention to themselves and their disgust. (I suppose they hoped to discredit me and my statements, but they were so obnoxious that many, who may not have been on my side to start with, wanted nothing to do with the position of these men, whatever it was. Intending to thwart my effectiveness, they were actually a big help.)

Interpretation A
This clam evolved over long periods of time.

Interpretation B
This clam died in Noah's flood, having descended from originally created clams.

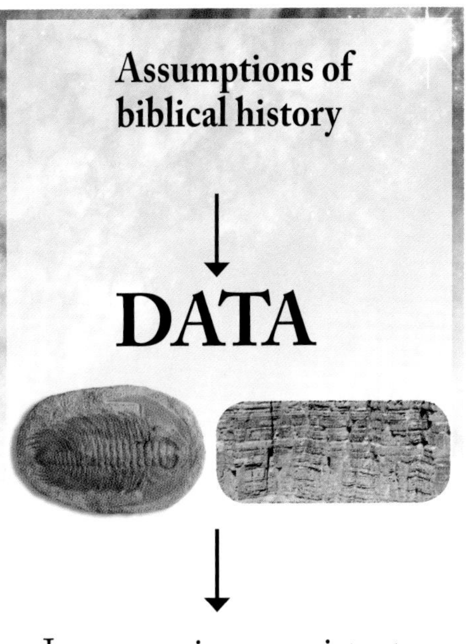

Interpretations consistent with the Bible.

As the lecture ended, many people gathered around to ask questions. The two atheists shoved their way to the front, and the younger man fired one question after another. He appeared to have been coached by the older. I tried to be polite, but each time he saw I had an answer for his last question, he interrupted and asked another. Finally, I challenged him (i.e., them) to give me his hardest question and then listen while I answered, if I could. The crowd hushed to hear his question, but it never came. Perhaps the older man's coaching had not prepared him to think for himself.

The older man, a professor with a long history of "fighting creationism" as he put it, stepped in to rescue his protégé from having to think for himself. He said he didn't like creationism because it disagreed with all the great scientists of our day — Stephen Gould, Carl Sagan, Isaac Asimov, etc. (atheists all). My view was different from theirs; therefore, I must be wrong.

But his main point was that my view mixed science and religion, and we all know that only naturalistic (read atheistic) evolution is science, but creation is religion.

Evidently he had not been listening to my lecture. Over and over again, I had insisted that the majority of university scientists did not hold my interpretations, and that I had specifically been giving another interpretation. I had pointed out that I did not disagree with scientific data, just the religious opinions (i.e., naturalistic opinions) of some scientists about those data and their reconstructions of unobserved history. I had specifically pointed out that the modern definition of science is improper, self-serving, and harmful. Furthermore, I had shown many data censored by my evolutionary colleagues, facts which do not fit an evolutionary view very well at all and which were therefore usually ignored. But I had not disagreed with the *facts*!

The place we differed was in the *interpretation* process. I had started from a different assumption set, performed good scientific research on the data, and derived an interpretation consistent with my world view. I had insisted that my presuppositions were different from those of many scientists. But, when I asked him to find fault with my interpretations given my assumptions, he got strangely silent. The only thing he would say was to repeat the oft-repeated charge that science has no room for the supernatural, and that I could not be a scientist if I believed in God.

He was unwilling to consider my assumptions as possibly legitimate, but admitted he couldn't fault my science or my interpretations. My heart ached, and still aches, for the millions of students brainwashed and badgered by religious evangelists of naturalism into accepting a wrong "religion" in the name of science.

Until a person is willing to think on an assumption or presuppositional level, there can be little movement on this issue. The facts are roughly compatible with both models of history. Both groups can do good science, and the resulting interpretations can be consistent within each model, although quite different from each other.

The schematic drawing on the previous page illustrates the point well. It actually works for many situations, even in the present. This is how you get political liberals and conservatives, for example.[4]

Where Are You Coming From?

As we have seen, the Christian's assumption set should come from a careful and honest interpretation of Scripture, guided by the Holy Spirit, and in submission to its teachings. The evolutionist's assumption set comes primarily from an unnecessarily high assessment of the ability of scientists to discern truth. Finite men who were not present to make the necessary observations, have access to only a portion of the total data and possess fallible logical tools, and therefore can hardly expect to fully understand the past. Humankind, created in the image of God, can do many things, but there are limitations.

Many evolutionists believe in evolution simply because that is the only concept they have ever been taught. Their mentors, from high school on up, have drilled into them the false notion that only ignorant fundamentalists — flat-earthers — believe in creation, so young evolutionists reject creation thinking without investigation.

They have never heard a credible case for creation, and so they perpetrate the lie that evolution is the only legitimate view. This fallacy is furthered by the redefinition of science as *naturalism*, which denies the possibility of creation.

Comets: Assumptions and Interpretations

Consider this interesting application of the two models. We observe comets in our solar system in elliptical orbits around the sun. We observe that on each swing around the sun, a comet loses some of its mass. By measuring the mass of the comets and the amount of loss over time, we can conclude that many comets (especially the short period comets which make frequent passes around the sun) are not extremely old.

Young-earth advocates have interpreted this to imply a young solar system. If the solar system were many millions of years old, the short-period comets would have all ceased to exist. But since those comets still exist, the solar system must be young. Seems simple enough.

But those who insist on an old solar system hold that position in spite of the evidence from comets. They acknowledge that the present comets must be young, but are convinced the solar system is old. They propose a hypothetical storehouse of comets in the outer reaches of the solar system, too far out to see with telescopes or to measure with any sensing device. They call this hypothetical (read imaginary) cloud of comets the Oort Cloud, after the man who first proposed it. Oort claimed that inter-stellar events occasionally dislodge a piece of material from this otherwise stable cloud, propelling it into a near solar orbit, furnishing our solar system with an inexhaustible supply of comets.

Did you follow the logic? Assumption: The solar system is old. Observation: Comets live for only a short time. Conclusion: Youthful comets are continually coming in from a faraway unseen source.

When young solar-system advocates bring up the age of comets, old solar-system advocates say, "Oh, we have solved that. Comets are replenished from the Oort Cloud." Thus, the observations play second fiddle to the assumptions. Without getting a person to question the assumption, you will seldom get him to question the imaginary Oort Cloud.

Resolution becomes even more difficult when dealing with proposed one-time events of the long-ago past, events outside the realm of scientific observation.

Unfortunately, evolutionists seldom admit they have presuppositions. They present their view of history and their interpretations as if they were observed facts. Students and laymen alike are either duped by authority or intimidated into acceptance of a world view with its philosophical and religious implications without even knowing what has happened. Simply put, most people believe in evolution because most people believe in evolution. It is all they have ever been taught. If creation is even mentioned, it is ridiculed and unfairly caricatured. Thus, evolution is assumed, not proved; and creation is denied, not refuted.

Observations made by careful observers in the past, such as Newton and Pasteur, for example, are legitimate within the limitations of the day. One must always discern the difference between scientific data and interpretations of those data, and the observed past and unobserved, inferred past. By the way, many of the founding fathers of science, including the two giants

4. I am indebted to my friend Dr. Donald Chittick for helping firm up my thinking in this area. This schematic is adapted from his excellent book *The Controversy* (Portland, OR: Multnomah Press, 1984).

mentioned above, were Bible-believing Christians and creationists and did their study from a scriptural world view. I recommend *Men of Science, Men of God*, by Henry M. Morris,[5] for brief biographies of many such scientists.

Nevertheless, comparison, evaluation, and rational discussion *are* possible if both parties recognize their own assumptions and interpretative process. You will not get very far with someone who will not even admit he has presuppositions. But let us look at how we can and should proceed to choose between the evolution and creation models of the unobserved past.

Predicting the Evidence

We first must agree on the basic nature of each model. Recognizing that there are many shades of opinion on many points within each view, let me first list the basic points about which we can agree.

Evolutionary theories generally start with either nothing or chaos. Something happens to cause matter to coalesce into particles, atoms, molecules, stars, galaxies, planets, and life. Over time, the life becomes more and more complex: single-celled organisms branch into plants and marine invertebrates, then into fish, amphibians, reptiles, birds, mammals, and finally, into man. All of life, modern and extinct, came from a common ancestor through innumerable stages, all by natural, unguided processes.

Biblical creation ideas start with nothing other than an omnipotent God, the God of the Bible. The state before creation is totally unknowable, but there came a point in which He called into existence the space-mass-time universe, out of His own inexhaustible power. He created light, water, the continents, the atmosphere, and stellar bodies, preparing earth for life. He created each basic category of life distinct from all others, complete with a means of replicating. He created man after His own image, separate from the animals. It was perfect at the start, but fell into disarray as man rejected God's authority.

Obviously, since both views deal with the unobserved and unobservable past, neither can be empirically proved. The best we can do is determine which view is best, and which we choose to believe.

Having completed the formal statement of each model, predictions can now be made. These are not predictions of the future, but, instead, predictions about the data. In effect, each adherent must say, "If my assumptions are correct, I predict that when we look at the data, we will see certain features." The model that better predicts the evidence is more likely the correct one, but neither model can be ultimately proved or disproved.

We evaluate the predictions by looking for internal inconsistencies. Is the model consistent within itself? Does the model need secondary modifications in order to be consistent? Furthermore, does it fit all the data? Are there facts that just do not seem to fit at all? Finally, on a more basic and

5. Henry M. Morris, *Men of Science — Men of God* (Green Forrest, AR: Master Books, 1988).

intuitive level, does the model in question work when applied in science and life? Does it make good common sense, or does it require imaginary components? Can I live with its implications? Does it satisfy my personal need for purpose and hope? Does it lead to a suitable and pragmatic philosophy of life? This process of evaluation allows us to select an appropriate model, one that works in science and in life.

I make three claims for the creation model. I do not claim it is *scientifically* proven, but I do claim that it (1) handles the data in an internally consistent fashion — it does not contradict itself; (2) does so in a way clearly superior to the evolution model; and (3) makes sense of life and forms the basis of a satisfying life.

PREDICTIONS OF THE EVOLUTION MODEL

1. Transitional forms
2. Beneficial mutations
3. Things getting better
4. New species

Marxist Assumptions

In 1990, I had the distinct privilege of journeying to Moscow on a lecture tour, speaking on university campuses and at scientific research institutes. I was there just before communism was displaced. Change was in the wind.

PREDICTIONS OF THE CREATION MODEL

1. Separate, distinct kinds
2. Intelligent design in nature
3. Tendency for decay
4. Extinction of species

I once gave a lecture to several hundred biology faculty and students at the University of Moscow. I had come to suspect that Russian students had one interesting advantage over American students. Whereas in America, students are all too often expected to memorize what the professor has taught and then to give it back on a test, Russian students tend to think presuppositionally. (Perhaps Russian students have grown up reading Tolstoy and playing chess, while American students read comic books and play video games.) Russians of that time openly admitted their atheism and their naturalistic view of science, while today, many American students and professors hold naturalism by default, without knowing it. Thus, to a greater degree than in America, Russians seem to be prone to think presuppositionally and to be less intimidated when confronted with another model.

However, at that time Russians were totally steeped in evolutionary thinking. Communism rests unalterably on atheism, and that is all this present generation had heard until the Communist government collapsed. Evolution provided the communistic world view with an air of scientific credibility.

Parenthetically, I remember one of my graduate students at the University of Oklahoma, who, as a young man growing up in Iran under the Shah's regime, had turned to communism. A leader in the Student Communist Party, he was taken to Moscow for a year's saturation in Communist thought. Do you know what they taught him? Not Marx. Not Lenin. For the whole year, they just filled him with evolution! Evolution is a necessary foundation for Marxism. According to Marxism, evolution is true, and all things come from natural processes (*materialism* is the Marxist word for this) and evolutionary progress through time is inevitable. Marxism claims to be the most highly evolved social and political system.

The Russian people tend to be very quiet, almost stoic in lecture settings, but certainly respectful of authority figures (such as a guest professor). I suspect that for 70 years they had not been allowed to show much emotion. The result was that I had little audience response during my lecture.

At any rate, my talk was focused on the presuppositional nature of science and the legitimacy of the creationist presupposition set and the scientific logic of its resulting interpretations. I used the schematic drawing of Assumptions A and B yielding Interpretations A and B respectively, and I could see they were listening intently although I got little response.

Until, that is, I showed them a revised schematic, with only one assumption set and only one interpretation. I pointed out that this was the way it was in Russia, this was how they were being taught. Remarkably, there were heads nodding all over the room. They recognized it!

Encouraged by this response, I claimed, through the interpreter, "This is not education; this is brainwashing!" Together they burst into a nervous laughter of recognition. Warming to the occasion, I blurted out, "This is adherence to the party line!" I thought they never would quit laughing and talking among themselves. They recognized their education and themselves in that chart and did not like what they saw. From then on, students and faculty alike listened intently to the presentation of a creationist world view consistent with itself and with the real world. Reporters thronged me as soon

as I was through and an article about my lecture and even my itinerary for the rest of the lecture tour was carried in *Pravda*, the first time such a thing had ever been done.

Incidentally, my tour was partially sponsored by the new and courageous Moscow chapter of the Gideons. They had just received their first shipment of Bibles — the book students had been warned about but had never seen.

As my lecture ended, having presented only logical and scientific information that pointed toward creation, the students and professors had thought it through. "With this evidence for creation, there must be a God. Who is this God? How can I know Him?" many called out. They rushed the platform with questions, nearly all of a spiritual nature. And the Gideons were there, opening boxes of Bibles and passing them out. The liberating light of creation has great power, even in the midst of darkness.

Conversely, evolutionary ideas have brought much bondage and sorrow. Without question, Marxism is founded on evolution and naturalism. Marx considered Darwin's book, *On the Origin of Species*, as the scientific justification for his view of evolution in the social realm. He offered to dedicate his book, *Das Kapital*, to Darwin. In the name of evolution, unthinkable evils have been perpetrated, especially in Marxist and totalitarian countries. Even many of our Western social ills are the result of a society that has adopted evolution, rejecting the Creator's authority over their lives and actions. "Ideas have consequences," as they say, even ideas about the past.

While most evolution teachers simply repeat what they have been taught, maybe even trying to do a good job, some understand the battle, and know what they are doing. Christ noted that while "light has come into the world," "men loved darkness rather than light, because their deeds were evil" (John 3:19). With that knowledge, the controversy comes into focus. Not only are thought systems at stake but lifestyles! Many would rather believe they came from a fish than acknowledge a Creator God to whom they are accountable for their choices and actions.

In 1993, I had occasion to speak to a packed crowd of 2,700 government bureaucrats, university students, and Communist Party officials in Beijing, China. Believe it or not, the government had requested Christian professionals to come and address the possible benefits of Christianity to China. The task of organizing the conference, identifying the lecture topics, and selecting the speakers had fallen to me. The others were to discuss education, economics, medicine, etc., while I was scheduled to expound the benefits to science of a creationist world view.

Throughout the months of preparation, the government canceled many of the presentations, including mine, on several occasions. But each time, mine was reinstated because of the primary role I was playing in conference preparations. They were quite concerned about my talk but were reluctant to lose face by canceling it. Finally, the night before the conference, it was canceled again. The Communist organizers deemed my talk a frontal assault on their world view, and rightly so.

Thankfully, in final negotiations, since I was already listed in the printed programs, they offered to let me speak if I refrained from mentioning creation, evolution,

Christianity, or the Bible. They approved me to lecture if I agreed to speak only about my own personal geologic field research. Since all the other talks of substance had been totally canceled, and this was the only opportunity to present anything, I agreed. I presented a slide lecture on the 1980 eruption of Mount St. Helens and its implications in interpretations of unobserved geologic events of the past. Some of these startling evidences are discussed later in this volume.

My presentation, however, included a little more than just interpretations of the past. I showed how my *American* education, at all levels up through my Ph.D. program, had been incomplete. Much information, such as we had discovered at Mount St. Helens, had been *censored* out of my education, indeed, out of all geologic education. These new ideas about catastrophes were proving quite helpful in geology. Censorship of information and ways of thinking from students produces harmful effects, both to the student and to the country involved in such brainwashing.

The Communist Party dignitaries on the front row knew what I was saying and to whom I was talking. They appeared furious, a fact that was later related to me in no uncertain terms. On the other hand, the students were delighted. They were hearing things that had been kept from them. As for the scientists, as soon as the lecture was over, I was surrounded by several, including the director of the Academy of Science, and questioned at length over these new ideas (which they themselves had never heard). They unofficially invited me back to speak at universities and even to join them on a field trip to Tibet to see if catastrophism would help in locating oil and minerals. The only ones who approve of censorship and brainwashing are those who have a world view to protect — in this case, an atheistic world view based on evolution.

We must get away from thinking of evolution as a science. Evolutionary naturalism is a philosophical world view about the past, loaded with religious implications, which historically and presently exists in a frantic attempt to explain the fact that we are here without accountability to a Creator/God. It results in bad science, a denial of true history, and much misery to people and nations who have adopted it.

May God grant all nations a return to light and logic.

THE MOST ASSERTIVE ANTI-CREATION ORGANIZATION TODAY IS THE BERKELEY, CALIFORNIA, BASED NATIONAL CENTER FOR SCIENCE EDUCATION. ITS DIRECTOR, DR. EUGENIE SCOTT, KNOWS THE TRUE RELIGIOUS NATURE OF THE ISSUE AND EVEN CALLS HERSELF A "PHILOSOPHICAL MATERIALIST" — A RELIGIOUSLY HELD COMMITMENT TO NATURALISM, THAT NATURE IS ALL THERE IS. THIS IS ESSENTIALLY THE SAME AS ATHEISM. UNFORTUNATELY, SHE AND HER RELIGION ARE WELCOMED AT SCHOOL BOARDS, LEGISLATURES, AND UNIVERSITIES NATIONWIDE, OFTEN IN THE NAME OF SEPARATION OF CHURCH AND STATE.

QUESTIONS

1. Rocks don't talk. They must be interpreted. What is the most important part of the interpretation process?

2. What are some limitations on our ability to accurately interpret the past?

3. How is each fact listed below an important part of the creation model?
   a. The creation in six days

   b. The Curse on all things because of sin

   c. The great flood of Noah's day

   d. Dispersion at the Tower of Babel

4. What is meant by the term "scientific model"?

5. How can a scientific model make "predictions"?

Chapter Two

WHAT DOES THE BIBLE SAY?

Many Christians would readily agree that large-scale evolution has not occurred in the basic plant and animal types, especially as it applies to the origin of mankind. Those who have carefully thought about it with an open mind can easily see that the fossil record gives no support to the concept of descent of all life from a common ancestor. Likewise, the trend of change is not toward innovation and introduction of more complexity in living things, but rather toward deterioration and extinction. It is inconceivable to most Christians that the incredible design and order that we see in the universe, especially in plants and animals, could have come about by mere mindless and random natural processes. Mutations (birth defects) could never produce the spectacular precision that life exhibits.

Furthermore, evolution is essentially the atheistic explanation for origins, doing away with the need for God. From Darwin to the present day, evolutionists use the theory to explain how we got here without a Creator, and therefore, to justify a lifestyle without accountability to God. Evolution relies solely on natural selection; there is no room for supernatural input. At best, evolution relegates God to inactivity. But to those who do not hold an atheistic world view, the exclusion of God from any involvement in earth history is unreasonable. Thus, most committed Christians tend to shy away from embracing naturalistic evolution too tightly. And, of course, Christians of all persuasions believe in Scripture (albeit in many varying degrees), and Scripture clearly presents God as Creator.

> A man who has no assured and ever-present belief in the existence of a personal God or of a future existence with retribution and reward, can have for his rule of life, as far as I can see, only to follow those impulses and instincts which are the strongest or which seem to him the best ones.[1]

But the issue of the age of the earth is a different matter. Somehow it has become acceptable for Bible-believing Christians to adopt the idea of a five-billion-year-old earth. Many evangelical Christians would claim that God *has* created, using special creative processes and that He did not use theistic evolution, a concept that relies on either totally natural processes, or on very minor input from God. But these Christians have also come to believe that God accomplished His work of creation over billions of years as supposedly documented in the rock and fossil record. This position usually accepts as authoritative the results of radioisotope dating, and either ignores the biblical genealogies and other passages which speak to the age question, or claims that they refer only to the relatively recent timing of the origin of true man (i.e., Adam, who they feel was the first living creature with an eternal spirit, unlike "pre-Adamic" hominids or supposed ape men).

This book contends that the earth is only thousands of years old, not billions, just as a straightforward reading of the Bible indicates, and that the rock and fossil evidence is fully compatible with the biblical teaching. Furthermore, since all Scripture is interrelated, the age of the earth has important theological implications, as we shall see.

Two Views Very Different

The old-earth and the young-earth views are extremely different in their conclusions. They simply are not saying the same thing. Attempts to straddle the fence and accept them both will be unsatisfying — scientifically and scripturally.

The Bible, if we allow it to speak for itself, tells of a creation period of six solar days, during which the entire universe was created in a "very good" state, only thousands of years ago.

Note: The term "solar day" needs some explaining. Strictly speaking, it refers to the time for one rotation of the earth on its axis, today approximately 24 hours, resulting

1. *The Autobiography of Charles Darwin,* 1887, as republished by The Norton Library, New York, p. 94.

in a day/night sequence. But according to Genesis 1, light and the day/night cycle were created on day one, whereas the sun was not created until day four, so there was no sun during the first three days. In Scripture, however, there is no differentiation between the length of the first three days and the last three, and the entire week is referred to as being six days long, followed by a day of rest. For convenience, therefore, I use the term solar day to refer to a day quite similar to ours.

This creation soon came under a death sentence, due to the rebellion of Adam against God's authority. Later, the earth's surface was restructured by the worldwide flood of Noah's day.

The Bible does not specify a precise date for creation. This is clearly discerned from the fact that nearly every scholar who has tried to calculate such a date from Scripture has arrived at a slightly different number. Perhaps the Bible does give such a date, but it has eluded us. But Scripture does give a ballpark age for the earth of just a few thousand years. Even if one inserts every possible time gap in the genealogies and elsewhere (which is clearly not warranted), the time of the creation of Adam would be no longer ago than, say, 12,000 years (most likely, closer to 6,000 years). Stretching the Bible beyond that leaves it with little meaning.

How Much Time Elapsed before Adam?

The length of time allowed by Scripture for the creation-week days has been demonstrated conclusively by many Bible-believing scholars to be only six solar days.[2] As has been pointed out, the Hebrew word *yom*, translated *day*, has a variety of possible meanings and sometimes can mean an indefinite period of time. The word occurs over 2,000 times in the Old Testament, and it is worth noting that this word almost always certainly means a solar day and always *could* mean a solar day. But, when uncertainty arises, the Bible must be used to interpret itself, most specifically noting the context of the word, other usages of the word, and other passages on the same subject. For the following several reasons, we know that the context and the way in which the word *day* is used in Genesis 1 implies a literal solar day.

When the Hebrew word *yom* is modified by a number, such as *six* days or the *third* day (as it is some 359 times in the Old Testament outside of Genesis 1),[3] it always means a literal day. Furthermore, the words *evening* and *morning*, which always mean a true daily evening and morning, define *yom* some 38 times throughout the Old Testament outside of Genesis 1. There are several good words in Hebrew which mean time, or an indefinite period, which the writer could have used; but *yom* was chosen — the only Hebrew word which can mean a solar day. Thus, in all cases, the use of the language implies a literal meaning for *yom*. Why would Genesis 1 be the exception? These facts, plus the general tenor of the passage, plus the summary verses in Genesis 2:1–4, will not allow any other meaning. Genesis 1:1–2:4 was obviously intended to give a chronology of events that really happened, just as written.

Moreover, to make sure we didn't misunderstand, God defined the word the first time He used it. Soon after calling the universe and earth into existence, God created light.

> Then God said, "Let there be light"; and there was light. And God saw the light, that it was good; and God divided the light from the darkness. God called the light Day [i.e., *yom*], and the darkness He called Night. So the evening and the morning were the first day (Gen. 1:3–5; NKJV).

Here we see the word defined as a solar day, or the daylight portion of a

2. For an excellent discussion of this topic, see *The Genesis Record* by Dr. Henry Morris, a scientist and careful Bible scholar. This well-received commentary on Genesis contains much insight into early earth history, both from the Bible and from science.

3. See, for example, the article in the ICR newsletter *Acts & Facts*, "The Meaning of 'Day' in Genesis," *Impact* no. 184. (A free subscription to *Acts & Facts* can be obtained from ICR at P.O. Box 2667, El Cajon, CA 92021.) Also see the same author's series of articles in *Creation Ex Nihilo Technical Journal*, published by Answers in Genesis, especially vol. 5, no. 1 (1991): p. 70–78.

day/night cycle. But it is also used for the entire cycle itself. We often use the English word day in both ways, too, relying on the context to make the meaning clear. While our English word can also mean a long period of time (e.g., in the day of George Washington), it clearly does not mean a long period in this passage.

Perhaps the most definitive passage defining *yom* was written by God's own finger on a tablet of stone so that we couldn't get it wrong. The fourth of the Ten Commandments regards resting on the Sabbath day:

> Remember the Sabbath day, to keep it holy. Six days shalt thou labor, and do all thy work: But the seventh day is the sabbath of the Lord thy God: in it thou shalt not do any work, thou, nor thy son, nor thy daughter, thy manservant, nor thy maidservant, nor thy cattle, nor thy stranger that is within thy gates: For in six days the Lord made heaven and earth, the sea, and all that in them is, and rested the seventh day: wherefore the Lord blessed the sabbath day, and hallowed it (Exod. 20:8–11).

In this passage, God instructs us to work six days and rest one day because He worked six days and rested one day — the week during which He created the heavens, the earth, the sea, and all things in them. The word *remember* in Hebrew, when used as a command, as it is in Exodus 20:8, always refers back to a real historical event. And *for* in verse 11 is usually translated *because.* It too refers back to a real historical event. Thus, the days of our real work-week are equated in duration to the real days of creation. The parallel usages of *day* in context provide certainty in its interpretation. In both places the same words are used with the same modifiers, in the same sentence, on the same slab of rock, written by the same finger. If words mean anything, and if God can write clearly, then creation occurred in six solar days, just like our days.

Furthermore, when the plural form of *yom* is used, *yamim,* as it is over 700 times in the Old Testament, including Exodus 20:11, it always means a literal, solar day. How could God, the author of Scripture say it any more plainly? He did it all in six solar days!

The passage in Exodus also clears up another mystery. "If God is omnipotent, surely He is capable of creating the entire universe instantaneously. Why did He take six days?" some ask. The answer is: to provide a pattern for our work week. We are to work six days and rest one, just as He did. The seventh day rest is a commemoration of His perfect work of creation.

How Long Is a Day?

- The word *day* (Hebrew *yom*) can have a variety of meanings.
  * A solar day
  * Daylight
  * An indefinite period of time
- It was defined as a literal day the first time it was used (Gen. 1:3–5).
- Occurring 2,291 times in the Old Testament, it almost always means a literal day.
- When used in the plural form *yamim* (845 times), it always refers to a literal day.
- When modified by numeral or ordinal in historical narrative (359 times in the Old Testament outside of Genesis 1), it always means a literal day.
- When modified by *evening* and/or *morning* (38 times outside of Genesis 1), it always means a literal day.
- The context of Genesis 1 is a tight chronology.
- It forms the basis for our work week of six literal days (Exod. 20:11).
- The proper interpretation is a solar day, not an indefinite time period.

Old-Earth Creationists

Many Christian writers who attempt to accommodate long ages into biblical history recognize the obvious meaning of *yom* as a literal day, but claim that science has proven the old earth and, therefore, Scripture must be interpreted to fit. Consider the testimony of old-earth advocate Dr. Davis Young, Christian geology professor at Calvin College:

> It cannot be denied, in spite of frequent interpretations of Genesis 1 that departed from the rigidly literal, that the almost universal view of the Christian world until the eighteenth century was that the Earth was only a few thousand years old. Not until the development of modern scientific investigation of the Earth itself would this view be called into question within the church.[4]

Recognizing that the historic view of the church was "young-earth creation," Dr. Young has chosen to hold a different view. He started out his career as a young-earth creationist, "evolved" into an old-earth creationist, then a theistic evolutionist, and now teaches that since the old earth and evolution have been proven by science, Scripture must contain little factual scientific or historic content. He recommends we even stop trying to incorporate evolution into Scripture, and adopt the "Framework Hypothesis," wherein one simply allegorizes those portions of Scripture that appear to present facts about the past. He now advocates gleaning only "spiritual" implications from Genesis, not historic or scientific implications.

4. Davis A. Young, *Christianity and the Age of the Earth* (Grand Rapids, MI: Zondervan, 1982),p. 25.

For in six days the Lord made heaven and earth, the sea, and all that in them is, and rested the seventh day: wherefore the Lord blessed the sabbath day, and hallowed it (Exod. 20:8–11).

In a summary statement of his position,[5] Dr. Young gives seven "Conclusions and Suggestions for the Future," of which some are given below:

> Literalism and concordism are failed enterprises that evangelicals should abandon [p. 291]. . . . In future wrestling with geologically relevant texts such as Genesis 1–11, evangelical scholars will have to face the implications of the mass of geologic data indicating that the earth is extremely old, indicating that death has been on earth long before man, and indicating that there has not been a global flood [p. 295].

> Approaches to Genesis 1 that stress the contemporary cultural, historical, and theological setting of ancient Israel are potentially fruitful [p. 302].

> I suggest that we will be on the right track if we stop treating Genesis 1 and the flood story as scientific and historical reports. . . . Genesis is divinely-inspired ancient near-eastern literature written within a specific historical context that entailed well-defined thought patterns, literary forms, symbols and images [p. 303].

Narrative or Poetry?

Some evangelicals refer to the Genesis account as poetry: an inspired saga written in flowery, emotive language that does not need to be taken literally. Poetic passages in Scripture do contain such figurative language, but how about Genesis 1? Is it poetry or prose? Do we need to take it literally or not?

Recently, ICR commissioned Dr. Steven Boyd of The Master's College to investigate the nature of Genesis 1. Is it really to be understood as a historical narrative, or is it poetic, not necessarily communicating accurate truth about creation? This project was a part of the RATE Initiative on Radioisotopes and the Age of the Earth, which will be described more fully in the following chapters. The scientists wanted to make sure their scientific conclusions were in harmony with Scripture; and Dr. Boyd, a physicist turned Hebrew scholar, had just the right background for the job.

Poetry may contain many truths about history, for God can write with flair if He chooses; but it is the narrative passages which provide the time, place, and details of the story, who is involved, and the sequence of events.

Dr. Boyd performed a comprehensive statistical study on numerous portions of Scripture of all types, and concluded that the verb tenses and forms used in narrative passages differ greatly from those used in poetry.[6]

Comparing Genesis 1:1–2:3 to obviously poetic passages dealing with creation such as Psalm 104 identifies the account of creation in Genesis as perhaps the most narrative passage in all of Scripture. There is no internal hint that it should not be taken as a straightforward recitation of the facts, or understood as anything other than brute history.

This study of verb tense usage was perhaps the most careful and applicable study ever undertaken to specify the difference between narrative and poetry in the Old Testament. It concluded that Genesis 1:1–2:3 is clearly narrative and not poetry, and was intended to convey historical truth. If we allow Scripture to speak for itself, our only valid conclusion is that God created all things in six literal days not very long ago.

Efforts to Avoid the Obvious

Next, consider the opinion of Wheaton College biologist Dr. Pattle P.T. Pun. Dr. Pun believes in creation (sort of) but advocates that God created over billions of years and claims to be among the most conservative professors on the Wheaton science faculty. Note what he says about the Scriptures:

> It is apparent that the most straightforward understanding of the Genesis record, **without regard to all the hermeneutical considerations suggested by science** [emphasis added], is that God created heaven and earth in six solar days, that man was created in the sixth day, that death and chaos entered the world after the Fall of Adam and Eve, that all of the fossils were the result of the catastrophic universal deluge which spared only Noah's family and the animals therewith.[7]

While Dr. Pun insists he believes in inerrancy, it seems obvious from this quote that Scripture cannot be trusted in a straightforward sense when it deals with earth's early periods. It must be understood within the hermeneutic of

5. Dr. Young's latest thinking is explained in his two-part series "Scripture in the Hands of Geologists," Parts One and Two, *The Westminster Theological Journal* 49 (1987): p. 1–34 and 257–304.

6. See Don DeYoung, "A Proper Reading of Genesis 1:1–2:3," chapter 10, in *Thousands . . . Not Billions* (Green Forest, AR: Master Books, 2005).

7. Dr. Pattle P.T. Pun, *Journal of the American Scientific Affiliation* (March 1987): p. 14.

secular science, even though it is obvious, even to him, that the author intended a literal interpretation.

Note: Hermeneutics is the methodology by which Scripture is interpreted. Conservative Bible scholars hold to a historical, grammatical hermeneutic which seeks to discern the actual meaning the author was communicating to the reader. Dr. Pun advocates one based on secular science for early earth history.

Old-earth advocates Bradley and Olsen also agree that the Scriptures, in context, seem to point to a young earth. But, as is apparent in the last sentence, they have adopted, for other reasons, the idea of the old earth. They imply that since science has proven the old earth, and since Genesis 1 and Exodus 20:11 are describing its creation, these scriptural passages that seem to be describing a recent creation should not be understood in a literal sense.

> The Hebrew word *yom* and its plural form *yamim* are used over 1,900 times in the Old Testament. In only sixty-five of these cases is it translated as a time period other than a day in the King James Version. Outside of the Genesis 1 case in question, the two hundred plus occurrences of *yom* preceded by an ordinal, *all* refer to a normal twenty-four hour day. Furthermore, the seven-hundred plus appearances of *yamim always* refer to a regular day. Thus, it is argued [by young-earth creationists, ed.] that the Exodus 20:11 reference to the six *yamim* of creation must also refer to six regular days.
>
> These arguments have a common fallacy, however. There is no other place in the Old Testament where the intent is to describe events that involve multiple and/or sequential, indefinite periods of time[8] [emphasis mine].

Recognizing that every rule of interpretation points to a literal meaning of *day* in these foundational chapters of Genesis, these scientists (sincere Christians and anti-evolutionists) insist that Genesis 1 and other creation passages are the only exceptions to the rule that the context defines the meaning of a word.

How do these authors know that Genesis 1 is describing "multiple and/or sequential, indefinite periods of time"? They do not develop that opinion from Scripture. They are convinced of it through the interpretations of scientific data by some secular scientists. Thus, they must force long ages into Scripture, placing opinions of scientists above the clear meaning (even to them) of God's Word.

But Scripture does speak clearly. The question is not what does it say, but does it really mean what it says, and will I believe it.

Most secular scientists think that young-earth advocates are wrong, but these secular scientists have little regard for Scripture and have probably never been exposed either to proper biblical interpretation technique or to good scientific data in support of the young earth. From their way of thinking, the old-earth idea must be true, regardless of what the Bible says. But what must they think when they see supposedly Bible-believing creationists distort the Bible and the normal Christian way of biblical interpretation in order to embrace something clearly refuted by God's Word? As the Hebrew scholar Dr. James Barr (who does not claim to be a Bible-believer) recognizes:

> Probably, so far as I know, there is no professor of Hebrew or Old Testament at any world-class university who does not believe that the writer(s) of Genesis 1–11 intended to convey to their readers the ideas that (a) creation took place in a series of six days which were the same as the days of 24 hours we now experience; (b) the figures contained in the Genesis genealogies provided by simple addition a chronology from the beginning of the world up to later stages in the biblical story; (c) Noah's flood was understood to be world-wide and extinguish all human and animal life except for those in the ark. Or, to put it negatively, the apologetic arguments which suppose the "days" of creation to be long eras of time, the figures of years not to be chronological, and the flood to be a merely local Mesopotamian flood, are not taken seriously by any such professors, as far as I know.[9]

Dr. Barr, recognized as being one of the world's leading Old Testament Hebrew scholars, makes no claim to believe Scripture in a historical sense, yet he forthrightly insists that any worthwhile scholar would rightly conclude that the Genesis narrative was intended to be understood literally and that it speaks of a recent creation and a global flood. If a non-believing scholar has such a high regard for Genesis, how much more should "Bible-believing" Christians take Genesis seriously?

"Long" Days Don't Help

To top it off, even if the days of Genesis were long periods of time, and if Genesis is giving, in any sense, a historical account of creation, the problem still remains to those who equate Genesis days with "geologic time." As it turns out, the order of creation given in the Bible differs markedly from the order of appearance of things in the view of mainstream scientists. The two are simply not telling the same story. Any attempt to harmonize the two always results in severe twisting of Scripture. Perhaps Dr. Young, quoted previously, is more consistent, arguing that the biblical Genesis account contains no actual historical information.

8. Walter L. Bradley and Roger Olsen, "The Trustworthiness of Scripture in Areas Relating to Natural Science," *Hermeneutics, Inerrancy, and the Bible* (Grand Rapids: Academic Books, 1984), p. 299.

9. Letter to David Watson from James Barr, April 23, 1984, quoted in Russell Grigg, "Should Genesis Be Taken Literally?" *Creation* 16 (1) (December 1993): p. 38–41.

Contradictions between the Biblical View and the Secular View

Biblical Order of Appearance	Evolutionary Order of Appearance
1. Matter created by God in the beginning	1. Matter existed in the beginning
2. Earth before the sun and stars	2. Sun and stars before the earth
3. Oceans before the land	3. Land before the oceans
4. Light before the sun	4. Sun, earth's first light
5. Atmosphere between two water layers	5. Atmosphere above a water layer
6. Land plants, first life forms created	6. Marine organisms, first forms of life
7. Fruit trees before fish	7. Fish before fruit trees
8. Fish before insects	8. Insects before fish
9. Land vegetation before sun	9. Sun before land plants
10. Marine mammals before land mammals	10. Land mammals before marine mammals
11. Birds before land reptiles	11. Reptiles before birds
12. Man, the cause of death	12. Death, necessary antecedent of man

Overlapping Days

Thus, we have a difficult time understanding and appreciating the lengths to which old-earth advocate and Christian astronomer Dr. Hugh Ross goes in his efforts to reinterpret Scripture to fit what some secular scientists insist is true. He proposes that the days of Genesis were not only long periods of time, long enough to allow for the billions-of-years-old universe and earth, but also overlapping. By this, he means that each day overlapped onto the days before and after it, and thereby he claims he solves the obvious mismatch between the order of creation as given in the Bible and the order of appearance of things according to the standard evolutionary chronology and geologic time scale.

For example, the Bible says that fruit trees bearing fruit were created on day three, while oceanic life, even the invertebrates, did not appear until day five. This order is opposite in evolution, in which marine invertebrates evolved early, while fruit trees are much more recent. By claiming that day five extended from day two through day six, and that day three extended from day two through day five, he can rearrange the order to fit. Some parts of day five came before some parts of day three. After undergoing such manipulative twisting, Scripture no longer has any meaning, for it can fit any reconstruction of the past. Dr. Ross's diagram, redrawn here, has proven offensive to many Bible-believers.

Dr. Young once proposed a similar scenario, and his graph of overlapping days is nothing short of repugnant. He evidently no longer holds this view, having given up on any idea of the historicity of Genesis; but it illustrates the lengths to which one must go to harmonize the Bible with evolution and the old earth.

Dr. Ross has even claimed that Scripture necessarily teaches the old earth, and he says that he decided to become a Christian only when he was satisfied that Scripture fits in with the big bang and old-earth ideas. (He now aggressively defends the big bang as God's method of creation, even though many secular astronomers are casting about for another theory that fits the observed evidence better.)

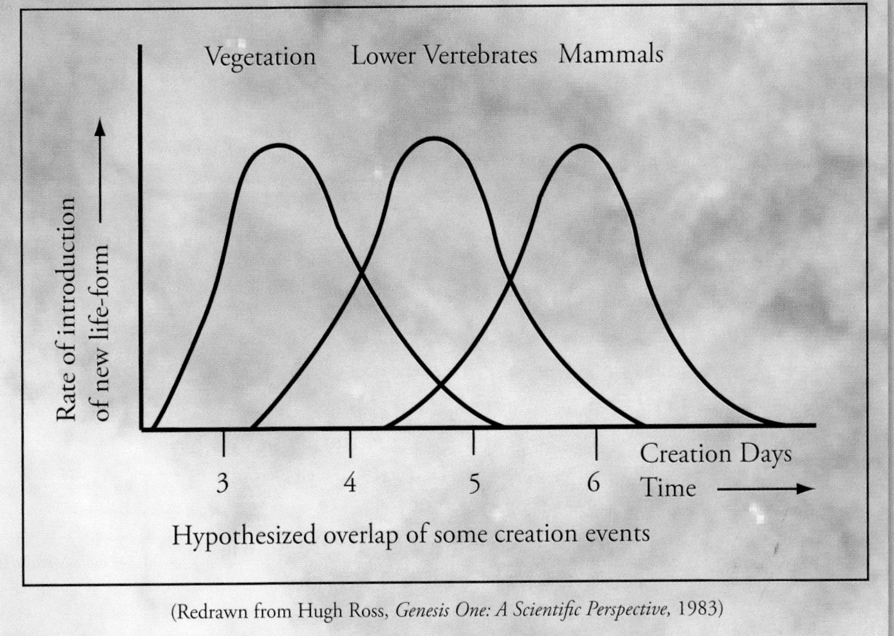

(Redrawn from Hugh Ross, *Genesis One: A Scientific Perspective*, 1983)

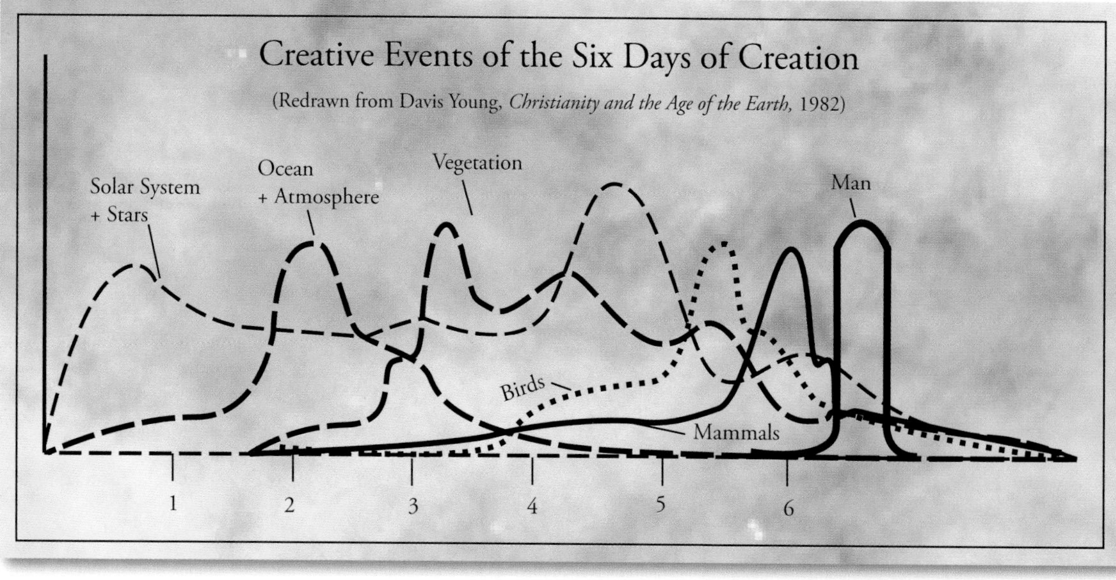

"scientific" opinion of the day.

The trap of twisting Scripture to fit one's preference can have grievous consequences. We shouldn't be looking to science to prove the Bible — the Bible does not need our help. Nor should we be looking to scientific opinion to interpret the Bible for us. The Bible will interpret itself. We just need to believe it.

Whatever the currently held majority view among secular scientists, some Christians, especially those trained in science, feel they must adopt it, because after all, how could science be wrong? Perhaps it is peer pressure, the desire to be accepted and recognized by one's colleagues. Perhaps it is a misplaced understanding of the abilities of scientists to reconstruct the past. But whatever the reason, many Christians insist on holding the mainstream viewpoint of science.

Unfortunately, it does not stop there. There are many essential doctrines of the New Testament, including clear teachings of Jesus Christ, which are undermined by adopting the old-earth view. These will be discussed in later chapters.

To the Bible-believing Christian, science must be compatible with Scripture, leading many to conclude the two must be combined somehow. As it concerns evolution and old-earth ideas, this combination takes the form of theistic evolution, Progressive creation, the gap theory, the day-age theory, or the framework hypothesis. In each case, it is Scripture that suffers and is made to bow to the opinion of secular scientists. But then, of course, scientists change their view, and Scripture must be reinterpreted.

How much better to recognize that Scripture is truth, and that incomplete scientific data must be interpreted within a scriptural framework. With Scripture as our presuppositional stance, we can do better science, guided by the witness of the Holy Spirit within us. But we still must acknowledge that precision in scriptural interpretation sometimes escapes us, and that scientific observations can help us understand difficult passages. By doing so, we can continue to improve our understanding of both Scripture and science as research continues. Even then there is no guarantee we will arrive at a full understanding, but at least this philosophy keeps the Christian from being held hostage by the changing

But if the Bible is true, it has got to work; the evidence must fit! And that's the contention of this book. We must use Scripture and a biblical understanding of the past to interpret scientific data. We should do all things in submission to God's Word, for when we do, we find that the evidence is not only compatible with Scripture, but also supports the Bible and encourages our faith.

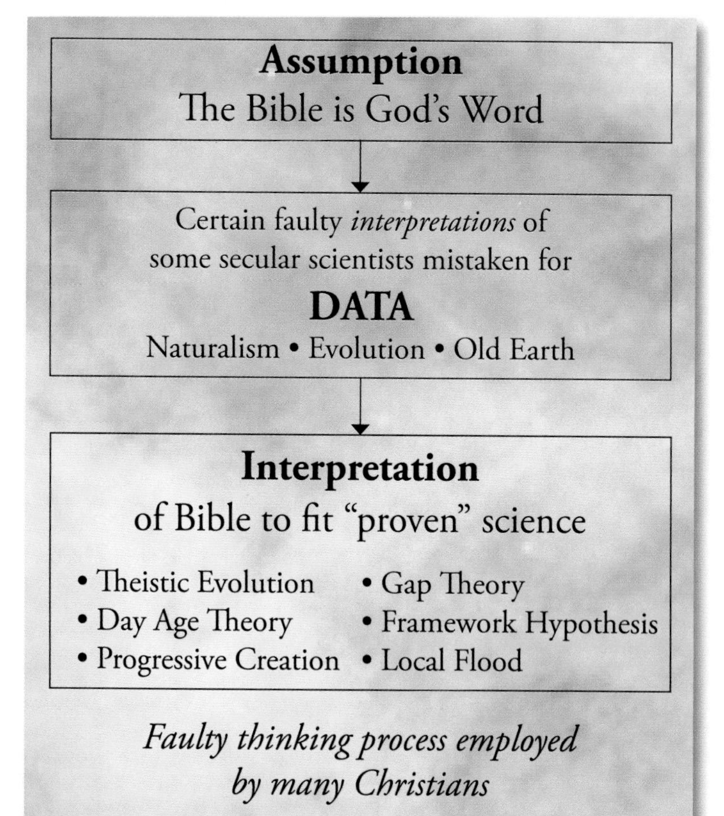

Faulty thinking process employed by many Christians

"For I am not ashamed of the gospel of Christ: for it is the power of God unto salvation to every one that believeth; to the Jew first, and also to the Greek" (Rom. 1:16).

QUESTIONS

1. List several ways in which the biblical model stands in contrast to the evolution model.

2. What is the best biblical evidence used by old-earth advocates that "day" in Genesis 1 means a long period of time? Give evidence that "day" means a solar day.

3. Why do some evangelicals resort to "overlapping days" in Genesis 1? What problem is this supposed to solve?

4. Twelve differences between the biblical order of creation and the evolutionary order of appearance are given. List several more.

Chapter Three

THE TWO VIEWS CONTRASTED

Despite pronouncements by Ross, Pun, Davis, and others, the old-earth/universe view differs markedly from the straightforward concept of creation as understood from Scripture alone. According to the big-bang concept (which is coming under more and more criticism these days), the universe began some 10 to 20 billion years ago with a big bang. Prior to that time, all the matter and energy in the entire universe was condensed into a super-dense "cosmic egg" about the size of an electron. Some cosmologists now claim that even the egg itself originated "as a quantum fluctuation in a vacuum."

At some distinct time, an instability arose and the egg exploded, first in a very short-lived cold big "whoosh" (called inflation) and then a hot big bang, initially producing sub-atomic particles and then fusing some particles into hydrogen (then some into helium) gas atoms. Eventually, the hydrogen gas, instead of expanding radially outward as would be expected from an explosion in a vacuum, began to coalesce into stars, galaxies, and super clusters of galaxies concentrating the still-moving mass into huge "lumps," leaving the majority of space quite empty.

Within the interior of stars, hydrogen and helium were supposedly fused into heavier atoms. In the course of time, some of these stars underwent nova and super-nova explosions, flinging the heavier elements into space. The exploded remnants of such stars eventually coalesced into "second-generation" stars containing minor concentrations of those heavier elements. In time, the process repeated. Our sun is thought to be a "third-generation" star, and the other planets and all people consist of leftover interstellar stardust, which escaped the sun's gravitational pull and remained in orbit. Our solar system dates back about five billion years, according to this view.

In this scenario, life arose spontaneously from non-living chemicals about three to four billion years ago, and multi-cellular life some one billion years ago. Life increased in complexity until man evolved around one to three million years ago. Modern man and civilization date back only a few thousand years — a seeming after-thought in the cosmic timetable.

Scripture and Genealogies

The Bible, on the other hand, places creation in six literal days only a few thousand years ago, with man, the "image of God," being the goal from the very start. This date derives mostly from summing up the time spans given in scriptural genealogies. By adding up the numbers found in the genealogy given in Genesis 5, as found in all English Bibles based on the Massoretic text, we find that only 1,656 years passed from the creation to the Flood. These genealogies consist of the age of each patriarch at the birth of his son through whom the patriarchal line was passed, the years the father lived after the son was born, and the summation of both, providing the total age of each father at death. Because of the correct addition of the numbers given and no hint elsewhere in Scripture that generations are missing, it is concluded by most conservative Bible scholars that the total of 1,656 years accurately reflects the time span between creation and the Flood, allowing for the possible rounding off of numbers and birthdays within a particular year.

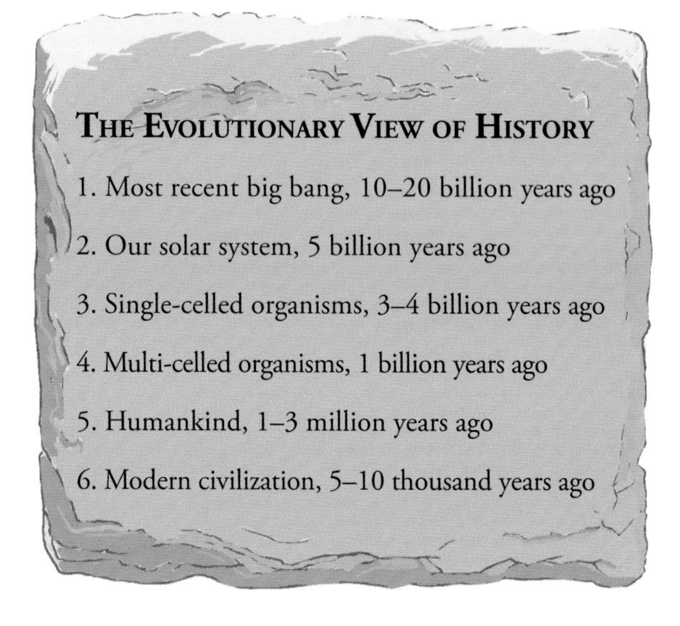

Time reckoned by the Jewish calendar provides a similar date. In it, this book, published in 2007, computes to being published in 5767. This is the Anno Mundi, or years since creation. This dating system is the work of Rabbi Jose ben Halafta in the 2nd century A.D., and is also based on the Genesis patriarchal ages. Differences in Jewish dates stem from the estimate of the destruction of the second Jewish temple. But using Anno Mundi yields a time of creation of 3760 B.C. Obviously, this falls within the same "ballpark," and for our purposes can be considered essentially the same.[1]

It must be admitted that the Septuagint text, the Greek translation of the Hebrew Bible used in Israel at the time of Christ, places the number of years at about 2,300. While both cannot be correct, for the purposes of old-earth/young-earth discussions, the difference can be considered trivial.

The various extant copies of the Masoretic text, from which our English Old Testament is translated, give exactly the same numbers in the genealogies of Genesis 5. The Septuagint, on the other hand, has numerous variants. Taking the maximum number for each link in the genealogy yields a maximum of 2,402 years between creation and Flood. Taking each minimum number gives a time span of 1,307 years. The most reliable Septuagint texts give 2,262 years. Josephus, the Jewish historian who lived at about the time of Christ, followed the most reliable Septuagint figures. The Samaritan Pentateuch, another ancient manuscript, yields a span of 1,307 years. Whichever manuscript is preferred, there is no support for adding millions of years to Genesis 5.

See Paul J. Ray, "An Evolution of the Numerical Variants of the Chronogenealogies of Genesis 5 and 11," *Origins* 12, no. 1 (1985): p. 26–37.

Noah to Abraham

The next two intervals are less well defined. Genesis 10 provides a list of the early descendants of Noah's three sons, Japheth (v. 2–5), Ham (v. 6–20), and Shem (v. 21–32). These are repeated exactly in 1 Chronicles 1:8–23. Genesis 11 amplifies and extends the lineage of Shem and furnishes age spans from Noah to Abraham (v. 10–32) (with the names exactly reproduced in 1 Chronicles 1:24–28). Adding up the numbers in Genesis 11 yields 292 years from the Flood to the birth of Abraham. But the total is not nearly as tight, lacking the summary totals of Genesis 5.

Furthermore, by comparing the list with that in Luke, we find one discrepancy in the line from Noah to Abraham, for in Luke 3:36 the name *Cainan* is added as Shem's grandson. Many scholars offer good explanations for the difference (most likely a late error in copying Luke's Gospel, with a scribe erroneously adding the name *Cainan*, properly found in Luke 3:37 to Luke 3:36, by mistake), but we must admit that the time span cannot be fixed with absolute certainty.

However, even if one puts a large gap of time between each father-son listing (i.e., say great-grandfather to great-grandson instead of father to son), it still does not stretch the total more than a few thousand years. Thus, it does not help solve the discrepancy between the secular view and the biblical view.

Abraham to David

The time from Abraham to dates well established in the Bible and in archaeology, say the time of David, is also somewhat subjective. Most scholars conclude that Abraham lived about 2000 B.C., but uncertainties in the date of the Exodus and the time of the Judges make it possible, as proposed by some, that either a somewhat shorter or somewhat longer time is implied. Indeed, an expanded chronology might seem to yield more compatibility with the scale developed by secular Egyptian archaeology apart from scriptural input. Please understand, I am not advocating a longer time span. I suspect that it is the Egyptian chronology that needs revision. However, although we must admit the possibility of some uncertainty as to the exact dates, the young-earth doctrine of Scripture is not in question here.

Even if we stretch it and stretch it to accommodate every possible longer period, the numbers only increase by a few thousand years, an insignificant increase as far as evolution is concerned.

Thus, we can derive a most probable range of dates, all of which fall into the young-earth position.

	Min.		Max.
From creation to the Flood	1656	to	2400
From the Flood to Abraham	300	to	4000
From Abraham to Christ	2000	to	4000
From Christ to present	2000	to	2000
Total Range of Dates	5,956	to	12,400

My own conviction is that the true age is probably on the order of 6,000 years or so. But in order to make a

1. See Stephen Rosenberg, "Happy 5767 — But How Did We Reach That Number?" *Jerusalem Post Online Edition* (Sept. 20, 2006), www.jpost.com.

As in Genesis 5, the Septuagint chronologies of Genesis 11 are varied. For the time span from the Flood to Abraham, they range from a minimum of 292 years (matching the Masoretic) to a maximum of 1,513 years — the most accepted variant registering 942. This figure matches that from the Samaritan Pentateuch and approximates that given by Josephus, 952.

See Paul J. Ray, "An Evolution of the Numerical Variants of the Chronogenealogies of Genesis 5 and 11," *Origins* 12, no. 1 (1985): p. 26–37.

correct statement, one in which we can have confidence, we should give the age of the earth as a range of approximate dates. Remember, even a 12,000-year-old earth is a young earth, as far as our discussions of creation/evolution, young-earth/old-earth are concerned. I think it sufficient to place the age of the earth in the 6,000–10,000 year range, and this is the figure often used by evangelicals.

But what can be made of the billions of years of history required by evolution and the big bang? Suffice it to say that if the Bible is right, the old-earth concept is wrong, and vice versa. If the earth is old, the Bible is wrong. The only point of general agreement between old- and young-earth views is that modern civilization began just a few thousand years ago, with the introduction of writing and recorded history (i.e., the only history we know is true).

Comparing the Two

These two viewpoints are so divergent and different in their predictions of the data that we ought to be able to test between them and see from the data which one is more likely correct, and I think we can.

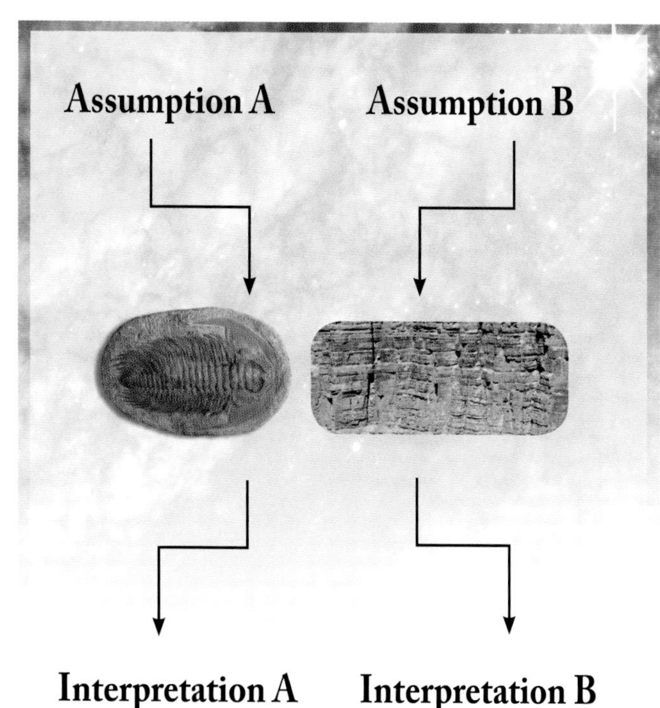

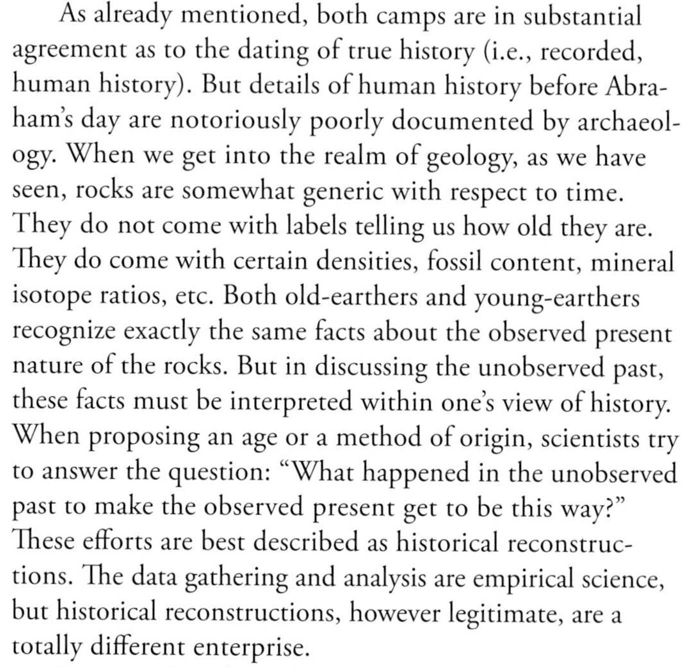

As already mentioned, both camps are in substantial agreement as to the dating of true history (i.e., recorded, human history). But details of human history before Abraham's day are notoriously poorly documented by archaeology. When we get into the realm of geology, as we have seen, rocks are somewhat generic with respect to time. They do not come with labels telling us how old they are. They do come with certain densities, fossil content, mineral isotope ratios, etc. Both old-earthers and young-earthers recognize exactly the same facts about the observed present nature of the rocks. But in discussing the unobserved past, these facts must be interpreted within one's view of history. When proposing an age or a method of origin, scientists try to answer the question: "What happened in the unobserved past to make the observed present get to be this way?" These efforts are best described as historical reconstructions. The data gathering and analysis are empirical science, but historical reconstructions, however legitimate, are a totally different enterprise.

It is true that the rocks and fossils can be interpreted within the old-earth viewpoint, with some degree of success. They can be made to fit. In fact, the rocks can fit within any number of old-earth scenarios. This is obvious when one recognizes that the accepted age for the earth in 1900 was only about 100 million years, and now evolutionists date it 50 times as great! No matter what the evidence and what the politically correct interpretation of the day may be, the rocks can be made to fit.

The rocks can also be interpreted, however, within the young-earth viewpoint. They are compatible with either (although less compatible with the old earth, I believe). Neither the old-earth idea nor the young-earth idea can be scientifically proven by geologic observations; and, likewise, neither can be disproved.

Many Bible-believing creationists, including myself, hold to the young-earth view. I am convinced that the Word of God specifically indicates that creation took place only thousands of years ago, and a worldwide flood subsequently restructured the world's surface in the days of Noah. If these events represent true history, any attempt to reconstruct history that denies these truths will surely fail.

Actually, the earth does not really look old at all. It does look cursed and flooded, however. It was shaped either by a lot of time and little water action, or lots of water and a little time.

While neither can be proven or disproven, these two views can be compared to see which one fits the data better and is therefore more likely correct. I am convinced that under comparison, the creation/Flood/young-earth model will be found not only to fit the data quite well, but it also will fit the data much better than does the old-earth/evolutionary model.

Those committed to a completely naturalistic viewpoint of history can perhaps be expected to adopt the old-earth model. But a Christian, one who believes in the existence of an all-powerful God and claims to believe in Scripture, should never feel compelled to adopt this naturalistic, unscriptural, and quite inferior way of thinking. Instead, a Christian should feel very uncomfortable relegating God to the long ago and far away and making Him responsible for the ages-long evolutionary process — as wasteful, bloody, and contrary to God's revealed nature as it is.

As always, if we begin our reasoning process with Scripture and interpret the scientific data from a scriptural perspective, we will find our interpretation not only scientifically compelling, but also personally satisfying, intuitively correct, and clearly preferable to those derived from a viewpoint which denies true history.

Importance of the Issue

Interestingly enough, the scientific view of biological creation (as opposed to evolution) does not necessarily depend on young-earth ideas. Many Christians who certainly do not believe that all life came from a common ancestor through descent with modification and that strongly hold that the Creator God specifically created each basic category of plant or animal have accepted the old-earth position. They are creationists (of a sort) but old-earthers. Unfortunately, this viewpoint entails many biblical problems and therefore should be rejected. Did death and bloodshed occur before sin? What was the omniscient God's purpose in creating dinosaurs and other now-extinct animal types if they were gone long before man got here? Furthermore, compromising on this issue does not yield acceptance among secular academics, for they demand strict naturalism. There is no benefit to the Christian in this compromise.

On the other hand, the old-earth concept is a necessary part of evolution. Everyone agrees that evolution is an unlikely process, involving millions and millions of favorable mutations, fortuitous environmental changes, etc. Only as one shrouds evolution in the mists of time does it become respectable. If the earth is billions of years old, there is enough time for unlikely events to occur, or so it is thought.

Consider this incredible quote from George Wald, a well-known evolutionary spokesman:

> Time is in fact the hero of the plot. . . . Given so much time the impossible becomes possible, the possible probable and the probable virtually certain. One has only to wait: time itself performs miracles.[2]

With new ideas coming along in astronomy to replace the big bang, essentially proposing an infinitely old universe, it would not be surprising if some major revisions in the age of the earth come too. But, not to worry, the rocks are generic enough to accommodate any new date. Not long ago the universe was thought to be about 20 billion years, but recently scientists have revised the age down to 12–14 billion years.

Time has become a vast carpet under which all the problems of evolution are swept. If someone brings up a problem — the lack of transitional forms, living or extinct; the paucity of mutations which could be called beneficial; the conservative nature of natural selection; the precise design of living things, far beyond the reach of unintelligent processes to produce; the downward spiral of the second law of thermodynamics vs. the upward trend of evolution; the lack of new species in the present but extinction all around — oh well, just wait; in billions of years nature will overcome them. Just sweep them under the carpet of time.

But a realistic look at the evidence insists that time does not perform miracles, nor has real evolution ever happened. The fossil record shows no evidence that any basic category of animal has ever evolved from or into any other basic category. The laws of statistics show that favorable mutations, which actually add genetic information to the genomes, are so improbable that they would most likely never happen even once in 20 billion years, let alone happen millions of times. The laws of science absolutely preclude evolution, pointing toward degradation of life's complex systems and not toward evolutionary integration. The more time there is, the more extinction and the more harmful mutations will

2. George Wald, "The Origin of Life," *Physics and Chemistry of Life* (New York: Simon & Schuster, 1955), p. 12.

According to evolution, early plants reproduced by spores, and seed-bearing plants are a late addition to the biosphere, long after even land animals appeared. Yet the Bible puts seed-bearing plants before everything else. The claim that the order of evolution and the order of biblical creation are the same must distort or ignore biblical details.

occur. De-evolution will occur, not evolution. Time is the enemy of evolution, rather than its hero.

But of course, if the earth is only thousands of years old, then evolution becomes even more foolish. Thus, the idea of the old earth is necessary for the evolutionary viewpoint, but the idea of the young earth is not absolutely necessary for belief in the special creation of plants, animals, and man. However, strictly speaking, belief in the young earth is necessary for a truly biblical point of view. The old-earth creationists, whose spiritual salvation is not in question here, embrace an inconsistent way of thinking about God, the Bible, and the past.

A Functionally Mature Creation

It has been pointed out that when God created, He must have created things with at least a superficial appearance of history. For instance, when God created fruit trees, they were mature fruit trees with fruit already on them (Gen. 1:11). When He created animals, they were able to swim or fly or walk (v. 14–25). When He created Adam, Adam was a mature, full-grown man, not a baby or an embryo. Indeed, it would be impossible to create functioning organisms that did not have a superficial appearance of a prior history. (Even an embryo has a history.)

The word *superficial* is important because if careful and objective scientists had been able to examine Adam immediately after he had been created, they might have been able to discern that he had just been created, that he had not lived a life of, say, 25 years or so. Certainly they would have found no decay in his teeth, no calcification in his bones, no cholesterol in his arteries, and no defective genes. Careful investigation might have shown that he could not have arisen by the normal processes we observe in the present. The only way he could be in that state was to be newly created, for he would have exhibited no objective evidence of deterioration caused by age. Superficially, he appeared to be a grown man. He was functionally mature, but only minutes old. The same could be said for the plants and animals.

Freshly created trees may even have had tree rings. The finished creation was "very good," you remember, and tree rings perform useful work today. They aid in transporting water up the trunk, and their presence adds great beauty to wood products. Without tree rings, living trees would be much weaker, and less stable and less able to grow to great height. Perhaps tree rings were a part of God's "very good" creative design.

Similarly, the stars were created to be seen on earth, to accomplish the purpose of measuring time (Gen. 1:14–19). In order for God's purpose to have been fulfilled, the light would have both been created en route and arrived immediately, or perhaps the speed of light was initially nearly infinite, or perhaps the stars were not so far away, or perhaps the structure of space has been changed. However it got here, the light from the sun and stars had to be here on earth by the end of day 6 in order for God's purpose in creation to be fulfilled.

ICR physicist Dr. Russell Humphreys has devoted years of study to the sticky problem of light from distant stars. He agrees that many stars are now billions of light years away. Restricted to the present well-measured velocity of light, it would take light much longer than a few thousand years to arrive on earth. Given the biblical doctrine of recent creation of all things, how do we see so many stars? Even supernovas (exploded stars), which are far away, can be seen. Did God create a stream of photons, a few thousand years of travel time long, ending in an explosion, when there never was a star at this location? Maybe, but Humphreys has proposed a more satisfying possibility.

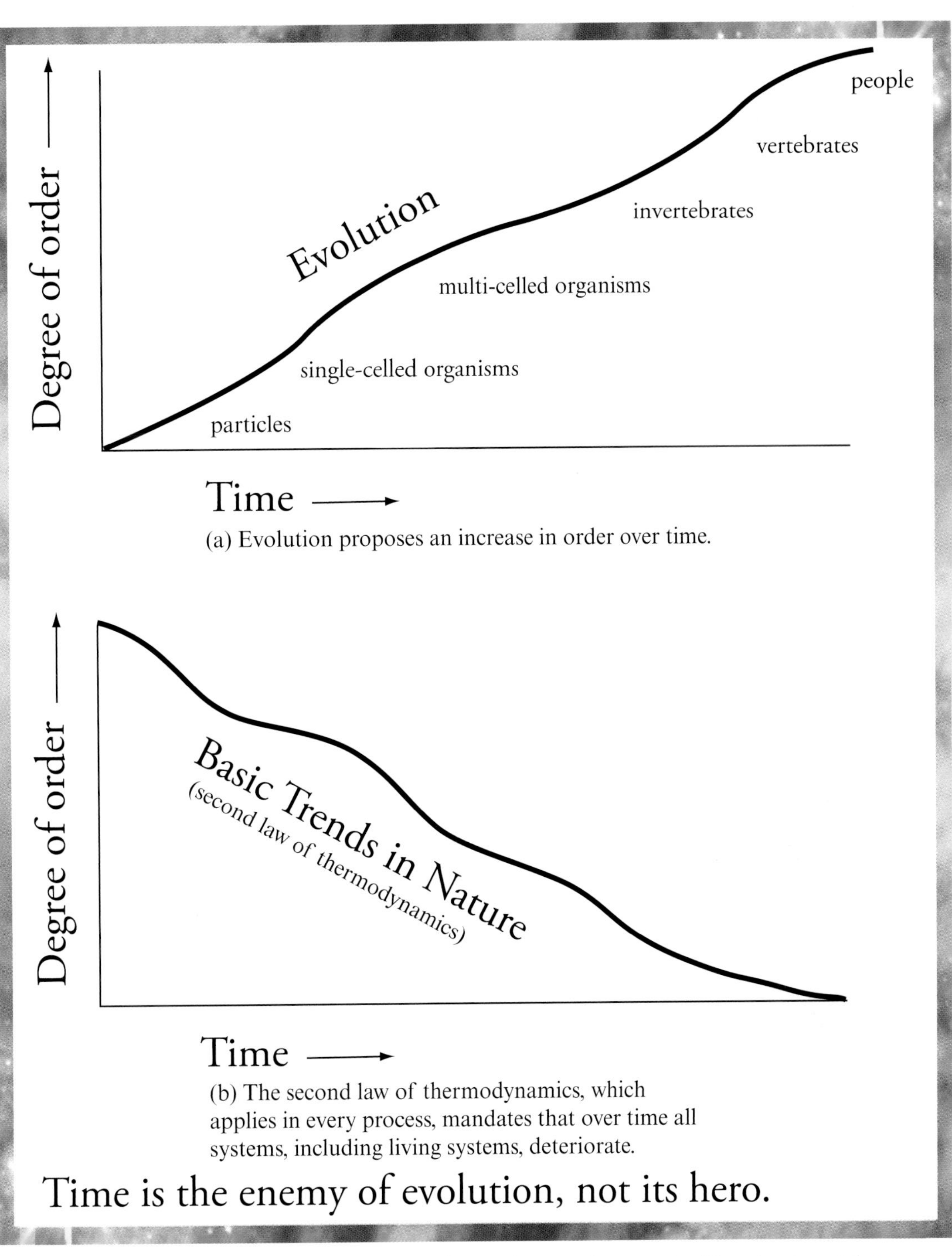

(a) Evolution proposes an increase in order over time.

(b) The second law of thermodynamics, which applies in every process, mandates that over time all systems, including living systems, deteriorate.

Time is the enemy of evolution, not its hero.

Most theories of cosmology assume the theory of relativity: the best approximation of reality modern physics offers. The relativity equations, which govern movement of anything in space, set several necessary boundary conditions. The equations assume that space is infinite and, obviously, there is no center of mass or anything else in infinite space. Yet the Bible seems to indicate that only God is infinite. Space may be very, very large but not limitless. Scripture also identifies earth as the center of God's attention. Here is where He put His image in man. Here is where His Son came to live and die and rise again. Here is where Christ will reign. Here is the site of the New Jerusalem on the new earth. The big-bang theory might assume that earth is a nowhere planet rotating around an average star in a feeble arm of a backwater galaxy, but to God, this place is special. It seems reasonable to conclude earth's location in space might also be special.

Using the same well-applied equations of physics, but with the boundary conditions of a finite (but very large) universe, and with earth somewhere near the center, everything changes. The equations predict that light emanating from anywhere in the known universe would be here in just two days — the length of time between the star's creation on day 4 and creation's completion on day 6! Adam could observe

Remember that Exodus 20:11 tells us God created everything, including the heavens, during the six days of creation, starting with earth on day 1. Old-earth/universe advocates such as Hugh Ross hold that the stars predate the earth by billions of years, even though Scripture reveals that stars were not created until day 4. The Hebrew construction, as well as the context, makes a straightforward understanding of Genesis 1 preferable. For a good discussion of this, see "Star Formation and Genesis 1," ICR *Impact* Article no. 251, May 1994.

the stars on the first evening, and use them for their intended purpose of timekeeping (Gen. 1:14). They could accomplish their very good purpose when creation was finished.

But of course, if God is capable of creating a star, He is also able to create light. There are many different types and sources of light besides a star's internal processes. Creating light would probably be an easier job than creating ripe fruit on a newly created fruit tree. For some reason, this issue remains a real problem to many Christians, who are willing to accept the creation of a fruit-bearing fruit tree but cannot conceive of the creation of stars with light already here or an ordered universe still under construction. But it should be no problem if we understand the nature of God and His creative power. This is not deceptive, as some have charged, but the inevitable result of the creation of a functionally mature creation. Furthermore, God told us when He created, in case we were inclined to make an error of judgment. In fact, if creation were really long ago, He deceived us, since in His Word He tells us He created things recently.

Most importantly, we dare not make the error of limiting God to that which we see occurring today. Creation week was different in every respect from today. The omnipotent, omniscient Creator was using creative processes that He is no longer using, and which are certainly not happening on their own. God even told us that His work of creation is finished (Gen. 2:1), no longer going on. The first law of science today, which has never been violated in the present, insists that nothing can be created. The very fact that the universe exists proves that some process not now occurring accomplished it in the past. Present processes cannot create. Perhaps some recognizable processes were occurring during creation week (e.g., gravity), but we cannot even limit them by today's experience. Christians need to rest in the certain knowledge that the creation episode is beyond our present experience, and the only way we can know about it is for the Creator to tell us. This He has done in His Book to us. We can study the results of creation, but we cannot study the actual event of creation or the processes used. By studying what God has accomplished, however, we can and are expected to discern the fact of creation and the nature of the Creator (Rom. 1:20).

At the end of Genesis 1, God declared His entire creation to be "very good" (v. 31). In order for it to have been so good, it would have to be functionally mature, ready to accomplish God's purposes in creation. As we study the results of creation today, we see that the evidence is perfectly compatible with the scriptural record. The data do not prove Genesis, but they do support and confirm it. In general, the facts of science fit quite nicely with what we would expect if Scripture is correct.

God knew that this superficial appearance of history might be misunderstood by those not having access to the originally created state or not having the patience to study it, so He told us in His Word when this was accomplished. Today, some scientists, attempting to discern the age of things, deny the possibility of creation, and having denied truth, come to a wrong conclusion. If one denies the possibility of a functionally mature creation, he or she will perhaps mistake that functional maturity for age.

Aspects of a Mature Creation

Partial List

- Continents with top soil
- Plants bearing seed
- Fruit trees bearing fruit
- Land with drainage system
- Rocks with crystalline minerals
- Rocks with various isotope ratios
- Stars visible from earth
- Marine animals adapted to ocean life
- Birds able to fly
- Land animals adapted to environments
- Plants and animals in symbiotic relationships
- Adam and Eve as adults
- All "very good"

QUESTIONS

1. Where does the biblical age for the universe of between six and ten thousand years come from? How is that derived?

2. What does the term "appearance of age" mean? Is this a solution to the conflict between evolution and creation?

3. A graphic is given listing aspects of a mature creation. List several more that could have been added.

4. How does the second law of thermodynamics contradict the evolutionary concept?

Chapter Four

DATING METHODS

In this chapter we want to answer questions raised by those newspaper and magazine articles, those television specials, and those classroom lectures that insist that a particular rock or fossil has been discovered which dates to 3 million years or 700 million years or 2 billion years. Few people stop to think about how these dates are derived. How do the scientists determine the supposed age of a rock and is this method reliable?

Not only are rocks and fossils dated, but many other systems are as well. Perhaps scientists want to date a river delta — how long it took sediment to accumulate. Perhaps we want to estimate past population growth or pollution build-up. The concept is quite useful to understand.

As we have seen, the order of the fossils found in rock sequences is concluded to be the evolutionary order and sequence, which in turn determines all other geologic dates. But the dates, right or wrong, come from somewhere. Let us see where they originate.

Actually, every dating method involves the same basic procedure, and the concept behind dating techniques is not difficult to understand. Keep in mind that rocks, fossils, and datable geologic systems do not come with labels on them revealing their age. The investigator must interpret the history of the phenomena. There may be, and in fact generally is, more than one legitimate way to interpret the data.

Under normal circumstances, the dating method proceeds in the following manner:

1. The scientist will observe the present state of the rock or system that is to be dated. (This is science, dealing with the present.)
2. The scientist will measure the rate of a process presently operating within that system. (This also is science.)
3. The scientist must then assume certain things about the past history of this rock or system. (This is model building, with assumptions being made in order to reconstruct unobserved history.)
4. The scientist can now calculate how long it would take for that present process, operating throughout the unobserved past at a rate comparable to today's observed rate, to produce the present state of things in that system. (This is interpretation of observed data based on assumptions about the unobserved past.)

A Parable

Let us illustrate this procedure with a parable. Parables can be used to shed light on complex concepts, and while the concept of dating is not terribly difficult, it is new to many people, making a parable appropriate. We will call this the "Parable of the Potato Basket."

Suppose that as a scientist you entered a lecture hall to attend a scientific lecture. As you arrived, you saw someone up on the platform with a basket of potatoes on the table in front of him (sketch 1). As you sat down, you noticed that as the second hand of the wall clock reached 12, this man reached into the basket, pulled out a potato, peeled it, and put it back in the basket. As the second hand reached 12 once again, he repeated the process. You observe him peeling potatoes at the rate of one per minute for ten minutes; and finally, you ask yourself, "I wonder how long this nut's been doing that?"

The question you have just asked is exactly the same question that a scientist asks when investigating the age of a rock or system. How old is this rock? How long has this tree been growing? How long has this river delta been building up? How long has this process been going on?

How are you going to determine the length of time the man has been peeling potatoes? Obviously, you would first come up and count the peeled potatoes. Suppose you count 35 peeled potatoes. You have thus observed the present state of the system (the number of peeled potatoes, 35), and you have measured the process rate (the rate of potato peeling, one per minute). Both of these observations are scientific observations, dealing with the present. You would

Sketch 1

likely conclude that the system has been in operation for 35 minutes.

Is That the Correct Age of the System? Well, Maybe.

Let us step back and think for a moment. In order to derive such a conclusion, you must make certain assumptions about the unobserved past. These assumptions are critical to your conclusion.

The first thing that you must assume about the past is that the rate of potato peeling has been constant throughout the whole history of the potato basket. Scientifically, all you really know is that the man has been peeling potatoes at one per minute for the last ten minutes. You simply do not know what the rate of potato peeling was before you came in. Perhaps the man is getting better at it and only now can peel a potato each minute, whereas before it took him longer. Or perhaps he is getting tired and slowing down. By observing the present rate, you do not necessarily know the rate in the past, and you have no firm basis on which to assume that the rate of potato peeling has been constant. Perhaps your assumption of constant peeling rate is reasonable, but is it correct?

You may recognize this first assumption as the principle of uniformity. Basically, it postulates that things have been uniform throughout the unobserved past, that no process has ever occurred dramatically different from present processes. It includes at least two parts: the uniformity of process and uniformity of process rate. We have already seen that the Scripture clearly teaches that the creative processes God was using during creation week have ceased. Creation was of the entire world, not too long ago. And Scripture also speaks of a great worldwide flood that restructured the planet! Where on earth could you go and not view a created and subsequently flooded terrain? Certainly the Flood employed present processes for the most part; but process rate, scale, and intensity were far different from similar processes today. The Bible speaks of catastrophism, not uniformity, in earth history.

Sketch 2

James Hutton in the late 1790s and Charles Lyell in the 1820s first proposed uniformity in science. Both had a desire to minimize the influence of Scripture in society and tried to marshal evidence for slow and gradual processes acting over immense time, thereby proving Scripture in error. Obviously, no one could really know the nature of processes of the past without traveling back in time to observe them. Nevertheless, this assumption of uniformity dominates science, especially the historical sciences. Scripture strongly warns against this idea, as will be discussed later.

Uniformity in the Historical Sciences

Biological uniformity — evolution

Astronomical uniformity — big bang

Geological uniformity — billions of years

Sketch 3

The next assumption you have to make or the question you must answer is, have any peeled potatoes been added to or taken away from the basket throughout its whole history? If so, then your calculation would be misleading. For all you know, someone has sabotaged the experiment by adding several peeled potatoes to the basket, so that some of the peeled potatoes now in the basket did not get there through the observed process of potato peeling (sketch 2). Likewise, you must assume that no one, including the government, has come in and removed some of the hard-earned peeled potatoes. Again, you have absolutely no way of knowing just by looking at the potato basket (sketch 3).

There is another question that you must answer, and that is, were there any peeled potatoes in the basket at the start? Perhaps when the basket was brought in, there were already several peeled potatoes in it, and therefore the time determination is incorrect. Again, you have no certain way of knowing, except by asking the man peeling or another witness who was present at the start, and then you would not really know if you were told accurate information or not (sketch 4).

These three assumptions, (1) regarding the constancy of the process rate, (2) regarding the degree to which the system has been isolated from the environment, and (3) regarding the initial conditions of the system, are inherent in any dating process. Correct assumptions in each area must be made in order to proceed to a correct answer, unless specific, accurate knowledge about the past is known.

We must continually remind ourselves of what is taking place in a dating process — any dating process. Strict scientific observation can only get us started. We are able to observe the present state of things. And we are able to measure the rate of a relevant process. But establishing a date for the unobserved origin of something requires making assumptions regarding unobserved history, to a great degree inaccessible to empirical science. It is legitimate for a scientist to speculate on such things, but it would be better for scientists to approach them with a little more humility. Unfortunately, the results of historic speculations are usually presented as unquestioned fact; and students, or tourists at the national parks, or interested persons watching a TV special or reading the newspaper are sometimes intimidated into accepting a politically correct view of history based on uniformitarian assumptions as if that view were scientific fact.

Trees and Tree Rings

Another more realistic illustration would be determining the age of a tree.

We all know that certain trees form tree rings at the rate of one per year, with very few exceptions. Much can be inferred from tree rings, based on years of careful study. For instance, in a wet year, the tree grows faster than in a dry year, leaving a wider ring. A year of disease or insect infestation will show up as an abnormal ring. Frost damage can be seen, and a protracted cold spell during the normal growth season may even produce a second ring in one year, but those are usually recognizably different from normal rings. By documenting weather patterns and other variable conditions and cataloging tree-growth responses in the observed past, scientists have developed confidence in deciphering the past of a particular tree.

Let us say that we examine a particular tree and find it has 250 tree rings.

Sketch 4

We document that no unusual atmospheric or geologic occurrences capable of altering normal tree growth are recorded in the most recent 250 years, and therefore the rate of tree-ring formation was likely constant, at one per year, throughout the life of the tree. We could even observe how the tree had responded to various known, historical episodes during its lifetime. Furthermore, we could properly assume that nothing had happened which had somehow robbed the tree of a tree ring, and that when the tree first formed as a seed, it had no tree rings present.

Because these assumptions are likely correct, we are justified in

Tree ring geometry can usually give an accurate picture of the tree's age and the history of its surroundings.

Dating Niagara Falls

Another less obvious example is the age of Niagara Falls. The waters of Lake Erie flow over the Niagara escarpment in spectacular falls that empty into Lake Ontario a few miles downstream. The falls are observed to be retreating toward Lake Erie as the cliff erodes, at a measured rate of four (or five) feet per year, forming a long gorge. This has been stabilized somewhat in recent years by artificial means, but the measurement reflects the natural erosion rate before engineers slowed it. Next, we notice that the falls are only seven miles (37,000 feet) from Lake Ontario.

Here is the question: How old is this system? How long has Niagara Falls been eroding the cliff in the upriver direction?

Simple division indicates that the system is on the order of 9,000 years old (i.e., 37,000 feet divided by 4 feet per year), but is that the correct determination? As we have seen, there are some assumptions involved, including a constant rate of erosion, no major alterations of the dynamics of the system, and that the erosion started at the end of the gorge, as the tilt of the land caused the water to run faster and do its erosive job.

But what if there were more water in the past? And what if the rock were more

concluding that the tree is 250 years old. But in a real sense, the only way we could know for sure is if someone gave us an accurate record of the date of tree-planting, and then we might still be somewhat uncertain of the total accuracy of the record. In this case, the age determination of 250 years is quite likely precise, but the point is that the past holds many uncertainties.

This aerial view shows the headward erosion of Niagara Gorge.

Niagara Falls

easily eroded? I suspect that in the centuries after the Flood there would have been much more water, and the (then) fairly recently deposited strata might have been softer, more easily eroded. And in all likelihood, the Ice Age followed the Flood, with major changes in precipitation and runoff as well as in acidity of the water. And do we really know where the original mouth of the gorge was? Very likely, the true age of this waterfall system is younger than the simple calculation indicates, but obviously we cannot truly know.

Interestingly enough, Charles Lyell visited Niagara Falls in 1841 while promoting his concept of uniformity of geologic processes throughout the past, a concept widely embraced by geologists for decades but largely abandoned by geologists today. He was anxious to find geologic features that would take more time to form than the Bible would allow. Although local residents who had lived near the Falls for years insisted that the Falls were retreating at a rate of at least three to five feet each year, he estimated the rate at only one foot per year, even though he observed it for only a brief time (much less than even one year). Thus, he charged that the Bible was in error, for Niagara Falls would take 35,000 years to form at the rate he claimed. Obviously, assumptions about the unobserved past dominated the dating process. In the chapters to follow, numerous evidences for the young earth are given. Even though certainty cannot be reached, the claim will be made that the evidence is much more compatible with the young-earth model than with the old-earth. Such is the case with Niagara Falls. The age calculated on sound observations is quite compatible with the biblical time scale, especially when factors concerning the recent Flood and subsequent Ice Age are considered.

The youthful age of the falls and its gorge does not support the concept of vast ages, despite the wishful thinking and dishonest calculations of adherents. The evidence fits with Scripture, while wrong assumptions must be employed to support long ages.

Unfortunately, Lyell's rigged calculations were believed by many, and played a significant role in the abandonment of the popular Ussher chronology[1] for Scripture. In a similar way, bogus claims abound today, and still lead to disbelief of the Bible — and even of God.

---

1. Bishop James Ussher was an outstanding scholar, linguist, and historian. His chronology was based on careful study of both the biblical and primary documents, many of which are no longer available today. His work, in Latin, is not inspired in the same way Scripture is inspired, but is much more scholarly than the efforts of his detractors today. A recent and accurate translation of his *Annals of the World* is available from Master Books or ICR.

QUESTIONS

1. The book gave the parable of the "potato basket." Devise your own parable to make the same point.

2. Consider how two trees growing at the same time and in the same forest might have different tree ring patterns.

3. Niagara Falls was mentioned as a possible young-earth indicator. Can you think of other geologic formations that would likewise be "datable"?

Chapter Five

RADIOISOTOPE DATING

Certainly many people think radioisotope dating has proven that the earth is billions of years old and that this family of dating methods can determine the age of ancient rocks. However, as seen in the potato basket illustration, the efforts suffer from various problems and disputable assumptions.

It must be stated before we begin to look at these methods that the only rocks which can normally be dated by radioisotope methods are igneous and metamorphic rocks, rocks which once were very hot, some even in liquid form, and which since have cooled into solid rock. This includes rocks such as basalt (a type of solidified lava) — rocks that are now quite hard, but once were in a hot, liquid or semi-liquid condition. Advocates propose that melting resets the age clock to zero and that the date given through this method reflects the time elapsed between the cooling of the rock and the present.

Generally speaking, sedimentary rocks, such as limestone, sandstone, and shale, cannot be dated with radioisotope schemes. (There are a few proposed schemes by which some scientists attempt to date certain minerals or crystals contained within sedimentary rocks, but these schemes are rarely used and not discussed here.) Sedimentary rocks, by definition, are laid down as sediments by moving fluids. These are made up of pieces of rock or other material that existed somewhere else and were eroded or dissolved and redeposited in their present location. In other words, the rock material itself is from a previously existing older source, and no dating would be accurate because of redeposition. This would be a contaminated specimen. Fossil-bearing rocks are dated ultimately by the index fossils contained within, which, of course, are organized, arrayed, and dated by the assumption of evolution (which is a false assumption). Often the sedimentary layers are assigned an age when a nearby igneous layer is dated by radioisotope means, but as we shall shortly see, these suffer many weaknesses.

The first radioisotope dating technique which was well studied and which has formed the basis for all of the others utilizes the fact that uranium-238, an unstable radioactive element, decays spontaneously into lead-206 through many intermediate isotopes. Old-earth advocates do not think that uranium-238 and other radioactive elements formed here on earth but instead result from the long-ago fusing together of smaller atoms in the interior of stars, and were slammed together and flung out into space during violent supernova events. Both larger and smaller atoms are presumed to be part of the inter-stellar stardust that coalesced to form the earth billions of years ago. Many of these larger atoms are unstable and change through radioactive decay into smaller, stable atoms.

As shown in the accompanying diagram, uranium-238 changes into thorium-234 through what is called alpha decay, in which the decaying atom loses mass and changes into a smaller atom. Other types of decay, including beta decay, do not substantially reduce the atom's mass. The alpha particle ejected in alpha decay actually consists of two protons and two neutrons, and its ejection decreases the mass of the uranium atom by four mass units, so that it equals the mass of thorium-234. Thorium-234 subsequently loses an electron and

Cardenas Basalt at the Grand Canyon

changes into protactinium-234, which changes into uranium-234, which changes into thorium-230, and on down the line, through various isotopes of radium, radon, polonium, lead, and bismuth, finally arriving at the stable atom lead-206. Each time an atom changes into another type of atom, it gives off a certain amount of energy that identifies the specific decay event that has occurred. Thus, uranium is called the *parent* material that transforms into the stable *daughter* element lead, after undergoing the various intermediate transitions.

The rate at which uranium changes into lead through its intermediate steps is measurable and has been accurately measured for the last several decades. It is referenced by its *half-life*, the time it takes for half of a given number of uranium-238 atoms to turn into lead-206 atoms. Actually, each of the intermediate steps also has its own characteristic half-life, but they are much more rapid, thus they are subsumed within the first step from uranium-238 to thorium-234. As we proceed, keep in mind that the measurement of half-life is not a measurement of time, but of the rate of decay.

Simply stated, when a scientist wants to age-date a rock, he or she can only measure the present state of that rock and the processes occurring within that rock. This means measuring the amount of each of the affected isotopes present in that rock, including the amount of uranium-238 and lead-206. This can be done with a great amount of precision. Since we already know the rate of decay of the parent uranium into the daughter lead, we can begin the process of answering the question, how old is this rock? How long, in other words, would it take for the measured quantity of decaying uranium to decay into the measured quantity of stable lead at the present rate of decay?

But do we thus derive the true age of the rock? As you might suspect, the calculated age depends critically on the validity of the assumptions that have been made. Remember the potato basket and the assumptions involved. Has the specimen been isolated with no contamination? What were the initial conditions? Has the process rate been constant through time? Unless all of the assumptions are correct, the calculated age will be incorrect.

For years, creationists limited their critiques of radioisotope dating to the assumptions regarding the openness of the system to the environment and the initial conditions. However, in 1997, the Institute for Creation Research launched an aggressive research initiative into radioisotope dating. Numerous experts in this field were recruited to participate in the basic research and to critically review the results. They were not only to investigate the veracity of radioisotope dating, but also to improve it if possible. One of their stated goals was to seek to understand why there are such large amounts of daughter elements in the rocks when the Bible indicates that the earth and cosmos are young. Could they have been produced by some other method? The project was labeled "Radioisotopes and the Age of the Earth," or RATE, and before it was over, it made several important discoveries, which will be woven into the discussion to follow. This author was not one of the primary investigators but was present at all the meetings from initial planning to conclusion

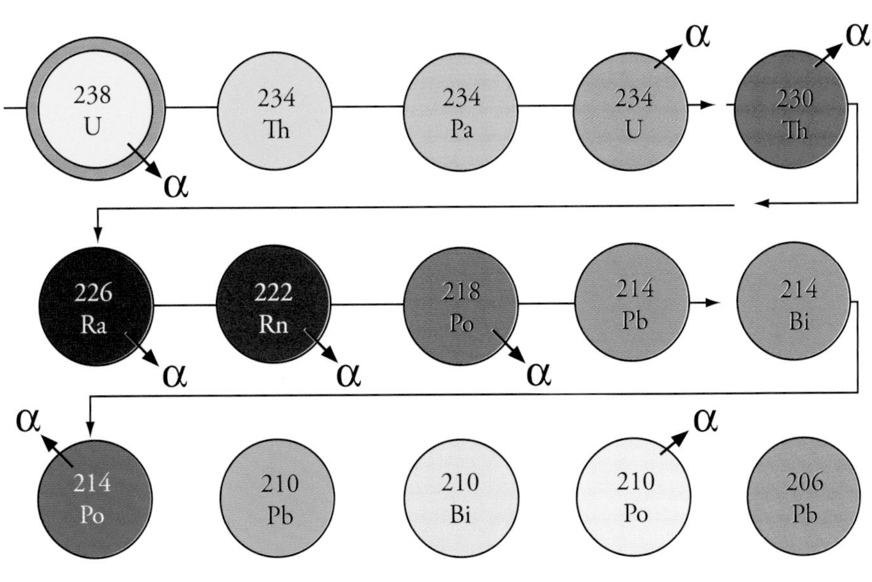

U^{238} Decay Series

The horizontally bedded sedimentary rock layers cannot be dated by radioactive dating methods. The tilted, dark layer intruded into the others, a diabase sill near Hance Rapids, is an igneous rock, and has been dated.

and can attest that the spirit and integrity of each scientist was above reproach.[1]

The First Assumption

Let us consider again the three main assumptions that underlie all dating methods. The first assumption which casts doubt on the results of radioisotope dating deals with the degree of isolation of the rock from its environment. This assumes that neither the parent nor the daughter concentrations (nor any of the intermediate products between uranium and lead, one of which is a highly mobile gas) have been altered throughout the entire history of the rock (except by radioactive decay) or that the amount of loss or gain can be known. Is this assumption free from question?

It is true that when scientists gather a specimen for analysis in a laboratory, they attempt to find one that shows no evidence of having been contaminated through leaching by groundwater movement or other processes throughout its history. Great care is taken in this. A specimen that shows such evidence would not be considered proper for analysis. One would hope that the results obtained on good specimens would be reasonable and consistent, since all questionable specimens were already screened out.

Nothing could be further from the truth. Many, many times, when specimens are dated, the resulting answers do not agree with each other or with any other estimate gained from the fossils or from stratigraphic position. If the results come back wrong, the results from the tests are thrown out, and a charge of contamination may be levied. But these are the results of tests run on specimens that have already been culled for any evidence of contamination or loss or gain of its constituents.

For instance, it is well known that either uranium or lead can easily be leached by ground water. Every municipal water supply must constantly monitor the presence of toxic heavy metals in their drinking water. When it exceeds a certain level, the water is undrinkable. It either must be removed or the system shut down.

Let me give an example of this occurring in a natural setting. Dr. Andrew Snelling, ICR geologist, studied the published dates and isotope ratios from a uranium deposit in Australia. He wrote:

1. Larry Vardiman, Andrew A. Snelling, and Eugene F. Chaffin, eds., *Radioisotopes and the Age of the Earth: A Young-Earth Creationist Research Initiative* (El Cajon, CA: ICR, 2000); Larry Vardiman, Andrew A. Snelling, and Eugene F. Chaffin, eds., *Radioisotopes and the Age of the Earth: Results* (El Cajon, CA: ICR, 2005); Don DeYoung, *Thousands . . . Not Billions* (Green Forest, AR: Master Books, 2005), see also companion documentary of the same name.

These observations alone demonstrate the open system behavior of the U-Th-Pb system that renders meaningless any "age" information derived. However, both Hills and Snelling have recognized that U and Pb also have migrated several times and on a considerable scale in the primary ore zone, with the latest redistribution having produced supergene uraninites, often with colloform banding, found as fracture and cavity infillings . . . and between quartz and gangue grain boundaries. . . . With such wholesale repeated migrations of U also, all attempts at "dating" must be rendered useless, especially when whole-rock samples, in which different generations of uraninites are lumped together, are used. Indeed, it must surely be virtually impossible to be certain of the precise status and history of any particular piece of uraninite selected for "dating." Even though every conceivable precaution is taken when selecting grains for "dating," how can we be sure that the U and Pb isotopes and isotopic ratios measured represent the "original," unaffected by the gross element movements for which there is such abundant evidence? The uraninite grains or ore samples "dated" always contain radiogenic Pb both within crystal lattices of minerals, and as microscopic inclusions or grains and veins of galena, but how can we be sure all the Pb was generated by radioactive decay from U *in situ*? In any case, the uraninite grains and veins do not have uniform compositions — either between or within grains — so that "dating" of sub-sections of any grain or vein would be expected to yield widely divergent U-Pb and Pb-Pb ratios and therefore "ages" even within that single grain or vein. Thus it is logical to conclude, as others have already, that U-Th-Pb ratios may have little to do with the "ages" of many minerals, rocks and ores. Not only then has open system behavior of these isotopes between demonstrated, as confirmed by the independent evidence of ore textures, mineral chemistry, supergene alteration, uranium/daughter disequilibrium, and groundwater and soil geochemistry, but apparent "isochrones" and their derived "ages" are invariably geologically meaningless. Thus none of the assumptions used to interpret the U-Th-Pb isotopic system to yield "ages" can be valid. . . . Creationists should therefore not be intimidated by claims that U-Th-Pb radiometric "dating" has "proved" the presumed great antiquity of the earth, and the strata and fossils of the so-called geological column.[2]

The above evidence conclusively demonstrates that the U/Pb system, including its intermediate daughter products, especially Ra and Rn, has been so open with repeated large-scale migrations of the elements that it is impossible to be sure of the precise status/history of any piece of pitchblende selected for dating. Even though geochronologists take every conceivable precaution when selecting pitchblende grains for dating, in the light of the above evidence, no one could be sure that the U and Pb they are measuring is "original" and unaffected by the gross element movements observed and measured. Those pitchblende grains dated have always contained Pb, both within their crystal lattices and as microscopic inclusions of galena, making it impossible to be sure that all the Pb was generated by radioactive decay from U. In addition, the pitchblende grains don't have uniform compositions so that "dating" of sub-sections of any grain would tend to yield widely divergent U/Pb ratios and therefore varying "ages" within that single grain. A logical extension of these data and conclusions is to suggest, as others already have, that U/Pb ratios may have nothing to do with the age of a mineral. So that in spite of the "popular" dating results looking sensible, the evidence clearly indicates that these dates are meaningless.[3]

My question is, if leaching and contamination can occur which cannot be visibly detected, how can we be sure they have not occurred in other clean-looking samples whose resulting dates happen to come back in agreement with what the examiner thought they should be?[4]

The Second Assumption

The second assumption is a true Achilles' heel of radioisotope dating. This is the one that considers the original quantity of the various isotopes, particularly the daughter product. If some of the daughter material is present at the start, the rock would already appear to be old, when in fact it was just formed. It would already have a superficial appearance of history.

This assumption can actually be tested for its reasonableness, because rocks that can be dated are forming now. We can gather samples, for example, from recent volcanic eruptions and date them. If the dating process is accurate, then the date derived should be almost equivalent to zero, or too young to be measured. In the scientific literature, research results have often been reported where rocks of known age have been dated. In almost every case, the age of these recent lavas has come back from the lab in terms of excessively high ages, not essentially zero, as one would predict.

Let me give a few examples. It is known that Sunset Crater in northern Arizona was formed by a series of recent

2. Andrew A. Snelling, "The Failure of U-Th-Pb 'Dating' at Koongarra, Australia," *Creation Ex Nihilo* 9, no. 1 (1995): p. 88, 91.

3. Andrew Snelling, "The Age of Australian Uranium," *Creation Ex Nihilo* 4, no. 2 (1981): p. 44–57.

4. John Woodmorrappe, "Radiometric Geochronology Reappraised," in *Studies in Floral Geology* (Santee, CA: Institute for Creation Research, 1993). See for a compilation of many unusable dating results.

volcanic eruptions. Indian artifacts and remains are found in association with the rocks formed by the most recent volcanic eruption, which first spewed out liquid lava, then cinder showers. Few of the inhabitants seem to have been killed by the eruption, but their villages and agricultural sites were buried. The Indians hastily moved to a safer location, but took with them the tale of the mountain's activity, some 940 years ago. Tree-ring dating accurately dates the eruption to about A.D. 1065, and it is instructive to compare this historical date with the radioisotope date obtained.[5]

Two of the lava flows were dated by the potassium-argon method. Much to everyone's surprise, the lava flows gave "ages" of 210,000 and 230,000 years![6] The explanation? The date falsely registers old because of excess argon. We know the rocks are not that old, but merely appear to be old. Well, it is true that higher levels of argon-40 are present than were expected, but that is not much of an explanation.

Consider another example. A coal mine in Queensland, Australia, required a vertical ventilation shaft to provide air to the miners. On the way down, the drill encountered a basalt layer, and underneath the basalt they found pieces of unfossilized wood. Multiple carbon dating studies of the wood fragments yielded an "age" of 30,000 to 45,000 years, while the basalt, using the potassium-argon method, dated 39–58 million years![7] The tests are designed to yield the highest quality results, but these mutually exclusive dates testify that something is wrong.

Speaking of "down under," Dr. Snelling dated rocks from a volcano in nearby New Zealand, Mt. Ngauruhoe. It has often erupted in recent decades, and it was these recently formed rocks that were gathered and dated by multiple methods. While K-Ar model ages dated from 270,000 years to 3.5 million, the Rb-Sr isochron dated over 133 million years, the Sm-Nd method nearly 200 million years and the lead-lead ratio method indicated a date of 3.9 billion years![8] All this from rocks less than 60 years old. Do radioisotope-dating results warrant our trust?

5. Steven A. Austin, *Grand Canyon: Monument to Catastrophe* (Santee, CA: ICR, 1994), p. 215–216.

6. G.B. Dalrymple, "40 Ar/36 Ar Analyses of Historical Lava Flows," *Earth and Planetary Letters* 6 (1969): p. 47–55.

7. Andrew A. Snelling, "Conflicting 'Ages' of Tertiary Basalt and Contained Fossilized Wood, Crinum, Central Queensland, Australia," *Creation Ex Nihilo* 14, no. 2 (2000): p. 99–122.

8. Andrew A. Snelling, "The Cause of Anomalous Potassium-argon 'Ages' for Recent Andesite Flows at Mt. Ngauruhoe, New Zealand, and the Implications for Potassium-argon Dating," in *Proceedings of the Fourth International Conference on Creationism*, ed. R.E. Walsh (Pittsburgh, PA: Creation Science Fellowship, 1998), p. 503–525; Andrew A. Snelling, "The Relevance of Rb-Sr, Sm-Nd and Pb-Pb Isotope Systematics to Elucidation of the Genesis and History of Recent Andesite Flows at Mt. Ngauruhoe, New Zealand, and the Implications for Radioisotopic Dating," in *Proceedings of the Fifth International Conference on Creationism*, ed. Robert L. Ivey, Jr. (Pittsburgh, PA: Creation Science Fellowship, 2003), p. 285–303.

A Sampling of Recent Volcanoes and their "Ages"[9]

Location	Known Age	Measured
Hualalai	200 years	1.6 my
Mt. Etna	2100 yrs.	.25 my
Mt. Etna	29 yrs.	.35 my
Mt. Lassen	85 yrs.	.11 my
Sunset Crater	950 yrs.	.27 my
Kilauea	<200 yrs.	21 my
Kilauea	<1000 yrs.	43 my
Kilauea	<1000 yrs.	30 my
Kilauea	40 yrs.	8.5 my
Mt. Stromboli	38 yrs.	2.4 my
Hualalai	200 yrs.	22.8 my
Rangitoto	<800 yrs.	.15 my
Mt. Erebus	17 yrs.	.64 my
Mt. Etna	37 yrs.	.7 my
Medicine Lake	<500 yrs.	12.6 my

Assumptions of Radioisotope Dating

1. No loss or gain of parent or daughter (closed system)
2. Known amounts of daughter present at start
3. Constant decay rate

The Third Assumption

The third assumption regards the decay rate of parent into daughter. Is it scientifically reasonable to assume that the decay rate has not changed over billions of years when we have only been measuring it in recent decades? To be sure, the decay rate has not changed since the early 1900s, when accurate measuring became possible. Scientists have performed all sorts of experiments trying to force the rate to change, applying parameters in ranges likely to occur in nature, but the rate has not changed more than by a very small fraction. But since the half-life of uranium-238 to lead-206 is 4.51 billion years (in other words, a very slow rate of decay), can we be confident in assuming that the half-life has remained unchanged throughout an assumed multi-billion-year past?

For all the early years of creationist work, the assumption of constant decay rates was not seriously challenged. Several creationist theorists, with good observational data and biblical hints to focus their research, have speculated on changing decay rates, most likely associated with the "stretching out of the heavens," mentioned often in Scripture, occurring during creation week, and possibly during the Flood. Non-creationists

9. Andrew A. Snelling, " 'Excess Argon': The 'Achilles' Heel' of Potassium-Argon and Argon-Argon 'Dating' of Volcanic Rocks," *Impact* 307 (January 1, 1999).

had speculated about it also. The RATE initiative (1997–2005) changed all that. Before it was over, at least three lines of evidence pointed to episodes of accelerated decay in the past, as well as speculations as to the physical nature of the change. One of these lines of evidence is especially interesting.[10]

After verifying that abundant radioisotope decay had indeed taken place, the RATE team began investigating the issue of when this decay had taken place. One project involved looking deeply into an unsolved mystery. In the 1980s, high levels of helium had been discovered in tiny crystals of zircon which were contained within deeply buried (i.e., ancient) granite rock; this zircon contained significant uranium. The granite was extracted from a hole drilled three miles deep in New Mexico. As uranium undergoes alpha decay, an alpha particle is given off which consists of two positively charged protons and two neutrons, essentially equivalent to a helium nucleus. Once in the surrounding medium, often the black, flakey mica mineral called biotite, it collects two negatively charged electrons and becomes a neutral helium atom. Helium is an extremely tiny atom, and being a noble gas it refrains from reacting chemically and combining with other atoms. Its small size and freedom as a non-reacting atom together with its high energy (amplified by the underground heat) allow it to migrate through the crystal, eventually escaping the lattice into the surrounding biotite and encasing rock. The decaying uranium cluster locked in the lattice continually produces helium, which begins its migration out. Given enough time, the rate of production should equal the rate of escape.

By measuring the amounts of uranium and lead in these crystals, previous investigators had determined the standard uranium-lead age of this rock to be about 1.5 billion years at today's rate of uranium decay. The amount of uranium and lead present was measured and therefore the amount of helium that should have been produced over this time at modern rates was also known. But when studied, the granite was seen to contain excessive amounts of helium, up to 80 percent of the total amount that had ever been produced! Very little had leaked out. Because helium moves so readily through most solids, especially at the elevated *in situ* temperatures measured in the granite, the RATE team realized such high retention levels were a strong indication that abundant nuclear decay must have occurred recently, over an interval of much less than 1.5 billion years,[11] or else much more would have leaked out.

RATE experimentally measured the helium diffusion rate for these crystals and found it pointed to a helium diffusion age of only 6,000 ± 2,000 years. Thus, within just the last few thousand years, 1.5 billion years' worth of decay (at today's rate of decay) took place. These data seem to demand such a burst of grossly exaggerated decay, not very long ago. Evidently the assumption of constant decay rates is in error.

10. D. Russell Humphreys, "Young Helium Diffusion Age of Zircons Supports Accelerated Nuclear Decay," in *Radioisotopes: Results* (see note 1), p. 25–100.

11. Humphreys, "Young Helium Diffusion Age," *Radioisotopes: Results* (see note 1), p. 25–100.

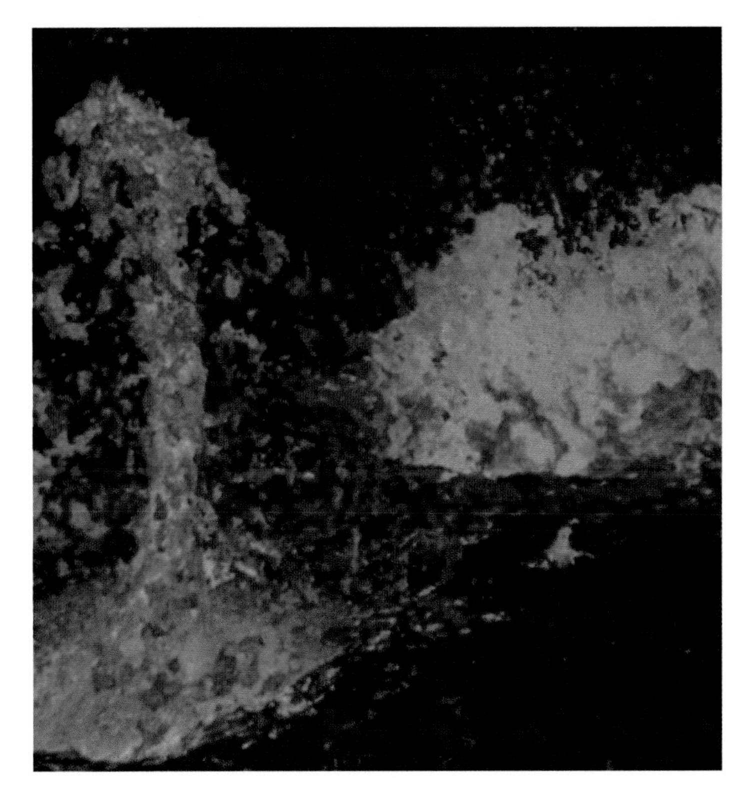

A volcanic eruption, bringing lava to the earth's surface

From a creationist standpoint, bursts of decay are biblically conceivable at the times of creation, the Curse, and/or the great flood of Noah's day when the Bible specifies that mere natural processes may have been supplemented or overridden by supernatural processes. Natural processes have operated throughout history and operate today according to natural law, but was it this way at the extraordinary times mentioned in Scripture? As creationists, we do well not to invoke miraculous intervention to explain things we do not fully understand except on the occasions the Bible reveals as miraculous. But we are warranted in appealing to the supernatural on those occasions when Scripture indicates special events actually occurred. Maybe God utilized other "laws" on those special occasions that He is not now using, or maybe recognizable laws operated on those special times at rates, scales, and intensities not seen today. Radioisotope decay seems to have been altered in the past. This idea will be verified by results from other RATE experiments to be discussed in the pages to follow.

As we have seen, assumption number one, regarding a closed system, is troublesome, because buried in it is the uniformitarian idea that nothing has ever happened to the earth's crust, which would have dramatically opened these rocks to environmental influences. But it would not be surprising if, during the time of Noah's flood, the earth's crust were in such turmoil that contamination or leaching would have been a very common occurrence. Is this assumption legitimate? Can it be assumed that catastrophes such as the great flood of Noah's day have not occurred? Even local catastrophes, which are now well accepted by all geologists, would disturb the uniformity of the geologic process in the areas affected.

Assumption number two, dealing with the initial conditions, fares poorly when tested and is probably wrong much of the time. It does not work whenever it can be checked, for essentially all recently formed rocks date old. How dare we assume this assumption is trustworthy when no checks can be applied? Furthermore, this assumption is essentially the denial of the possibility of creation! It claims knowledge that we do not have, and limits the range of God's options to things within our experience.

A Denial of Creation

Let me further illustrate how assumption number two involves a denial of the possibility of creation. The Bible says that on day 1, "God created the heaven and the earth" (Gen. 1:1). On day 3, the continents were called forth from the world ocean (v. 9). Certainly, rocks came to be which were either created directly by God or formed quickly during these early processes.

If a scientist were to come along on day 8 and gather a specimen of this newly created rock, the rock would actually be only a few days old. If the rock were then taken into a laboratory and dated with the set of assumptions discussed above, how old would that rock appear to be? The question could be rephrased, when God created the earth, were there any lead-206 atoms present? Or was the concentration of lead abnormally high? What processes were occurring within the minerals and at what rate? Did the isotopic levels remain static after the rocks first appeared and how long would they continue without change? When did isotopes begin to decay? Obviously, the rock might possess a superficial appearance of history from the very start, if one assumes that lead-206 comes only from uranium decay that has always occurred at the present rate. Such a perceived history would not be a history that actually occurred but was imposed by man's limited experience and observation.

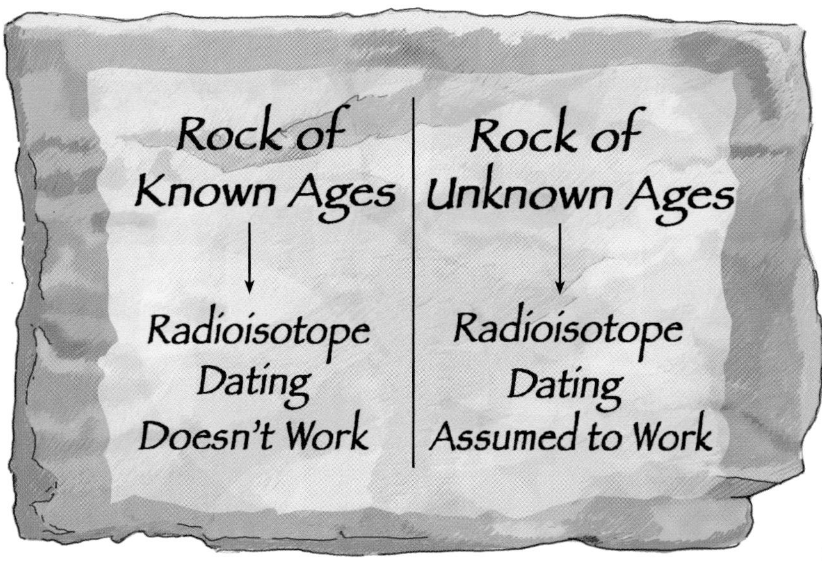

The Bible says that at the end of the creation period all was "very good." Would lead atoms have been present? Probably. The various isotopes of lead are indeed quite useful; in fact, lead has had many more uses for civilization, ancient and modern, than uranium has, which has been deemed useful only in recent decades. In order for the earth to be very good, it would certainly include lead and likely the various isotopes of lead as well. I suspect the rocks would appear old (using these questionable assumptions to date them), even though they were newly created.

This is not an act of deception on God's part, as some have charged. The Bible is very clear that creation took place only several thousand years ago, just in case we are inclined to misinterpret the array of isotopes. And, as already stated, if the earth is truly very old, then God has deceived us, for His revealed Word teaches plainly that His world is young! And His revealed Word communicates with much greater clarity than do the rocks. But keep in mind that the radioisotope-dating concept assumes that many, if not all, of the daughter isotopes came from parent decay and thus denies the power of God to create a variety of isotopes. In other words, it denies truth and therefore can only arrive at error.

The Fourth Assumption

There is another assumption that is an overarching backdrop for the whole method, and that is the assumption that the earth is at least old enough for the present amount of radiogenic lead in a specimen to have been produced by present rates of uranium decay. If we knew that the earth was old, the possibility exists that radioisotope dating could help us determine exactly how old, but it is useless in testing between old earth and young earth. It assumes an old earth.

To sum up, the concept of radioisotope dating assumes uniformity. It assumes that there has never been any world-restructuring catastrophe. It assumes there has never been any supernatural creation, and it assumes the earth to be old.

Since these are all questionable and biblically incorrect assumptions, one might suspect that the results so obtained would not be very useful; and indeed they are not. Many times the laboratory results are found to be bizarre: not agreeing with what was expected, not agreeing with each other, not agreeing with the ages of nearby fossils, and not agreeing with stratigraphic analyses. Even believers in radioisotope dating often discard such results as unusable.

Stratification in the Grand Canyon

Grand Canyon Dating

Let me illustrate from an area of interest to all scientists, and in particular to those of us at the Institute for Creation Research — the Grand Canyon.[12]

The most noticeable layers in the Grand Canyon, and of great notoriety, are the horizontal, fossil-bearing sedimentary layers. Being made of eroded material from a previous source, they are contaminated, and not datable by radioisotope methods. But there are several igneous layers that are potentially datable by the family of radioisotope techniques, which include not only the uranium/lead method, but also potassium/argon, rubidium/strontium, samarium/neodymium, and related other techniques.

Three particular rock layers in the Grand Canyon can be and have been dated extensively by these methods and to them we will give special attention. One is called the Cardenas Basalts, a sequence of basaltic lava layers that is thought to be among the oldest rocks in the canyon. It has been assigned to the Precambrian system, lying stratigraphically below the fossil-bearing Tapeats Sandstone of Cambrian age, which is assumed in evolutionary thinking to be about 550 million years old. The Cardenas Basalt layers are even older.

12. See Steven A. Austin, *Grand Canyon: Monument to Catastrophe* (Santee, CA: ICR, 1994).

Volcanoes up on the plateau above the canyon have extruded a much younger suite of basaltic lavas. Uniformitarians have concluded that the entire canyon was forcefully eroded by rapidly moving water within the last million years or so, and these volcanoes erupted after the canyon had been carved, because lava flowed down the canyon walls and even blocked the river for a time. Native Americans, in all likelihood, witnessed some of these eruptions, probably within the last few thousand years. Being on top of all the other rock units, these lava rocks are relatively younger. But how much older or younger, and what ages make sense?

In addition, dikes and sills of molten material have been squeezed (or intruded) into underground vertical or horizontal cracks between layers or into the rocks themselves. The intruded equivalent of basalt, these dikes and sills can be dated too, at least theoretically. Obviously, intruded material must be younger than the rock into which it is injected. But again, how much younger and how old?

All have been well studied, with results published in the geologic literature. In addition, the RATE team has gathered fresh samples in an attempt to reproduce the original results, as well as extend the studies. In each study, accepted radioisotope methods were used, employing the (questionable) assumptions discussed earlier. This extensive study thus provides a good test case. Do radioisotope methods accurately determine the ages of rocks?

Cardenas Basalt and the Colorado River

The Cardenas Basalt

The usually deeply buried Cardenas Basalts were first dated in 1972 by the potassium-argon (K-Ar) method,[13] deemed proper for this type of rock. The isotopic array published was used to calculate an age of 853 ± 15 million years, using recently revised values for the decay constants. A later study yielded ages of 820 ± 20 and 800 ± 20 million years.[14] Further study produced ages of 791 ± 20 and 843 ± 34 million years.[15] Thus, the range of dates, including uncertainties, would place the actual age somewhere between 771 and 877 million years. In each of these tests, only a single isotope analysis of each rock was obtained. The results are referred to as model ages. Results from model age studies are often recognized as *discordant*, not agreeing with other analyses obtained by using a different radioisotope method, or not even agreeing with the results of the same test run on a different specimen of the same rock. Other times, the derived isotope dates are *discrepant*, not agreeing with dates obtained by stratigraphic or fossil studies. Frequently, a date will simply be *discarded* if it does not fit, and never published at all.

In recent years, an effort has been made to minimize the effects of both variations in makeup throughout the rock and uncertain assumptions inherent in the model age method. Efforts have also attempted to reduce scattered estimates of the age to a single figure upon which more reliance could be placed. Thus, the isochron technique was developed, based on multiple analyses of various specimens of both rocks and minerals, all from the same geologic unit. In theory, this method would not only give the true age of the unit but also determine the amount of daughter material present initially. The result is considered valid when the various data points plot along a straight line. Supposedly, the slope of the line gives the age, and the intercept gives the initial daughter amount.

The five model ages given can now be reformatted as an isochron. To seeming approval, they plotted along a straight line. The straight line plotted indicates an age of only 715 ± 33 million years, and the intercept of the line with the axis allows the initial amount of argon-40 to be found. Remember that the model ages are calculated using the assumption that no argon was present at the start. But the newer and better-trusted isochron method revealed that this assumption

Igneous intrusion. Cutaway illustration of the features produced when rising magma (molten rock) intrudes into existing rock. Clockwise from upper right: a volcano, formed when magma erupts through a conduit to the surface as lava; a stock or batholith, formed when rising magma replaces or forces aside existing rock; ring dikes, concentric vertical intrusions which cut through existing rock layers; sills, intrusions which run between the existing layers; and radial dykes, another form of vertical intrusion which may run for hundreds of miles. At bottom is a magma chamber.

---

13. T.D. Ford and others, "Name and Age of the Upper Precambrian Basalts in the Eastern Grand Canyon," *Geologic Society of America Bulletin* 83 (January 1972): p. 223–226.
14. E.H. McKee and D.C. Noble, "Age of the Cardenas Lavas, Grand Canyon, Arizona," *Geologic Society of America Bulletin* 87 (August 1976): p. 1188–90.
15. D.P. Elston and E.H. McKee, "Age and Correlation of the Late Proterozoic Precambrian Grand Canyon Disturbance, Northern Arizona," *Geologic Society of America Bulletin* 93 (August 1982): p. 681–699.

Rock Unit	Location	Conventional Age	RATE Age Results (Millions of Years)						
			Model Ages		Whole Rock Isochron Ages			
			K-Ar		K-Ar	Rb-Sr	Sm-Nd	Pb-Pb
			Min.	Max.				
Recent Mt. Ngauruhoe Andesite	New Zealand	Historic 1949, 1954, 1975	<0.27	3.5±0.2	-	133± 87(7)	197±160(5)	3,908± 390(7)
Uinkaret Plateau Basalt	Western Grand Canyon, AZ	<1.16±0.18	1.19±0.18	20.7±1.3	-	1,143± 220(7)	916±570(6)	-
Mesozoic Somerset Dam Gabbro	Queensland, Australia	216±4 225±2.3	182.7±9	252.8±9	174±81(15)	393± 170(14)	259±76(13)	1,425±1,000(13)
Precambrian Cardenas Basalt	Eastern Grand Canyon, AZ	1,103±66	577±12	1,013±37	516±30(14)	892± 82(22) 1,111± 81(19)	1,588±170(8)	1,385± 950(4)
Bass Rapids Diabase Sill	Grand Canyon, AZ	1,070±30	656±15	1,053±24	841.5±164	1,007± 79(7) 1,055± 46(11) 1,060± 24(7) 1,075± 34(12)	1,330±360(9) 1,336±380(7) 1,379±140(7)	1,250± 130(11) 1,327± 230(6) 1,584± 420(10)
Apache Group Basalt	Central AZ	1,100	513±13	968.9±25	-	2,295± 300(5)	-	1,304± 69(18)
Apache Group Diabase Sill	Central AZ	1,120±10 1,140±40	267.5±14	855.8±17	-	2,067± 380(16)	-	1,142± 98(19) 1,146± 59(18)
Brahma Amphibolite	Grand Canyon, AZ	1,740-1,750	405.1±10	2,574.2±73	-	840± 86(25) 1,240± 84(19)	1,655±40(21) 1,678±60(24)	1,864± 78(27) 1,883± 53(20)
Elves Chasm Granodiorite	Grand Canyon, AZ	1,840±1-	-	-	-	1,512± 140(7)	1,664±200(7)	1,933± 220(7)
Beartooth Amphibolite	Northeast WY	2,790±35	1,520±31	2,620±53	-	2,515± 110(5)	2,886±190(4)	2,689.4± 8.6(5)

was in error, even though the significantly older dates had previously been accepted. Some daughter has been present at the start.

More accurate determinations for this rock type are thought now to result from use of the rubidium-strontium isochron method, which has become quite popular in recent years. Six specimens gathered from the same basalt strata[16] yielded an isochron date of 1.07 ± 0.07 billion years, much older than the previously accepted K-Ar isochron of 715 million years,[17] even though both of them plotted along straight lines. Obviously, they cannot both be correct. The geologic community has now generally accepted the Rb-Sr isochron as correct and discarded the younger K-Ar dates, calling it a pseudo-isochron.

When the RATE scientists got involved, they extended our understanding quite a bit. By this time, the accepted date was 1,103 ± 66 million years, based on a published Rb-Sr isochron.[18] Yet the model ages from K-Ar gave ages ranging from 577 ± 12 million years to 1,013 ± 12 million years, while the whole-rock isochron analyses ranged from 516 ± 30 million years to 1,588 ± 170 million years for the various methods.[19] Each method produced a different age, in ascending order, with K-Ar yielding the least pseudo age, with Rd-Sr next, then Sm-Nd, and Pb-Pb being the highest.

Diabase Sills and Dikes

The same scatter of results can often be seen. It seems that when a rock, properly screened and prepared, is subjected to multiple tests, dating results seldom agree. The RATE team not only documented inconsistent outcomes, it also tried to find an underlying pattern and cause. For the dikes and sills, keep in mind that they must be younger than the rocks into which they are intruded. The process of intrusion transpired quickly and thoroughly mixed the molten magma. Thus, the

16. McKee, "Age of the Cardenas Lavas," p. 1188–90.
17. Austin, *Grand Canyon: Monument to Catastrophe*, p. 120–122.
18. E.E. Larson, T.E. Patterson, and F.E. Mutschler, "Lithology, Chemistry, Age and Origin of the Proterozoic Cardenas Basalt, Grand Canyon, Arizona," *Precambrian Research* 65 (1994): p. 255–276.

19. S.A. Austin and A.A. Snelling, "Discordant Potassium-argon Model and Isochron 'Ages' for the Cardenas Basalt (Middle Proterozoic) and Associated Diabase of Eastern Grand Canyon, Arizona," in *Proceedings of the Fourth International Conference on Creationism* (see note 8), p. 35–51; A.A. Snelling, "Isochron Discordances and the Role of Inheritance in Mixing of Radioisotopes in the Mantle and Crust," in *Radioisotopes: Results* (see note 1), p. 393–524.

dates obtained for the whole rocks should agree with dates derived from the individual minerals as well as the isochrons.

The Bass Rapids Sill outcrops along the river west of Grand Canyon village. RATE obtained both model and isochron ages for the sill from whole rock study as well as individual minerals, a breadth of information seldom gathered from any outcrop. Predictably, the results were discordant and often meaningless. K-Ar model dates ranged from 656 ± 15 million years to 1053 ± 24 million years. Multiple isochrons were plotted, using a variety of elements, including K-Ar, Rb-Sr, Sm-Nd, and Pb-Pb; all resulting in straight line plots, seeming to indicate trustworthy ages. Each technique's results were acceptably consistent within itself but inconsistent with the others. Their results varied from 841.5± 164 million years (K-Ar) to 1,379 ± 140 million years (Sm-Nd) with absolute values in the same order as before. Interestingly, the method using the longer half-life element gave the older age in every case.[20]

All of the results are listed in the table on the previous page. It may be that Institute for Creation Research scientists have done more radioisotope dating on Grand Canyon rocks than anyone else.

Basaltic Rock Layer

six K-Ar model ages................ 0.01 to 17 million years
five Rb-Sr model ages .... 1,270 to 1,390 million years
one Rb-Sr isochron age.................. 1,340 million years
one Pb-Pb isochron age.................. 2,600 million years

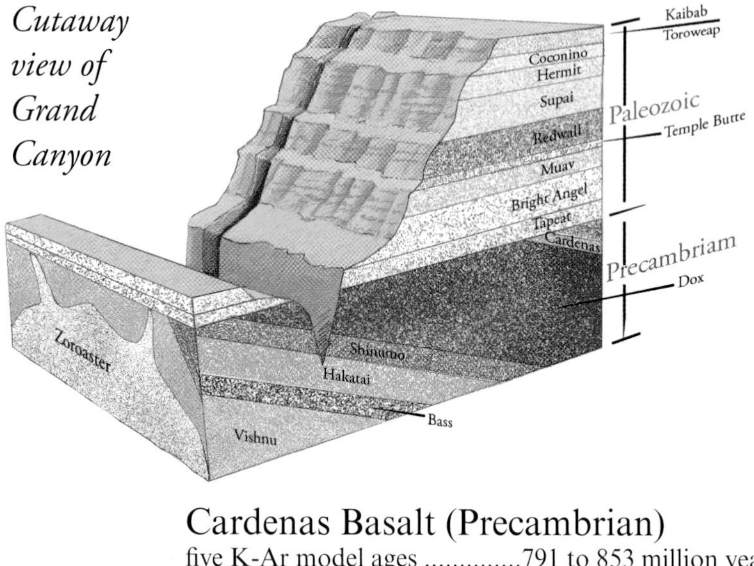

Cardenas Basalt (Precambrian)

five K-Ar model ages ....791 to 853 million years
six Rb-Sr model ages...........980 to 1,100 million years
one Rb-Sr isochron age..................... 715 million years
one Pb-Pb isochron age.................. 1,070 million years

RATE conducted a similar study on rocks from the Beartooth Mountains of Wyoming. From a single specimen of amphibolite, a metamorphic rock, three discordant mineral isochron ages were obtained using the same three different methods, and again the results were in the same order. Each radioisotope pair appears to yield concordant ages internally between whole-rock and individual minerals.[21] This is taken by advocates to imply accurate results, but the "accurate" methods disagree with one another. The RATE team suggested the possibility that decay rates have indeed changed in the past, but changed differentially for each unstable isotope.

Basalts on the Canyon Rim

Now let us apply the same suite of methods to the recent volcanic rocks on the canyon's rim. Remember that these plateau basalts are extremely fresh looking and are lying on top of all other rocks in the canyon. Some even erupted after the canyon was eroded. Perhaps witnessed by Native Americans, they are easily the most recent rock units in the Grand Canyon.

As mentioned before, one K-Ar model date stands at 10 thousand years, but another K-Ar model date of an olivine mineral from the same rock dated at 117 ± 3 million years.[22] (Some have proposed that this mineral was from an older pod that may have been incorporated into the later lava flow.) Other nearby specimens were dated by this method to be 3.67, 2.63, and 3.60 million years old.[23]

When RATE researcher Dr. Steve Austin conducted Rb-Sr studies on five specimens gathered from obviously recent (Quaternary) lava flows in the same area, he obtained a straight-line isochron age of 1.143 ± 0.22 billion years![24] Obviously, this isochron is discordant with the K-Ar dates and discrepant with the stratigraphic control, which places the entire suite of rocks at less than a few million years old, most likely in the low thousands of years.

Furthermore, these lava flows could not possibly be older than the Cardenas Basalts, even though both rock strata produced equally good isochron plots. Evolutionists would call the Rb-Sr isochron of the plateau basalts a fictitious isochron, with the isochron slope having no relationship to real time. Could the isochron (accepted as accurate) that was

20. Steven A. Austin, "Do Radioisotope Clocks Need Repair?" in *Radioisotopes: Results* (see note 1), p. 325–92; Andrew A. Snelling, "Isochron Discordances," in *Radioisotopes: Results* (see note 1), p. 393–524; Andrew A. Snelling, Steven A. Austin, and William A. Hoesch, "Radioisotopes in a Diabase Sill (Upper Precambrian) at Bass Rapids, Grand Canyon, Arizona: An Application and Test of the Isochron Dating Method," in *Proceedings of the Fifth ICC* (see note 8), p. 279–284.

21. Steven A. Austin, "Do Radioisotope Clocks Need Repair?" in *Radioisotopes: Results* (see note 1), p. 325–392.

22. P.E. Damon and others, "Correlation and Chronology of the Ore Deposits in Volcanic Rocks," *US Atomic Energy Commission Annual Report*, No. C00-689-76 (1967).

23. Reynolds and others, *Compilation of Radiometric Age Determinations in Arizona* (Tucson, AZ: Arizona Bureau of Geology and Mineral Technology, 1986), p. 14, 16.

24. Andrew A. Snelling, "Isochron Discordances and the Role of Inheritance in Mixing of Radioisotopes in the Mantle and Crust," in *Radioisotopes: Results* (see note 1), p. 393–524.

similarly derived for the stratigraphically lower Cardenas Basalts likewise be fictitious? And how does one know? How could you know?

Problems with the plateau basalts are magnified when a technique employing the ratio of lead isotopes is used. Fifty-five specimens were analyzed[25] from numerous lava flows throughout the plateau. When the lead-lead results were plotted, they yielded an isochron age of 2.6 ± 0.21 billion years! This is the oldest figure ever derived, yet it is for the youngest suite of rocks! These specimens came from numerous sources; but they plotted along a straight isochron line, attesting to their similar time of origin, usually thought to demonstrate the acceptability of results. Dr. Austin reproduced this trend.[26] Surely fictitious isochrons are real, but neither they nor the accepted isochrons seem to be giving the true age of the rocks in question.

It must be admitted that rocks lower in the strata column usually (but as we have seen, not always) date older than rocks found higher in the column. The true ages are not discerned, even when the results are selectively reported; but something is going on which is not yet fully understood by creationists or evolutionists. Uniformitarians, in their zeal to establish the old-earth position, misinterpret this enigmatic array of isotopes as evidence for great age. When the RATE scientists attacked this issue, they found that, in general, those isotopes which decay by emitting an alpha particle (i.e., U-Pb; Sm-Nd) tend to yield older ages than those isotopes that decay by emitting a beta particle (i.e., K-Ar; Rb-Sr). Furthermore, those isotopes that are heavier, thus having a larger atomic number, also tend to give greater dates than the lighter isotopes. Following the lead of RATE, a number of creationists are attacking this problem, and more answers may be forthcoming; but until then, surely the Bible-believing Christian need not be intimidated by radioisotope dating.

Age of Meteorites/Earth

Over the years, estimates of earth's age have varied dramatically. It was "proven" to be about 2 billion years old in the 1930s, but has more than doubled in recent decades, as radioisotope techniques were employed. The accepted age for the earth now rests in the neighborhood of 4.6 billion years. From where did this number come? Obviously, it came from some form of radioisotope technique, but what rock was dated? What rock was here at the formation of the earth, such that it could give the earth's age?[27]

Theories on the formation of the earth vary; but all (except special creation) hold that the earth was at one time, either during or after its formation, a molten fireball. No solid material was present. Whatever rocks were present in those early days would have undergone intense metamorphism, so that no dating effort could be certain of anything before the alteration. The oldest known earth rocks are now claimed to be up to 3.8 billion years or so. So where did the 4.6 billion years come from?

The answer? Meteorites — rocks that fall from the sky. Sometimes these meteorites date at 4.6 billion years or so, usually when the age is obtained by the lead-lead isochron method.[28] This age is then transferred to the earth.

Theories on the origin of the solar system propose that the sun and its planets condensed out of interstellar stardust at about the same time. Meteorites are thought by most to be remnants of either "planetesimals" that slammed together to form planets or of a planet that broke up after coalescing. Therefore, meteorites are of the same age as the earth. To date a meteorite is to date the earth, or so it is claimed. Now, obviously, some things are being assumed here, things that are not known.

A Meteorite Called Allende

A meteorite that has received much attention is a stony meteorite called Allende *(a-yen-day)*. This extraterrestrial rock has perhaps been studied more than any other rock on earth. Numerous radioisotope techniques have been employed in determining its age, but it is the lead-lead dating result which has yielded the date of 4.6 billion years for the meteorite, and thus for the earth. But what does this meteorite really tell us? Do the different determinations agree? As you might suspect, not at all.

25. J.E. Everson, "Regional Variation in the Lead Isotopic Characteristics of Late Cenozoic Basalts from the Southwestern United States," (Ph. D. diss., California Institute of Technology, 1979), p. 454; C. Alibert and others, "Isotope and Trace Element Geochemistry of Colorado Plateau Volcanics," *Geochimica et Cosmochimica Acta* 50 (1986): p. 2735–2750.

26. S.A. Austin, "Isotopic and Trace Element Analysis of Hypersthene-normative Basalts from the Quaternary of Uinkaret Plateau, Western Grand Canyon, Arizona," *Geologic Society of America Abstracts with Programs* 24 (1992): p. A26 1; Austin, *Grand Canyon: Monument,* p. 125–126.

27. Stephen G. Brush, "The Age of the Earth in the Twentieth Century," *Earth Sciences History* 8, no. 2 (1989): p. 170–182. See for a good history of dating efforts.

28. Faure, *Principles of Isotope Geology*, p. 311–12. See for a review of this evidence and technique.

Perhaps the most extensive dating effort[29] studied the results from several radioisotope methods, including Pb-206/U-238, Pb-207/U-235, Pb-207/Pb-206, Pb-208/Th 232, and Sr-87/Sr-86. For each of these methods (and others which did not give meaningful data), the authors identified the ages of the whole rock, as well as at least 50 different inclusions (mineral grains of a particular chemical composition) and of the rock matrix itself.

The U-Th-Pb suite of tests on the inclusions yielded much scatter, from 3.91 billion years to 11.7 billion years. The matrix results varied from 4.49 to 16.49 billion years, with 13 out of 18 ages being impossibly high, even though estimates of the amount of original daughter isotopes were subtracted out. This subtraction amount was based on the lead content of the mineral troilite (iron sulfide) in yet another important meteorite, the Cañon Diablo meteorite. No isochron was possible.

The Cañon Diablo troilite has been accepted as containing a representative ratio of radiogenic to non-radiogenic lead, and thus establishes the amount of original daughter material to be subtracted from the total. Of course, the individual atoms are identical and cannot be differentiated by simple inspection. The theoretical amount of original daughter material in all meteorites is simply accepted from the Cañon Diablo troilite ratio, the correct ratio in turn determined by its concordance with the accepted age of the solar system.

But the fact remains, there is a seeming excess of lead in meteorites, or a deficiency of uranium and thorium. Typically, there is too much lead for it to have been derived from decay of the uranium and/or thorium present. Thus, some estimate of the original daughter material must be made. Once done, meteorites still tend to give excessively high ages.

For Allende, the Rb-Sr suite of techniques yielded differing results. (The Sr-87/Sr-86 was the only technique discussed in the report — the results of other methods were deemed too unreliable and were not supplied.) The inclusions yielded ages from 0.70 billion years to 4.49 billion years, with most being significantly lower than expected. The matrix ages were reported as 4.60 and 4.84 billion years, even though the best estimates of original daughter material were taken into account. No isochron was possible.

Although the dating of mineral inclusions is considered standard procedure and the results accepted on many occasions, it is conceivable that discrepancies might arise. Thus, the whole-rock model age would take precedence. As can be seen from the following table, no agreement was reached, with many other values being greater than the assumed age of the solar system — an impossibility.

In the discussion portion of the article by Tatsumoto and coworkers, the authors gave reasons for the varied results,

29. M. Tatsumoto, D. Unrch, and G. Desborough, "U-Th-Pb and Rb-Sr Systemetics of Allende and U-Th-Pb systematics of Orgueil," *Geochemica et Cosmochimica Acta* 40 (1976): p. 616–634.

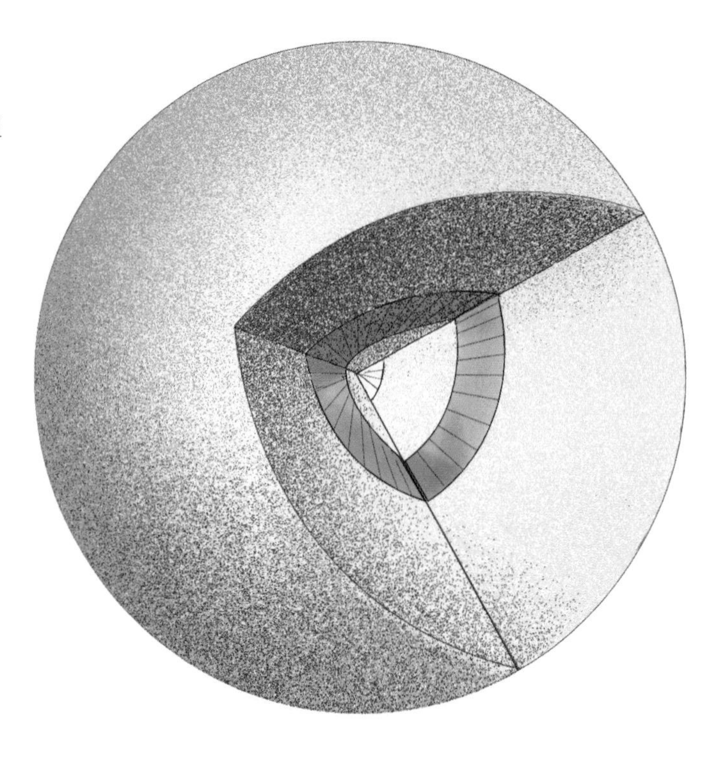

A radioactive inclusion produces damage in the form of concentric spheres, with each diameter recognizable as the decay of a particular isotope.

including anomalous concentrations in the original solar nebula, removal or enrichment of certain isotopes by later disturbance events, movement of mobile elements Rb and Pb from the matrix into the inclusions, large variations of isotope ratios in the individual inclusions, ratios affected by impact on earth, and original isolation from the solar nebula. If the results do not fit, explain them away! But how could a 20th-century investigator possibly know what was happening in an isolated corner of the solar nebula five billion years ago? How could anyone have confidence in the few dates accepted? Perhaps they too are contaminated, and the true date is unknown. As it stands, the dates are accepted or rejected based on their agreement with an unproven and unprovable idea about solar-system formation. The scatter, which is very real, seems more impressive and important than the forced agreement with the theory.

"Age" of Allende

Pb-207/Pb-206	=	4.50 billion years
Pb-207/U-235	=	5.57 billion years
Pb-206/U-238	=	8.82 billion years
Pb-208/T-232	=	10.4 billion years
Sr-87/Sr-86	=	4.48 billion years

Other investigators conducted a potassium-argon based effort of Allende, but it yielded no help. This study of the same mineral inclusions gave apparent ages averaging 5.29 billion

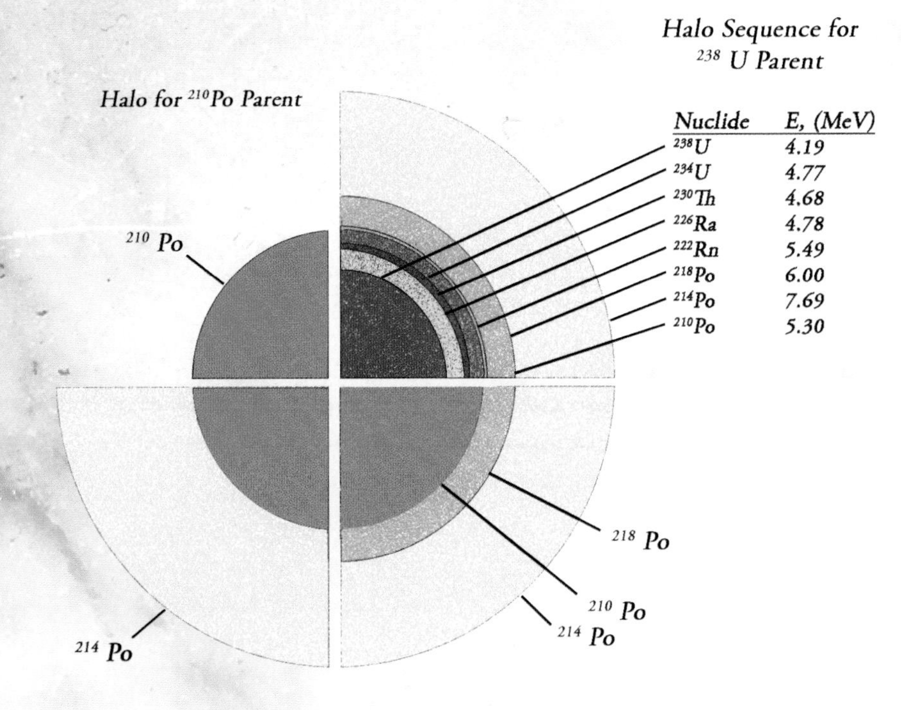

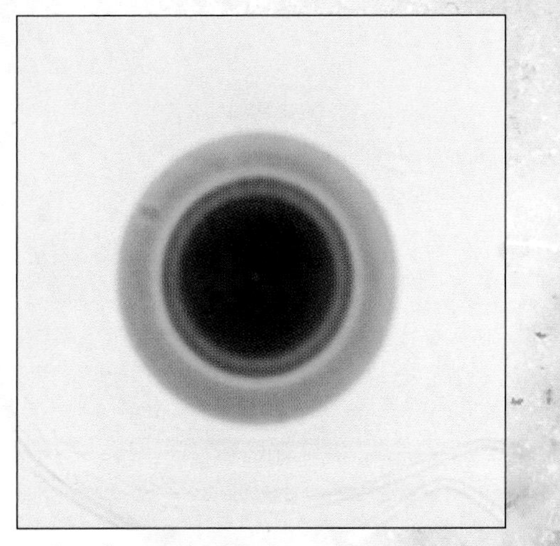

Pleochroic halo showing several individual rings

years, again older than the assumed age of the solar system.[30] The suspected cause is potassium loss in the solar nebula.

At the very least, we can say that the isotope ratios of meteorites do not demonstrate conclusively that the earth's age can be known. Even some evolutionists are inclined to agree. Note this concluding quotation:

> We suspect that the lack of concordance [scatter in the data] may result in some part from the choice of isotope ratios for primitive lead [the original amount assumed for daughter material based on the Cañon Diablo troilite], rather than from lead gain or uranium loss. It therefore follows that the whole of the classic interpretation of the meteorite lead isotope data is in doubt, and that the radiometric estimates of the age of the earth are placed in jeopardy.[31]

But there is also much selectivity in reporting the data. Many results are discarded, but to the extent that "independent" methods show similar isotope ratios compatible with a young age; this could mean that the universe is all the same young age, all created at about the same time, fully functional, with a God-ordained "very good" array of isotopes.

Radiohalos

Consider another very intriguing piece of evidence from radioactive elements. In recent years, creationist physicist Robert Gentry called our attention to an unusual phenomenon, which he interpreted as pointing to the instantaneous creation of granites. His conclusions have been published in scientific journals and in his book *Creation's Tiny Mystery.*[32] The RATE group confirmed his findings and greatly extended them, and thereby answered many unanswered questions.

Scientists have long known that when each particular radioactive atom decays, it gives off energy at a characteristic level. For an alpha decay episode, this energy burst damages the mineral matrix in which the atom rests; and the size of the damaged zone reflects the level of energy released. Because uranium atoms (for purposes of this discussion) are usually found in clusters containing billions of atoms (which themselves occupy a very tiny point of space) within certain minerals, the decay of these unstable atoms over time produces a sphere of damage around the radio-centers.

As mentioned before, uranium decays to lead through a series of intermediate steps, each of which has its own characteristic energy level upon decay. If the tiny uranium-containing crystal resides in a well-formed crystalline structure, as is common in the mineral biotite (a form of mica frequently found in granitic rocks), the damage will appear as a series of concentric spheres around the cluster, corresponding to a series of concentric circles, which are visible when one views a slice of the sphere through a microscope. These circles have come to be known as pleochroic halos, or radiohalos. Each element has its own characteristic halo size produced by its distinctive alpha decay energy. By observing the particular set of halos, one can deduce the identity of the original radioactive element and the intermediate daughter elements it produced.

Several of these intermediate decay steps have extremely short half-lives. For instance, when radon-222 (half-life of

30. Heinrich D. Holland, *The Chemical Evolution of the Atmosphere and Ocean* (Princeton, NJ: Princeton University Press, 1984), p. 6. See for a discussion of the study by T. Kirsten, 1980.

31. N. Gale and others, "Uranium-Lead Chronology of Chondrite Meteorites," *Nature (Physical Sciences)* 240, (November 20, 1972): p. 57.

32. Robert Gentry, *Creation's Tiny Mystery*, 2nd ed. (Knoxville, TN: Earth Science Associates, 1988).

Conventional age of rock	Number of rock samples (Number of slides prepared)	Number of halos counted				
		Po-210	Po-214	Po-218	U-238	Th-232
Tertiary 1 Ma–65 Ma	8(400)	9	0	0	2	0
	Average number of radiohalos per slide = 0.028					
Paleozoic-Mesozoic 70 Ma–490Ma	70(3,485)	15,847	1,350	426	11.092	286
	Average = 8.32					
Precambrian 600Ma–2,900Ma	31(1,510)	1,788	23	2	510	3
	Average = 1.54					
Metamorphic Rocks 100Ma–1,750Ma	21(1,051)	8,999	53	11	2,971	3
	Average = 11.45					

3.82 days) changes through alpha decay into polonium-218 (half-life of 3.05 minutes), it almost immediately changes again, into lead-214. Likewise, when bismuth-214 (half-life of 29.7 minutes) changes through beta decay into polonium-214 (half-life of 1.6×10^{-4} seconds), the polonium-214 rapidly changes into lead-210. Furthermore, when bismuth-210 (half-life, 5 days) decays through beta decay into polonium-210 (half-life, 138 days), the polonium-210 rather quickly reaches the stable lead-206 form. Obviously, the atom does not linger very long in any of these three polonium states before it decays into the next isotope in the decay chain.

Amazingly, the set of halos characteristic of polonium isotopes is sometimes found without the apparently more slowly forming uranium halos, showing no evidence of parent uranium but only parent polonium. There never was uranium present at these precise locations. Somehow, the short-lived polonium must have gathered there before quickly decaying, producing these polonium halos.

Granite is conventionally thought to require many thousands of years to cool from originally melted rocks in order for its several types of mineral crystals to form, although the individual minerals, especially when concentrated, can rather quickly solidify once the temperature drops to the crucial points. Even pegmatite, a coarser-grained version of granite, frequently occurring as veins within granite, does not require an appreciable length of time to solidify. Since polonium isotopes have such very short half-lives, it would be incredibly unlikely for the polonium halos to occur by themselves with no evidence of their parent material. There are only two possibilities. Either the granites were instantaneously created in a hardened condition with polonium inclusions present, which subsequently decayed to form halos; or somehow the polonium or its ancestors migrated to the decay centers in a very short period of time, after which the decay occurred and the halos were preserved.

The first possibility was fully falsified by the RATE investigations.[33] Many of the granite hosts of the halos obviously formed sometime after creation and are even found amid sediments deposited by the great Flood. Somehow the concentrations of polonium gathered after granite solidification, all the while decaying rapidly. The granite must have been solid when the polonium decayed, in order for the crystals to bear evidence of the zones of damage, and it must not have been heated to an elevated temperature after the spheres of damage formed, else the heating would have erased the halos. The granite cools too slowly, and the polonium decays too rapidly to accomplish this in any scenario other than extremely rapid implacement and cooling, or so it apparently seems. Evolutionists have come to call this a tiny mystery.

What is the solution to the mystery? Obviously, we cannot know for sure. God has not given us all the details. But the polonium halos do exist in abundance and must be explained. The only hope for a true interpretation necessitates going back to Genesis for our basic model. Sticky points include the fact that all of these polonium halos are of the element polonium, which is in the decay chain of naturally occurring uranium and thorium atoms. Also, why are fully formed uranium halos almost always found in the same crystals as the nearby polonium halos? The full uranium halos, which consist of numerous rings reflecting the multiple step decay chain, would seem to take a much longer time to form.

33. Andrew A. Snelling, "Radiohalos in Granites," in *Radioisotopes: Results* (see note 1), p. 101–208.

The RATE investigators, led in this project by Dr. Andrew Snelling, who performed yeoman's work, collected scores of granite samples from many locations on several continents, and counted halos in each one. Some samples were from Precambrian sources, considered to date from creation week. Paleozoic and Mesozoic rocks were certainly from the Flood, while Tertiary rocks were likely post-Flood. The RATE team found abundant halos in rocks from every designation except the Tertiary (post-Flood). As seen in Table 3.3, by far the largest concentrations were from Flood rocks. Fully developed uranium halos, which require long periods of time to form at today's decay rates, were always found near the rapidly formed polonium halos. On first blush, finding the two together seems impossible, for they require incompatible histories. The only sequence of events that explains the facts is rapid movements of radioactive atoms coupled with accelerated decay episodes.

At the center of each U-238 halo now there is still a crystal containing uranium and lead atoms. But at the center of the polonium halos are empty holes, evidence that it was only a liquid or gas that migrated there. One of the intermediate decay chain isotopes is a mobile, inert gas. Also, polonium is known to have an attraction for sulfur and chlorine, and usually traces of sulfur and chlorine were found nearby too, in the mineral hosting these halos. Evidently the migrating fluids and radioactive gas were pulled into central locations (or centers) where they subsequently decayed.

Subsurface, fast-moving hydrothermal (hot water) fluids are known to exist within cooling granite. In all likelihood, it was by this mechanism that atoms of radioactive elements were moved into place as they were decaying. Remember, one of the gaseous intermediate links can easily migrate, and note that all radiohalos are found along cleavage (splitting) planes within crystals and/or near tiny fractures in the minerals. These migrating fluids may have also played an important role in conveying excess heat away from the rock. This stunning evidence from radiohalos invalidates two of the assumptions of radioisotope dating: that of a closed system and that of constant decay rates. It also partially solves the heat problem.

As encouraging as these findings are, let me not leave the impression that radioisotope dating has been overturned. It has been called into question, flaws in its foundation exposed, and its results shown to be inconsistent. In short, it is in trouble, but it is still a very formidable concept in the minds of many. Much research needs to be done and is being done at ICR and elsewhere.

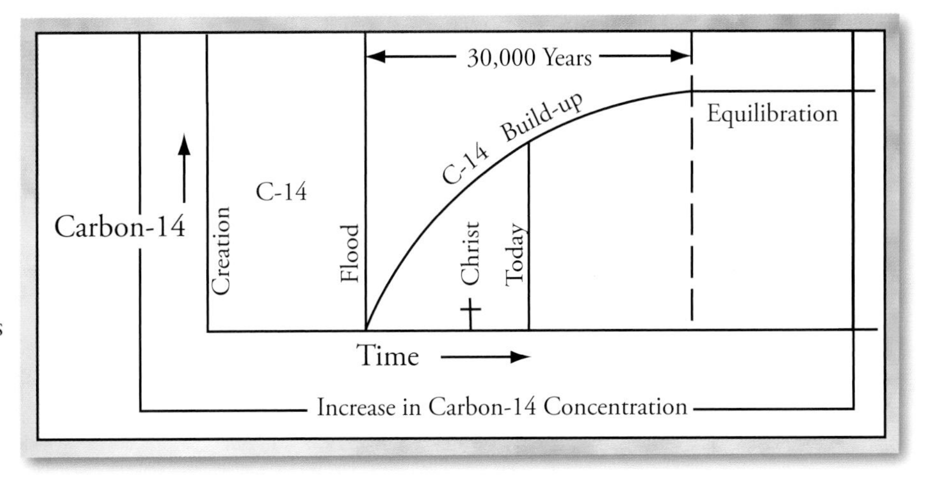

Carbon-14

Many people have the mistaken notion that the carbon-14 dating technique places the age of the earth at billions of years and various rocks at millions of years. But, in reality, the carbon-14 method is valid only for "recent" times. Carbon-14's half-life is only 5,730 years, meaning that much decay has occurred within human history. After ten half-lives or so (57,300 years), there should be essentially no C-14 left. Even the most devoted advocate would not claim that C-14 dating has any relevance beyond about 100,000 years before the present time, and its inaccuracies are well-known. It decays so rapidly that even if the entire mass of the observable universe was packed with carbon-14 atoms, after just 1.5 million years there would not be a single C-14 atom left. If any C-14 is present in a specimen it must be younger than that.

Thankfully, the carbon-14 technique does have some application in the most recent few thousand years. If the standard assumptions are valid (i.e., that the rate of carbon-14 decay is constant, that there have been no additions or deletions of parent or daughter materials in a specimen, and that the amount of the daughter material present at the start is known), then the method can perhaps tell us something about the specific dates of historical artifacts. Its only real application is in archaeology, not in geology.

First, know that carbon-14 dating is only applicable for carbon-based material. It is not helpful in dating inorganic rocks, but, rather, carbon-based, once-living remains such as bone, plant material, or fleshy parts. For instance, a tree buried by a lava flow can be dated by C-14, but the hardened lava itself cannot be dated by this method.

Next, a short description of the concept of C-14 dating is in order. Carbon-14 is formed when nitrogen-14 interacts with a cosmic ray-produced neutron in the upper atmosphere. This rate of formation is known. This radioactive isotope of carbon comprises only a minor percentage of total carbon. Only one atom of carbon-14 exists per one trillion atoms of stable carbon. This ratio of radioactive carbon (C-14) to stable carbon (C-12) can be measured in the environment today. The ratio changes as C-14 decays back to nitrogen-14. It would only take about 30,000 years for the rate of C-14

Bristlecone pine tree

that the C-14 concentration is currently increasing. Thus, the carbon-14 age must be adjusted, using a calibration curve derived by dating objects of known age.

Unfortunately, many times even adjusted C-14 dates on objects do not agree with historically derived ages. I remember talking once with a famous archaeologist from the University of Pennsylvania doing an excavation in the country of Turkey. He had discovered an ancient tomb with wooden timbers. I asked if he had sent timber samples off for dating through the carbon-14 method. His reply and candid admission shocked me. He had, of course, sent samples off for dating, but claimed he would never believe anything that came back from a carbon-14 lab. Nor was he aware of any archaeologist in the world who would accept such dates. If the date agreed with what he knew it should be historically, then the data would be published; if not, it would be ignored. He was obliged to carbon-date artifacts to keep his grant money coming, and he always did so; but he did not trust the method or its results.

buildup to equal the rate of its decay, so it is usually assumed that the atmosphere must be in carbon-14 equilibrium, with equal amounts of C-14 being formed and decaying.

Both forms of carbon are found distributed throughout the atmosphere, oceans, and earth. When a C-14 atom becomes part of a carbon dioxide molecule, it enters the food chain, first through plants, then into animals that eat the plants, and then into carnivores. Once the plant or animal dies, it ceases to interact with the environment by breathing, eating, and/or absorbing. Thus, it ceases to take in the normal ratio of C-12 to C-14 atoms, and the unstable C-14 atoms begin to decay back into N-14, thus changing the C-12/C-14 ratio over time. By measuring this ratio at any time after death, one can get an idea of when the plant or animal ceased taking in C-14 from the outside and through this derive the time since its death.

Many processes, such as ground-water leaching, bacterial action, etc., can alter the concentrations of the parent or daughter material; and so care must be taken, and usually is taken, to date only those specimens that give no appearance of having been contaminated or leached. Carbon-14 decays at a rather stable rate and has been further calibrated by comparing its results with historically known dates; but the assumption of the original concentration is once again a weakness of the technique.

Remember, it would take only 30,000 years or so to produce an equilibrium state between C-14 formation and decay, starting from an atmosphere with no C-14. Normally, the assumption is made that such an equilibrium has existed throughout the past, since most think the earth's atmosphere is much older than 30,000 years. This assumption of equilibrium provides a value for the concentration of C-14 at death; however, this assumption has now been disproved. It is now known to all investigators that C-14 is not in equilibrium,

On another occasion, I was debating an evolutionist at the national convention of the American Archaeological Society when dating processes came up. I chided the archaeologists present by insisting that they should be honest and admit that they never trust carbon-14 dates. There was nervous laughter throughout the audience, but no one even attempted to contradict me.

This total distrust of the method is, of course, an overstatement. There are many who do take the results from carbon-14 dating seriously. But only on very rare occasions does anyone take it as definitive, particularly when the date cannot be verified by another technique, usually a historical dating method.

The salvation of the carbon-14 technique has supposedly come through calibration by dendrochronology (tree-ring dating). By comparing the C-14/C-12 ratios in tree rings stretching back into the past, a calibration curve can be drawn. This is believed to give the researcher information on the precise carbon inventory in the atmosphere at the time the tree-ring formed and, therefore, makes possible the dating of other objects that died that year which presumably possessed the same C-14/C-12 ratio at death.

The technique is very precise and persuasive, but it also has a serious weakness — one that has not been resolved involving the reliability of dendrochronological methods as developed by researchers. The oldest living tree is thought to be on the order of 4,500 years old, yet advocates claim tree-ring chronology extends roughly twice that. Obviously, since no single tree lived throughout the entire time, dendrochronologists must match up tree-ring patterns from trees whose life spans are thought to have overlapped in order to extend the series far back into the past. This, of course, is fraught with difficulty and subjective analyses. Even trees living today in the same forest do not always show the same tree-ring patterns. Variations are seen from tree to tree due to distance from water source, prevailing sunlight direction, nutrients in the soil, storm patterns, etc. Investigations look for shorter sequences within the pattern thought to be unique, and thus can be used for correlation. Much care is taken, but problems still exist. The overlapping sequences are never perfect.

> Among the pines [the bristlecone] is, if anything, even more undependable than the Junipers. . . . We have many cores from bristlecones growing in the White Mountains of California, east of the Sierra Nevadas, at altitudes of 10,000 feet, where the rainfall is low and erratic. There are also a number of cores from bristlecones growing at high altitudes in southwestern Utah and on the San Francisco Peaks at Flagstaff, Arizona. Comparison of charts of measured rings shows no similarity whatever.[34]

> The construction of a definitive bristlecone chronology was, however, not without its difficulties. The trees grow extremely slowly and examples showing 40 rings per centimeter are common. With such narrow-ringed material, years of particular stress result in rings being locally absent. In fact, in any one core as many as 5 percent of the total number of rings may be missing. In order to overcome this problem there was a strong need for multiple cores and for replication between trees.[35]

Both the dendrochronology and the C-14 scales depend very much on at least pseudo-uniformity in the environment throughout the time spans covered. This, of course, would be impossible, given the biblical Flood. If the Flood really occurred the way the Bible says, no tree could have survived. Furthermore, the Flood would have drastically altered the carbon inventory in the world as it laid down the vast limestone deposits (calcium carbonate), coal deposits, and oil shales. At the time of the Flood, great amounts of carbon were removed from the atmosphere and oceans and were no longer available for ingestion or absorption into animals or plants, thus destroying any semblance of uniformity in nature and also any hope of a calibration curve going back before the Flood. Nor would such a calibration be possible for the first few centuries following the Flood, during which time things re-stabilized. As mentioned, the carbon-14 built up in the atmosphere has not yet even reached equilibrium with its decay.

Ancient tomb with wood timbers

We do not know all that happened to the available carbon at the time of the Flood and the years soon after. Nor do we know precisely what happened to the environment. In all likelihood, there were intense weather patterns and numerous volcanic events for hundreds of years. It would not be surprising if unstable and extreme weather conditions, particularly during the Ice Age that followed Noah's flood, might have caused numerous tree rings to develop in any one year. Furthermore, extensive volcanism late in the Flood and after the Flood could have released much primordial CO_2 in the atmosphere that would have had little C-14. Trees incorporating into themselves this unnaturally low ratio of C-14/C-12 in the atmosphere would have an elevated C-14 age. These conditions, combined with the magnetic field struggling to regain equilibrium and causing unpredictable fluctuations in cosmic ray influx, could very well result in a varying rate of C-14 formation. Cross correlation between ring arrays from different trees would be impossible.

C-14 in "Ancient" Rocks

But the story does not stop there. Over the years there has been a growing awareness that "ancient" carbon-bearing rock formations contain some C-14. According to conventional dating methods, they are so old they should be carbon-14 dead. For instance, coal is essentially made of

34. Harold S. Gladwin, "Dendrochronology, Radiocarbon and Bristlecones," *Anthropological Journal of Canada* 14, no. 4 (1976): p. 5.
35. M.G.L. Baillie, *Tree-Ring Dating and Archaeology* (Chicago, IL: University of Chicago Press, 1982), p. 36.

Table of C-14 Results			
Coal Location & Geologic Era	Coal Seam	Conventional Geologic Age (Millions of Years)	C-14/C-12 (pMC ± 1σ)
Cenozoic			
Texas	Bottom	34–55	0.30 ± 0.03
North Dakota	Beulah	34–55	0.20 ± 0.02
Montana	Pust	34–55	0.27 ± 0.02
Mesozoic			
Utah	Lower Sunnyside	65–145	0.35 ± 0.03
Utah	Blind Canyon	65–145	0.10 ± 0.03
Arizona	Green	65–145	0.18 ± 0.02
Paleozoic			
Kentucky	Kentucky # 9	300–311	0.46 ± 0.03
Pennsylvania	Lykens Valley #2	300-311	0.13 ± 0.02
Pennsylvania	Pittsburgh	300–311	0.19 ± 0.02
Illinois	Illinois #6	300-311	0.29 ± 0.03
Average percent modern carbon for the ten coal samples is 0.247 ± 0.025			

carbon. Limestone's chemical formula is CaCO3, or calcium carbonate. When limestone undergoes heat and pressure it becomes marble. In each case, the formations are thought to be far too old to have C-14 remaining, but over the years, investigators have noted C-14 present, particularly in coal. The scientists were not actually "dating" the coal, for they thought they already knew the age, but on occasion they conducted isotopic analyses and listed carbon-14 as a minor constituent.

Previously, the device used to determine atomic makeup lacked the ability to identify extremely small quantities of C-14 in older specimens. In recent years, highly sensitive accelerator mass spectrometer (AMS) tests have routinely discovered the presence of C-14. Many subsequent tests were run in an attempt to find out how C-14 "contamination" had taken place. They never found a contamination source, but their published results are instructive.

In each case, when "ancient" sources containing carbon were analyzed, they were found to contain C-14, even though they should have been C-14 dead. Samples from all layers of the geologic column, from Precambrian marble and graphite to Paleozoic limestone, wood, and even Mesozoic dinosaur bone were all found to contain C-14. Typically they dated from 30,000–60,000 years, using uniformitarian calibration curves, not "too old to measure" as was expected.

The RATE team collected all the published data and verified the ones on coal by doing their own tests. They acquired samples of numerous coal seams from North America, gathered by government researchers in such a way as to minimize contamination and maintained in pristine condition. These samples were subjected to AMS analysis; and in each case, the "very old" specimens (varying from 50–300 million years old in conventional thinking) contained C-14. Every coal seam, the ones ICR dated and the ones others dated, contained short-lived C-14, indicating they were only a few thousand years old at most![36] (See chart.)

Couple these findings with results revealing C-14 in various fossils, from whalebone to shells of invertebrate animals to foraminifera (tiny sea fossils). Each specimen was thought to be of great age, but each dated only a few thousand years old. Nothing that was studied was C-14 dead; and therefore, no specimen was as much as 100,000 years old! This fact is unthinkable for an evolutionist.

Recently it has been determined that numerous dinosaur bones have retained their boney material. Some even have parts that are soft and pliable. These have not been carbon dated by their evolutionary discoverers, but I hope they soon are.

36. John R. Baumgardner, "C-14 Evidence for a Recent Global Flood and a Young Earth," in *Radioisotopes: Results* (see note 1), p. 587–630.

Evidences of Accelerated Decay Discovered by RATE

- **Helium atoms trapped in zircon crystals**
  - **Rock dated at 1. 5 billion years showed evidence of 6,000 years of diffusion**
- **Uranium and polonium halos found together**
  - **In rocks of all ages, including Flood rocks**
  - **Rapidly moving fluids transported atoms to decay centers where they quickly formed halos.**
- **Ancient carbon-bearing rocks contain C-14**

However, over the last several decades, some creationists have dated dinosaur bones, ancient wood, etc., but the newer AMS was not yet in use. I worked for several years documenting dinosaur footprints and other markings in the Glen Rose limestone of central Texas. This limestone formation, which is thought to be 100 million years old, contains abundant wood fragments. Over the years, the other researchers and I dated several specimens, and each one dated only a few thousand years old.[37] While these data are not of the same caliber as the more recent AMS findings, each specimen dates only a few thousand years old! No specimens were carbon-14 dead. The results are compatible only with a recent origin of the strata. And since the layer of rock studied covers much of the American southeast and give evidence of rapid deposition in order to preserve the footprints, the great flood of Noah's day comes to mind as a likely depositional event.

37. John Morris, *Tracking Those Incredible Dinosaurs* (Nashville, TN: Thomas Nelson Publishers, 1980).

Diamonds: A Creationist's Best Friend

There is another form of carbon that RATE studied — one that had never been dated. Diamonds are a crystalline form of carbon, thought to have formed in earth's earliest days under extreme conditions. Because of their supposed great age, inorganic origin, and complete impermeability, no one had ever even suggested they might contain C-14. Until RATE, that is. Under this program, diamonds from several varied sources were obtained and tested. Once again, each specimen contained measurable C-14 and dated just thousands of years old.

Country of Origin	Diamond Location	C-14/C-12 (pMc ± 1σ)
Botswana, south-central Africa	Orapa mine	0.06 ± 0.03
	Orapa mine	0.03 ± 0.03
	Lethakane mine	0.04 ± 0.03
	Lethakane mine	0.07 ± 0.02
South Africa	Kimberley mine	0.02 ± 0.03
Guinea, West Africa	Kankan placer	0.03 ± 0.03
Namibia, southwest Africa (six diamond samples)	Placer deposits	0.31 ± 0.02
		0.17 ± 0.02
		0.09 ± 0.02
		0.13 ± 0.03
		0.04 ± 0.02
		0.07 ± 0.02
Average percent modern carbon for the 12 diamonds is 0.09 ± 0.025		

this period), and C-14 began to build up once again in the upper atmosphere. The biblical Book of Job was written during this chaotic period and it often mentions ice and snow in the northern regions, (e.g., Job 38:22–23, 29–30) as well as cave men (Job 30:1-8) and dinosaurs (Job 40:15–41:30). We have yet to understand all the ramifications.

Dr. Larry Vardiman of ICR is researching similar unsettled conditions recorded in ice cores extracted from the ice sheets of Greenland and Antarctica. Glacial ice forms as excessive

Consider the options. Was there contamination? Impossible, for diamonds are the hardest natural substance, completely impenetrable. Could the C-14 have spontaneously formed from N-14 within the diamond? Perhaps, but this has never been observed to happen and demands special conditions. Furthermore, even if C-14 formed, it would be subject to spontaneous decay, just like all C-14 atoms. In just a few half-lives it would all be gone. Is there a continuing source of radiation that would continually produce more C-14 internally? If so, how could it last, and how could we ever date any specimens, if C-14 can spontaneously form *in situ*? Under any possible scenario, C-14 dating of anything is invalidated! It would be more reasonable if there was an episode of accelerated decay sometime recently. Can it be that the earth formed not too long ago and that diamonds that date from creation contained some C-14, and there has not yet been enough time for it all to decay? That seems to be the best option, most consistent with the data.

POST-FLOOD CATASTROPHISM

The "very good" environment in the world's beginning ceased when Adam sinned. "Cursed is the ground" as a result of what you have done (Gen. 3:17), he heard the Creator say. Nevertheless, things still functioned well until the time of the Flood when everything changed. The fountains of the great deep spewed forth their contents and the windows of heaven opened. The created equilibrium was no more. It no doubt took several hundred years for the earth to settle back down into the relative equilibrium we now enjoy. In those transition years, earth's magnetic field fluctuated, weather patterns varied wildly (the Ice Age occurred in

Assumptions of Radioisotope Dating versus Reality	
Closed System	**RATE discovered many ways by which a rock remains open to contamination. Steam generated by the hot rock may be more efficient at moving isotopes than ground water. Discordant dates were common.**
Initial Conditions	**RATE collected dates from many historic lava flows. Virtually all of them indicated daughter products were present at the start.**
Constant Decay Rate	**RATE discovered three clear indicators that decay rates had changed in the past.** **• Helium produced by uranium decay was extensive but had not had time to escape.** **• Radiohalos of short-lived polonium were found adjacent to uranium halos which under today's decay rates would require a long time to form.** **• Dating results from multiple methods on the same rock show alpha-decay accelerated more than beta-decay episodes, as did heavier isotopes.**

Glaciologists taking ice cores in Sweden. Individual storm patterns are often misinterpreted as annual layers.

snow accumulates and compacts tightly into ice. Often the ice contains horizontal bands looking somewhat like tree rings, which uniformitarian researchers claim represent many winter/summer patterns. If each couplet is interpreted as one year, the total time indicated extends back for tens of thousands of years. But Dr. Vardiman's research indicates that the evidence better points to a time of intense volcanism and erratic storm patterns for only several hundred years, with frequent dynamic storms creating many pseudo-winter/summer patterns each year. This, of course, would be the Ice Age, caused by the Genesis flood. Evidently, the earth's processes were so destabilized by the global flood cataclysm that the earth took several hundred years to restabilize.[38] The Ice Age occurred during this time. What would this environmental crisis do to trees and their tree rings?[39] Are multiple trees rings possible per year?

Some creationists have investigated the tree-ring and carbon-14 calibration problems and have concluded[40] that even if one accepts standard tree-ring chronology, the only way to make sense out of the C-14 data is to accept a world-restructuring event no longer ago than about 12,000 B.C., which completely altered the world's carbon balance. While that date may be high, note that the C-14 data is not compatible with any sort of an old-earth model. We do not have all the answers yet, but the evidence is strongly in favor of the overall young-earth/Flood model. Research needs to continue, particularly on the tree-rings and C-14 calibration. Of all the radioisotope dating methods, carbon-14 is one of a very few which could potentially tell us something about true history. The rest have essentially little or no sensitivity below several million years.

Again, please do not get the impression that radioisotope dating has been disproved, because it often does yield results which are consistent with the standard old-earth paradigm. The make-up of the early earth and the dynamics of the Flood and the centuries following are still not completely understood, either; and until more is known, we cannot fully understand what these isotope ratios are telling us.

However, as we have seen, we can be confident that the radioisotope dating methods are not as accurate as we are told and need not be intimidating to the advocate of the

38. Michael Oard, *An Ice Age Caused by the Genesis Flood* (El Cajon, CA: ICR, 2002).
39. Larry Vardiman, *Ice Cores and the Age of the Earth* (Santee, CA: ICR, 1993). See this monograph by Dr. Vardiman.
40. Gerald Aardsma, *Carbon-14 and the Age of the Earth* (Santee, CA: ICR, 1991).

young earth. This is especially true as we recognize the basic assumptions of all such techniques, which in essence involve denial of the biblical facts of creation and the Flood. Our distrust of these methods even increases when we recognize that the methods frequently give discrepant, discordant, or fictitious dates and are frequently, if not usually, discarded.

The troubles of the radiocarbon dating method are undeniably deep and serious. Despite 35 years of technological refinement and better understanding, the underlying assumptions have been strongly challenged, and warnings are out that radiocarbon may soon find itself in a crisis situation. Continuing use of the method depends on a "fix-it-as-we-go" approach, allowing for contamination here, fractionation there, and calibration whenever possible. It should be no surprise, then, that fully half of the dates are rejected. The wonder is, surely, that the remaining half has come to be accepted.

No matter how "useful" it is, though, the radiocarbon method is still not capable of yielding accurate and reliable results. There are gross discrepancies, the chronology is uneven and relative, and the accepted dates are actually selected dates.[41]

41. Robert E. Lee, "Radiocarbon, Ages in Error," *Anthropological Journal of Canada* 19, no. 3 (1981): p. 9, 29.

Biblical Arguments for a Global Flood

The depth and duration of the Flood **— The Flood waters covered the mountains to a depth of at least the draft of Noah's ark (Gen. 7:19–20). Today's mountains in the Ararat region include Mount Ararat, which rises to 17,000 feet in elevation. The Flood lasted for a year, peaking 150 days after it started (7:11, 8:3–4), then it began to abate. A year-long mountain-covering Flood is not a local Flood.**

The physical causes for the Flood **— The Bible explains that the breaking open of "all the fountains of the great deep" and the "windows of heaven" (7:11) were the primary causes. The "deep" is the ocean; thus the "great deep" could hardly be the cause of a limited local Flood. The "windows" seem to refer to the "waters above the (atmospheric) firmament" (1:7). These were global causes, producing a global effect.**

Many expressions of the Flood's global nature **— An honest look at the Flood account uncovers an abundance of terms and phrases, each of which is best understood in a global sense. Taken together as forming the context for each other, the case is overwhelming. An abridged listing follows:**

Genesis 6 — "Multiply on the face of the earth" (v. 1). "Wickedness of man was great in the earth" (v. 5). "Made man on the earth" (v. 6). "Destroy man whom I have created from the face of the earth, both man, and beast, creeping thing and birds of the air" (v. 7; not just herds of domesticated animals as claimed). "The earth also was corrupt before God" (v. 11; how much can God observe?). "The earth was filled with violence" (v. 11); "God looked upon the earth" (v. 12). "All flesh . . . upon the earth [not just humans]" (v. 12). "The end of all flesh" (v. 13). "The earth is filled with violence" (v. 13). "Destroy them with the earth" (v. 13). "Floodwaters on the earth" (v. 17). "To destroy . . . all flesh" (v. 17). "Which is the breath of life" (v. 17; not just domesticated animals). "From under heaven" (v. 17; not just the atmosphere above Mesopotamia). "Everything that is on the earth shall die" (v. 17; animals at a distance would have been unaffected by a local Flood). "Every living thing of all flesh" (v. 19; couldn't be just Noah's herds). "To keep them alive" (v. 19). "Birds . . . to keep them alive" (v. 20; birds could certainly survive a local Flood).

Genesis 7—"To keep the species alive" (v. 3). "On the face of all the earth" (v. 3). "All living things that I have made" (v. 4). "Destroy from the face of the earth" (v. 4). "The flood of waters was upon the earth" (v. 6). "Because of the waters of the flood" (v. 7). "The waters of the flood" (v. 10).

QUESTIONS

1. List the three major assumptions of radioisotope dating and show how they compare with the potato basket illustration and your own illustration.

2. What would cause a volcanic rock of recent, known origin to date as if it were extensively old?

3. Why are the rocks commonly found in the Grand Canyon not datable using radioisotope dating methods?

4. Give a summary of the helium escape dating method proposed by the RATE Project.

5. Summarize the finding from the carbon-14 investigations through RATE.

6. The discovery of the recent apparent age of diamonds through carbon-14 is impressive. How do the three assumptions of radioisotope dating bear on the effort to date diamonds?

Chapter Six

HUMAN HISTORY AND THE YOUNG EARTH

Of all the dating techniques available to us, only a few tend to give ages on the order of millions or billions of years, namely those radioisotope dating techniques (with the exception of carbon-14) discussed previously and a few others that are not included. There are, however, many other techniques available to date the earth and its various systems, many of them based on much sounder science than radioisotope dating. Although employing the same uniformitarian assumptions critiqued in this book, the vast majority of these dating methods give maximum ages for the earth that are much too low to have allowed for evolution to occur.

All dating techniques are based on careful measurements and sound theory, but they share a common weakness in that they all employ the same uniformitarian, naturalistic assumptions inherent in radioisotope schemes, and therefore give questionable results. However, many such methods are more reliable than radioisotope schemes, even though these methods are not necessarily correct either. Rocks and other earth systems are not at all reliable for dating the earth, whether individual rocks or entire physical systems, simply because dating methods rely on unprovable assumptions which are in some instances biblically incorrect. But the methods explained in this chapter and the next involve less objectionable applications of these assumptions than radioisotope dating. They rely to a greater degree on true history — written and observed history — and are thus more reliable.

An effective debating technique is to show that the assumptions used by one's opposition lead to illogical conclusions, conclusions that even they do not like. In that spirit, we can use the set of assumptions employed by old-earth advocates and demonstrate internal inconsistencies in that way of thinking. When we do this, the weight of the evidence, even using their assumptions, points toward a young earth. Most of the evidence implies that the earth is far too young to be compatible with the evolutionary world view.

That is the key. Since the rocks themselves are not definitive as to age, the most we can hope for is to show that rocks and systems are not compatible with a particular world view. Having said that, we must acknowledge that, to some degree, the radioisotope techniques are loosely compatible with the view that the earth and its systems are millions or billions of years old, all the while recognizing that questions regarding them give us reason to distrust their conclusions. But there exists a large body of evidence that does not fit at all with

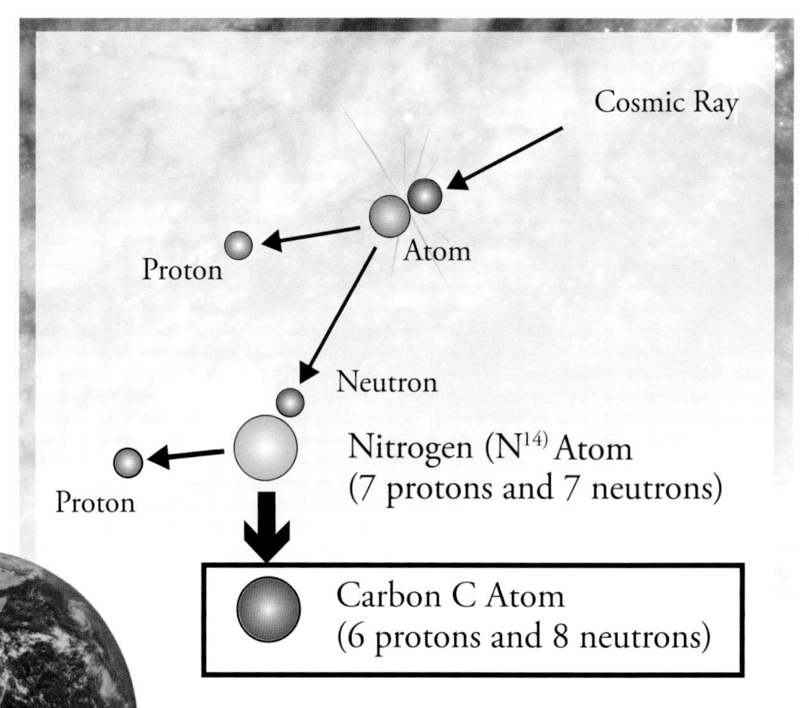

Currently C^{14}/C^{12} = 1/1,000,000,000,000
Small amount of carbon is radioactive

old-earth ideas, although derived by using uniformitarian techniques. In fact, we cannot fully disprove old-earth ideas, but we can show internal inconsistencies within that model.

Some of these alternative dating techniques point to an age of only thousands of years, while others give ages in the low millions. Remember that all these techniques involve assumptions that largely exclude the possibility of creation or Noah's flood. But even given those invalid assumptions (i.e., the same assumptions evolutionists use), the weight of the evidence is much more compatible with the young-earth position than with the old-earth position. The data cannot specifically tell us one way or the other, but the young-earth position appears to be favored. This chapter and the following chapters give several of these specific chronometers (or means of determining time) that point toward the young earth — an earth too young to have allowed for evolution. We will first look at some involving human civilization.

Recent Dating of Civilization

Several writers have advocated various dating methods, which, even if not definitive, are compelling.[1] One involves the fact that civilization dates to only five thousand or so years ago, at the beginning of written history. Evolutionary ideas, however, would insist that humans diverged from ape-like ancestors some three million years ago and through a gradual increase in culture developed into Stone Age people and then Bronze Age, Iron Age, and up into the modern era. This gradual increase in technology and cultural levels should be reflected in archaeological discoveries.

In reality, this is not borne out. Archaeologists have shown that in a variety of places around the world, very advanced, modern cultures sprang up suddenly, almost simultaneously. These were complete civilizations, each possessing a complex language, sophisticated culture, agricultural knowledge, rather impressive technology, and many times a written language. These cultures were able to devise elaborate calendars and build pyramids, impressive buildings, and seagoing vessels. Most eventually lost their advanced technology, and only in the last few hundred years has mankind begun to regain it. This early technology, even more advanced in some cases than modern technology, is not what would be expected if humans had recently been beetle-browed, stoop-shouldered, long-armed knuckle-walkers, hunting and gathering for their daily food.

Yet, true history — that is, written history — relying on human observation and authentication agrees remarkably with that suggested by biblical history. According to Scripture, human culture from its very start was advanced, and humans have always been intelligent. The only claims which disagree with this perspective are those derived from the illegitimate use of dating techniques as described before, as well as from the evolutionary assumption of human development. But evidence for primitive cultures can be more easily understood in terms of isolated language groups of intelligent people, migrating away from the Tower of Babel, having been separated linguistically, and no longer having access to the broad array of technology available to other groups. "Primitive" people groups were those which totally lost their technology from misuse or hardship, and who did not compete well against larger, better-situated, and advanced language groups.

Metal spike embedded in fossilized wood in rock dated 60 million years

Anthropologists have noted remarkable similarities between the historical folklore of nearly all cultures. Hundreds of widely dispersed people groups have a similar legend of a flood, sent by God because of man's wickedness, but survived by a favored righteous family, who built a huge boat for survival which eventually landed on a high mountain. Their common themes speak of a common ancestry that alone survived the Flood and passed the story of it on to their descendants.

Less well-known are the common creation legends, again held by groups in all corners of the globe. Typically, the legends tell of a great golden age in which food was abundant, life spans were long, and the language was the same. This wonderful situation was lost due to disobedience and punishment, eventually leading to a great watery cataclysm. A smaller but not insignificant number of legends tells of a God-induced dispersion of tribes, followed by migration and reestablishment of civilization. The similarities with Genesis are obvious, and fit the thesis that all people alive today descended from Noah, and remember their legendary histories. Indeed, the creation, Fall, Flood, and dispersion are all such monumental events they would be hard to forget, and remain by having been passed down through the generations. The stories have all changed somewhat in the telling and retelling, but their essence remains. This is what we would expect if biblical history is true.

Population Statistics

Observation of the earth's population and population growth likewise supports the young earth. Given the total number of people on earth today, now over 6 billion, and the present rate of population growth of about 2 percent per year, it would take only about 1,100 years to reach the present population from an original pair. This is of the same order of magnitude as the time since Noah's flood — at least it is within the right ballpark.

1. See for example, Henry M. Morris, *Biblical Basis for Modern Science* (Green Forest, AR: Master Books, 1984), p. 414–426.

Human remains are rarely buried complete, except by purposeful burial. Fragile remains are seldom preserved.

But suppose man has been around for one million years, as evolutionists teach. If present growth rates are typical, there should be about 10^{8600} people alive today! That's 10 with 8,600 zeros following it! This number is obviously absurd, and no evolutionist would claim it to be accurate. But it is an example of uniformitarian thinking in action.

Of course, the assumption of stable population growth throughout the past might seem unreasonable because of famines, plagues, and wars. However, the last few centuries, which have seen interdependent societies, mass weaponry, and crowded cities develop, have also seen the most brutal genocides, rampant abortion rates, the worst wars, the worst famines, and the worst plagues, in which multiplied millions have died. And yet the population growth rate has not changed much.

The Fossil Record

- 95% of all fossils are marine invertebrates, mostly shellfish.
- Of the remaining 5%, 95% are algae and plant fossils (4.75%).
- 95% of the remaining 0.25% consists of the other invertebrates, including insects (0.2375%).
- The remaining 0.0125% includes all vertebrates, mostly fish. Very few land vertebrates have been found, and almost all of them consist of less than one bone. (For example, many dinosaur bone fragments have been discovered, but only about 1,200 dinosaur skeletons.) 95% of the mammal fossils were deposited during the Ice Age, following the Flood.
- Essentially all marine fossils are today found on the continents, in great fossil graveyards. There are almost no marine fossils found in the oceans.
- The fossil record is best understood as the result of a marine cataclysm that utterly annihilated the continents and land dwellers (Gen. 7:18–24; 2 Pet. 3:6).

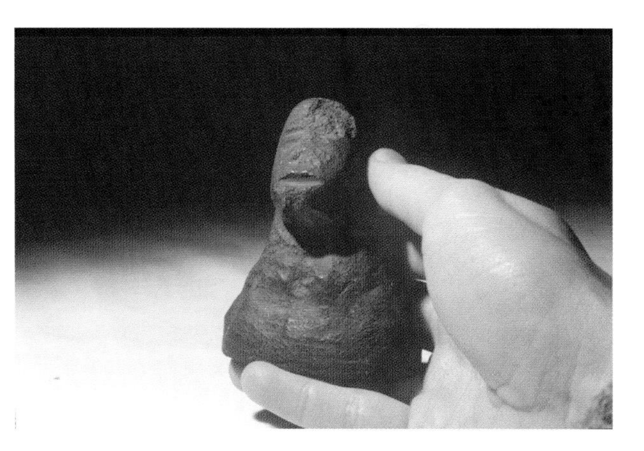

Carved bust resembling ape, found in rock dated about 50 million years

But let us assume man has been here for one million years. We can calculate the population growth rate necessary to produce today's population in that length of time from an original pair, and we find it to be only 0.002%, quite different from known measured rates throughout recorded history.

Even so, starting one million years ago, with an excessively low growth rate of 0.002%, and a present population of 6 billion, can you guess how many people would have lived and died throughout history? The number is so large it is meaningless, and it is approximately the number that could just fit inside the volume of the entire earth! If all these people lived and died, where are their bones? Why are human bones so scarce?

The numbers do not get any better when we consider only the Stone Age, in which the evolutionists tell us that Neanderthal and Cro-Magnon civilizations dominated.[2] These people groups even buried their dead, increasing the chances that bones and teeth would be preserved. If the Stone Age really lasted 100,000 years and supported a population of between 1 and 10 million individuals, they should have buried about 4 billion bodies in the uppermost soil layer! We find only a very few.

This argument applies even more so for all the other plants and animals which have comprised a much greater volume over a much longer period of time. Plant and animal remains, as well as human, decompose, are eaten, are recycled, and take unusual conditions to be preserved; but surely such conditions would sometimes occur. Actually, fossil remains are abundant, especially for marine organisms buried catastrophically in sedimentary rock units on the continent. But these trillions of fossils do not compare to the trillions of trillions that should have lived throughout the supposed billions of years. The present fossil array (consisting almost entirely of marine fossils) is more compatible with the idea that the world at one time contained abundant life, which was buried essentially simultaneously by a cataclysmic flood. Where is the fossil evidence of billions of years?

These calculations do not allow any firm conclusions. Too many conditions are subjective. But we can say that the earth and its fossil contents are quite compatible with the Flood and young-earth model, and not at all compatible with an old-earth model. Population calculations and volumetric quantities can only be made compatible with the old earth by adopting unusual conditions and unrealistic assumptions about the past.

Why Are Human Bones So Scarce?

- Fossils are formed when buried in sediment beneath moving water.
- Land vertebrates, especially mammals, bloat when dead and float in water.
- Land vertebrates dismember easily and fairly quickly disintegrate or are scavenged in a water environment.
- The processes acting during the Flood would tend to destroy soft-bodied organisms and preserve those with hard outer shells.
- Of all living things, humans are among the least in number. (Some estimate that only about 350 million people died in the flood of Noah's day, although there could have been many more.)
- The destruction of mankind was the primary goal of the Genesis flood.
- Human bodies have a low fossilization potential.
- Even if all were preserved and evenly distributed throughout the world's 350 cubic miles of Flood sediments, the chance of exposure, discovery, recognition, and reporting of even one human fossil would be extremely remote.

Lessons from the Genome

Recent research at ICR has inadvertently discovered a powerful new young-earth argument. Each plant or animal type has its own unique genetic code, the DNA. The information-laden code consists of myriads of "letters" which the rest of the cell can read and understand. The code tells each cell how to operate, grow, and reproduce. In reproduction, the DNA copies itself, causing the offspring to grow into the same kind of living thing. Alterations in the letters (mutations) pass on different information to the next generation. Evolution relies on these emerging differences to evolve the different kinds of plants or animals.

Yet the DNA code contains precise information. It is more than just order or design; it is intelligent, written information! Mutations in this written information produce "misspellings." How many misspelled words can a code absorb before it ceases to contain useful information? Eventually the organism and population of organisms will be unable to function and/or reproduce and go extinct.

In recent years the entire human genome has been decoded, and was found to consist of about 3 billion "letters" or

Bell found in coal from Pennsylvania, dated at around 250 million years old

2. See J.O. Dritt, "Man's Earliest Beginnings: Discrepancies in the Evolutionary Timetable," *Proceedings of the Second International Conference on Creationism* 1 (1991): p. 73–78.

Iron pot taken from coal seam in Oklahoma, dated at 250 million years old

nucleic acid base pairs. In 2006, scientists announced the decoding of the nearly complete chimp genome (about four billion base pairs long). It had been claimed that the human and chimp genomes were up to 99 percent similar, proving they came from a common, ape-like ancestor, and it is held that mutations in their supposed original DNA must have produced both. Careful analysis now reveals that they are much more different than claimed.

The Institute for Creation Research has inaugurated a major research effort into this potentially fruitful area. Preliminary analysis has revealed that chimp and human DNA are much more different than claimed by the evolutionary spin-doctors. Furthermore, each is rapidly accumulating mutations today. These changes in the genomes cause damage to the genome and result in birth defects, not evolution. In fact, the genomes seem to be deteriorating so rapidly that eventual extinction of both is only a matter of time.

The largely intact genomes of chimps and man imply that the creation of both was not very long ago, or neither would still exist. Thus, the evidence supports the biblical truth of recent creation. Chimps were created "after their own kind," while humans were created "in God's image." They did not descend from a common ancestor. At this writing the research has only begun, with tantalizing initial results. This may become one of the very strongest arguments for the young earth. Stay tuned.

Some Interesting Human Fossils

While the conditions for preservation of human fossils would have been rare during the Flood, it does seem possible that human artifacts might have survived. Genesis 5:22 mentions that people before the Flood employed objects made of both brass and iron. Metal implements would readily sink, even in turbulent water, and might be buried in Flood sediments. Few would ever have been exposed, and few have been claimed. But there are several which have been discovered that might just be from before the Flood. None were well documented before being removed from the surrounding sediments, so doubters may discount them; but they do exist and are reported by reliable witnesses to have come from rock supposedly millions of years old. They are included here both for interest's sake and to encourage those who know of other such objects to share them.

Keep in mind that nearly all sedimentary rock is of marine origin, and the fossils contained therein are marine fossils. Hardly any land remains are to be found, and most of them are surrounded by marine fossils and sediments or entombed in volcanic deposits. Land environments simply did not survive intact, with one exception.

We get the impression that before the Flood the biosphere was abundant. Vast forests covered the lowlands, perhaps partially floating in water. These verdant habitats were inundated and ripped up by Flood waters, but would have floated and perhaps stayed together with intertwined roots. Eventually, these would have decayed away or beached themselves as the Flood waters abated. They have become the immense coal seams of our modern world. Internal layering reveals volcanic clay and marine fossils, rather incongruous with a land-based environment. Occasionally, land fossils are found in coal seams, giving a hint that animals were clinging to the floating mass in a futile attempt for survival.

But it is in this environment that the rarely discovered human artifacts are sometimes found. Coal mining has excavated great volumes of coal. In years past, mining was by hand and reports of fossils trickled out, but today's mechanized techniques increase the possibility that an artifact would be destroyed. Nevertheless, some finds have been reported, although none have been properly documented and are minimally useful.

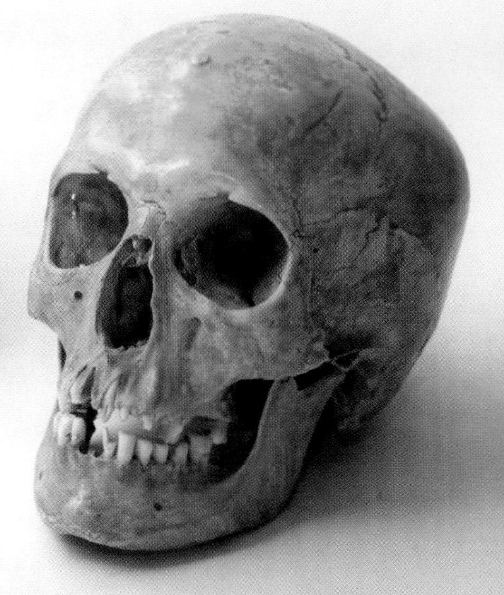

QUESTIONS

1. How far back in time does written human history go?

2. Starting with two people and given a population increase rate equivalent to that of today, how many people would be alive today?

3. Why don't we find human bones with dinosaur bones?

4. Describe the "real" fossil record. Why should it be that way?

Chapter Seven

WORLDWIDE PHYSICAL PROCESSES

As already mentioned, radioisotope schemes are not the only way we can date the earth or its systems. In fact, there are hundreds of clocks. Many of these physical processes or systems seem to imply that the earth is far too young to allow for evolution. These clocks are evaluated in exactly the same conceptual way as radioisotope clocks but differ widely in scope. When using radioisotope techniques, an individual rock or set of rocks is examined and dated. But a rock can, of course, be contaminated and altered in its mineral and chemical make-up. With the following techniques, the entire world is the sample. Since it is nearly impossible to alter the entire world's chemical make-up to any significant degree, these processes should be given more weighty consideration.

One of these worldwide processes has already been mentioned — the global build-up of radioactive carbon. Remember that C-14 is extremely rare compared to C-12. Given the present rate of cosmic-ray influx (which causes C-14 to form), when build-up equals decay, the global amount of C-14 should be about 75 tons. Calculations show that at present production rates the C-14 equilibrium can grow no larger than 75 tons, since the C-14 is continually decaying back into nitrogen. At present, only about 62 tons exist, but the total is climbing.

Recognizing that the C-14/C-12 ratio has not yet reached equilibrium but is still building up, we can calculate backward to the time when no carbon-14 should have been present. This calculation has some uncertainty, but it yields a maximum age for the earth's present surface layers (including oceans, atmosphere, and land surface) of approximately 10,000–15,000 years. However, the surface layers might be much younger. If the earth's surface is any older than 10,000–15,000 years, some environmental crises must have severely depleted the environment of C-14. Now, evolutionists might claim that the present rate of C-14 production reflects a temporary fluctuation in cosmic-ray influx, but certainly this is little more than ad hoc wishful thinking. As far as we know from scientific observation, the rates of cosmic-ray incidence and C-14 production are constant.

The concept of "maximum age" needs a little explaining. Recall that assumptions about the unobserved past are easily the most important aspect of the age determining process. Uncertainty in the assumptions employed in any dating technique makes it impossible to derive a truly accurate age. In this case, the calculation assumes that there was no carbon-14 present when the atmosphere formed. This, of course, is reasonable only if there was a time when earth had no atmosphere, or, in regards to C-14, a time when an event stripped the earth of its atmosphere during which all or almost all of its oceanic and atmospheric C-14 was removed. While the uniformitarian outlook cannot comprehend such an event, I suspect the intense and prolonged rain during the Flood mega-storms, coupled with deposition of limestone and other carbon-bearing deposits by ocean waters, would have stripped the earth of most of its C-14. However, in all likelihood there were still a minimal number of C-14 molecules in the environment at the end of the Flood. Since not all C-14 molecules were generated by post-Flood cosmic ray bombardment, the maximum age of the present atmosphere

- Only igneous rocks can be dated by radioisotope dating techniques.
- Fossil-bearing rocks are dated by the fossils they contain.
- Fossils are dated by the false assumption of evolution.
- The igneous rocks on the rim of the Grand Canyon date "older" than the igneous rocks at the bottom, according to radioisotope dating.

that would be needed to produce the present amount lessens somewhat.

As an interesting sidelight, only about one carbon atom in a trillion is of the C-14 isotope. The various carbon isotopes are equally likely to combine with other atoms to form larger molecules, such as CO_2. From studying certain chemicals and minerals in sedimentary rocks, it has been determined that much higher concentrations of CO_2 existed throughout the past, when the partial pressure[1] of CO_2 was up to 16 times higher than at present![2] Since CO_2 in the atmosphere seeks equilibrium with CO_2 in the oceans, and since animals emit CO_2 as plants assimilate it, a much larger concentration of CO_2 would imply that a much larger biomass could likely have been sustained in the past. This supports the impression we get from Scripture that the pre-Flood world was a well-designed place that could support abundant life, an idea equally well supported by studies of the fossil record.

Earth with magnetic field

For purposes of our discussion, let us assume that the concentration of atmospheric nitrogen and the rate of cosmic ray influx was the same before the Flood as it is today, and thus the maximum amount of C-14 would be the same as today (i.e., about 75 tons). But in the pre-Flood case, only one carbon atom in 16 trillion would be of the C-14 variety, due to the greater presence of carbon in the atmosphere as CO_2. The same amount of C-14 plus a higher amount of C-12 would yield an unnaturally low (by today's standards) C-14/C-12 ratio, both before the Flood and in the centuries following. This would tend to give older C-14 "dates" than would be suspected by assuming uniformity throughout the past. Again we see that the biblical model adequately handles the C-14 data, while the old-earth model does not handle it nearly as well.

Many similar chronometers, or earth clocks, could be discussed, using the entire world as a specimen. Most of these give young ages, far too young to have allowed for evolution.

Decay and Reversals of Earth's Magnetic Field

Dr. Thomas Barnes, formerly dean of the ICR graduate school and late emeritus professor of physics at the University of Texas, El Paso, performed the pioneering work on the classic geochronometer of earth's magnetic field, in the ICR technical monograph *Origin and Destiny of the Earth's Magnetic Field* (2nd edition, 1983). More-recent studies have extended Barnes's seminal work, to deal with the large amount of new data gathered since Barnes proposed his original straightforward concept.

As we know, the earth has a dipolar magnetic field with north and south poles. The earth is not permanently magnetized like a metallic magnet (permanent magnetism is destroyed by heat and the earth has an extremely hot interior), but rather, its field is due to an electromagnet, produced by electrical currents in the earth's interior.

Observations have shown that the earth's magnetic field has been measurably decaying over the last century and a half. Precise measurements of the field's intensity, or strength, have been made on a worldwide basis since 1835 that have allowed us to know the state of the field at any point in time since then. The intensity represents that force which attracts ferromagnetic particles, including those in a compass needle, turning it northward.

1. Partial pressure is the contribution any single gas in a mixture of gases makes to the total pressure of the mixture.

2. Crayton J. Yapp and Harold Poths, "Ancient Atmospheric CO_2 Pressures Inferred from Natural Goethites," *Nature* (January 23, 1992): p. 342–344.

Measurements of Magnetic Field over Time

Year	Magnetic Moment in amp-meter^2 x 10^{22}
1835	8.558
1845	8.488
1880	8.363
1880	8.336
1885	8.347
1885	8.375
1905	8.291
1915	8.225
1922	8.165
1925	8.149
1935	8.088
1942	8.009
1945	8.065
1945	8.010
1945	8.066
1945	8.090
1955	8.035
1955	8.067
1958	8.038
1959	8.086
1960	8.053
1960	8.037
1960	8.025
1965	8.013
1965	8.017
1968	7.985
1975	7.939
1975	7.927
1980	7.906
1985	7.871
1990	7.841
1995	7.812
2000	7.788
2005	7.768

Ref : Figures from 1835 to 1965 reprinted from Barnes's monograph supplemented by Humphreys.

From these measurements, we can ascertain that the field's overall strength has declined by about 7 percent since 1829. Such a phenomenal drop in historical recent history cannot be ignored! These measured data-points plot along a curved line, which best fits that of exponential decay, typical of many natural processes.[3] From the measured decay, it can be calculated that the half-life of the magnetic field's strength is approximately 1,400 years. If this half-life did not change with time, the field must have been much larger in the past and will be much smaller in the future.

3. By exponential decay, it is meant that the quantity lessens by a certain fixed percentage each year, and that this yearly decay percentage stays the same over time.

If we apply the same uniformitarian assumptions used in radioisotope dating to the magnetic field, the consequences of its decay in the future are significant. The measured half-life of 1,400 years implies that 1,400 years from today, the magnetic field will be one-half the strength that it is now. It will continue to decay at this rate, with half of its strength decaying every 1,400 years until sometime in the future, say A.D. 10,000, when it will, for all practical purposes, cease to exist.

But a robust magnetic field is important for life as we know it, because the field forms a protective shield around the earth, which deflects back into space much of the harmful cosmic radiation continually bombarding the earth, preventing the radiation from impacting the earth's atmosphere and surface and causing mutations in living things. Without a magnetic shield surrounding the earth, life would be rather harsh.

There are also implications of the decay rate for the past. If the earth's magnetic-field intensity was twice as strong every 1,400 years as you go back in time, only 100,000 years ago the magnetic field would have been incredibly strong, comparable to that of a neutron star. The heat generated by resistance to the electrical currents in the molten core required to produce such a large magnetic field would have had dire consequences. Barnes speculated that in the not-too-distant past, life would have been nearly impossible, and some 20,000 years ago, the heat produced would have disrupted the earth's internal structure. This may be an over-simplification, but you get the picture.

Furthermore, since cosmic-ray bombardment generates carbon-14 in the outer atmosphere, a stronger field, which would deflect more cosmic energy, would dramatically decrease the carbon-14 inventory in the past and, therefore, the results from using C-14 to date things would be even more uncertain.

From seismic studies, scientists are fairly certain of the overall makeup of the globe. It appears that the earth possesses an outer "crust" on its surface, which, while thin (about 20 miles thick on average), has never been completely penetrated by drilling. Below the crust lies the very thick (about 1,760 miles) mantle of the earth, consisting primarily of solid materials. The pressure in the mantle region is excessive and the temperature is quite high, but acting together, the pressure and heat maintain the mantle material in solid form. The very center portion of the earth is called the core, which is divided into the outer and inner portions. The outer core (1,400 miles thick) is even hotter than the mantle and in a fluid state, and is thought to consist primarily of molten iron and nickel. The inner core (with a radius of 780 miles) is solid once again, but hotter, with even greater pressure. (Near the boundaries of these zones, subdivisions are proposed, but for our purposes here, only the main divisions are considered.)

What Causes the Magnetic Field?

There are only two models (with variations of each) that have been proposed to account for the magnetic field as it exists. Uniformitarian scientists have proposed a self-exciting "dynamo" in the core, with a slowly circulating fluid flow of molten iron and nickel in the earth's outer core, capable of generating electric currents that have sustained and added to the magnetic field for billions of years. The energy fueling this movement is thought to be from the earth's rotation and its internal heat. Somehow, this energy is converted into magnetic energy without an overall energy loss. This dynamo concept has many problems, most particularly that there is no known way under reasonable conditions to either start or maintain the complex movements needed. (For comparison, consider the complicated electric path necessary in an electrical generator. Similar complex flow patterns are necessary in the earth, yet such paths are totally unnatural.) Many geophysicists, nevertheless, favor this concept, for it alone has the promise of maintaining itself over billions of years (in theory, anyway).

Drawing of earth's interior

The alternate idea to the magnetic field being generated by fluid currents in the outer core is that the field is generated by circulating electric currents in a rather stationary core fluid, decaying in intensity over time. Such electrical currents are known to exist, and due primarily to electrical resistance would decay in a manner consistent with the known field decay rate. Thus, the freely decaying electric-current theory fits modern observations of the decay rate quite well.

Next, consider the fact that abundant evidence exists that the earth's field has reversed its polarity many times in the past, as inferred from measurements and samples taken from archaeological sites, sedimentary rocks, lava flows, etc. The most important reversal data come from measurements of reversely magnetized rock on land, and to a lesser degree, from mid-ocean ridges.

The self-starting and self-exciting dynamo theory proposes that reversals occur when the fluid motions cause the electrical currents to slowly decay all the way down to zero, then build up again in a reversed orientation. Such a dynamo, theoretically, could account for reversals. As mentioned, this theory has serious problems, but it can accommodate reversals.

On the other hand, creationists of the 1970s theorized a smoothly decaying magnetic field without reversals, insisting that consideration of the overall field decay, as measured, took precedence over the measured reversed

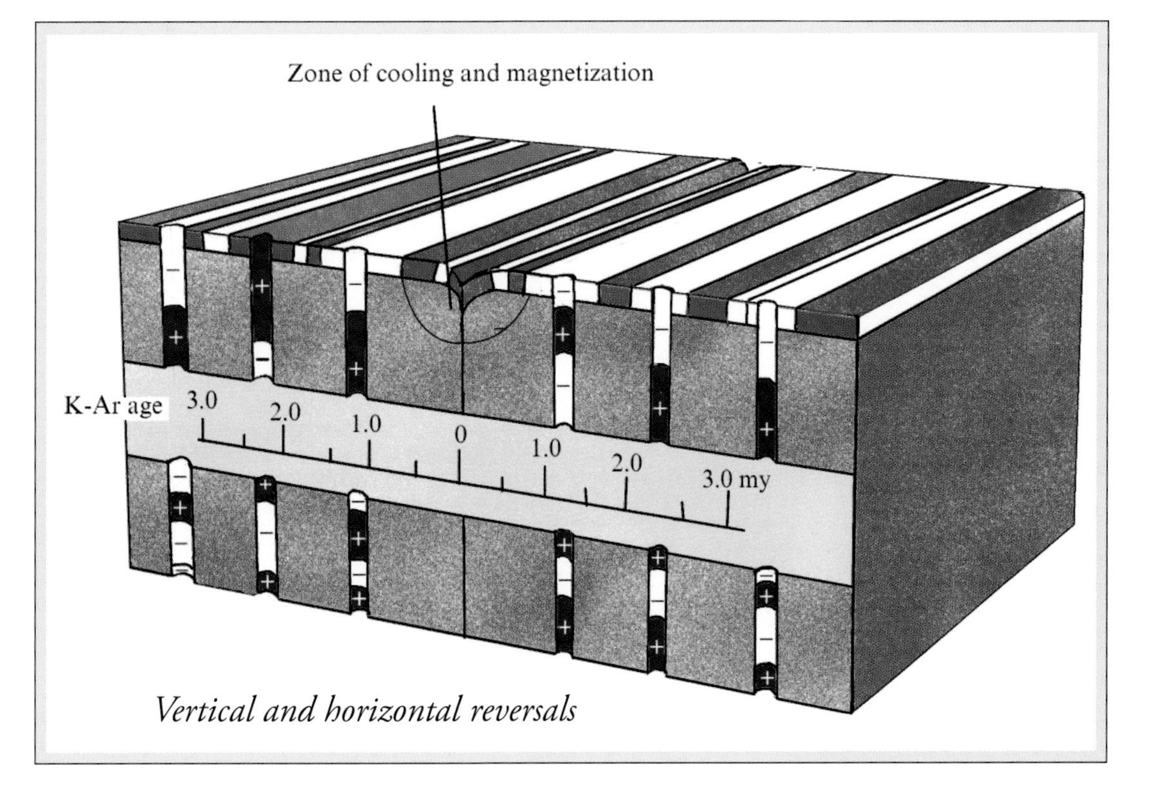

Vertical and horizontal reversals

orientation in some rocks, relegating those measurements to local causes. But ongoing research developed much confidence in the idea that whole-field reversals did occur. Thus, the early creationist concept was deemed inadequate to explain the evidence. As it turns out, rapid and complicated reversals are an essential part of the free-decay theory also, once the effects of Noah's flood are considered.

The reversal concept derives from the measured orientation of magnetic particles in rock, called remnant magnetism. This can be measured in a laboratory for an oriented specimen, or it can be recorded using a magnetic sensor towed along the ocean bottom, measuring the magnetic field recorded in basaltic rocks along mid-ocean ridges. Here it appears that large sections of the earth's crust (called plates) have spread outward from the ridges, being formed as emerging lavas cool into basaltic rock; the rocks which make up the plates acquire the magnetic signature of the magnetic field at the time and place they cool. These rocks sometimes show alternating positive and negative magnetized bands, roughly paralleling the ridge, and are interpreted as showing many reversals throughout the past. This evidence of spreading has been considered proof of continental separation.

There are many problems associated with this evidence. To start with, the gathering of the data is done by those who know what they are looking for, and the measurements which do not seem to fit preconceived notions are frequently discarded. One of my former colleagues on the faculty at the University of Oklahoma had been a researcher aboard a scientific vessel in the mid-Atlantic. Although he was a devoted advocate of plate tectonics, he grew skeptical of the sea-floor magnetic evidence, because he saw the selective manner in which it was being gathered. Likewise, a former graduate student of mine acquired a laboratory job at the university, measuring the remnant magnetism in individual specimens. He had never thought to question the theory, but he was puzzled to find how often discrepant readings were discarded by the scientist in charge. If the readings matched the theory's predictions, they were kept. Abnormal readings were culled out. Once he and I discussed the scientific problems with the theory, he understood better.

To make matters worse, there are seven different types of remnant magnetism, only one of which is associated with the earth's magnetic field, and there are four theoretical types of self-reversal possible.

When analyzing specimens, investigators attempt to erase or estimate the improper signals by subjecting the specimen to a series of heating cycles below the melting temperature, thus isolating the true paleomagnetic signal related to the earth's field at the time the magma cooled. Researchers have, in recent years, developed good techniques for evaluating such signals and have determined that self-reversal would be extremely rare, but you can imagine the difficulties and possibilities for error, especially in the early, formative days of this theory, during which many of the ideas of plate tectonics and paleomagnetic reversals were developed, ideas still popular today.

Another problem stems from the fact that in the lab, an individual rock's magnetic signature is thought to represent the field for the entire earth. Measurements from many specimens are averaged to minimize the effect of variant readings, but small errors in measurement may yield large errors in the estimation of overall field strength and orientation.

The drill ship JOIDES Resolution

This is not to say that the theory and measurements are without merit. Far from it. I feel that both are quite valuable, now that many of the problems (such as those alluded to above) have been solved. I recently toured the Deep-Sea Drilling Project research vessel, the *JOIDES Resolution,* when it was being refitted in San Diego. The sophisticated equipment on board and the professionalism of its staff were quite impressive. At issue is not the accuracy of the measurements, but the choice of investigations, the value placed on individual measurements, and the interpretation of all.

Make no mistake, reversals did occur. But I am convinced that the rocks have recorded events which are much more complex than is frequently admitted, and that the data's complexity is sometimes obscured or denied in order to support the standard dynamo theory.

Plate Tectonics

Plate tectonics is the idea that earth's surface is divided into numerous "plates" which move relative to one another, which is sometimes called continental drift. These continent-bearing plates are thought to spread apart, converge, or slide past one another. While no one observed the proposed separation of the world's landmass into the present-day continents, the evidence that supports this movement is strong. Not only does the rather amazing fit of the continents support the idea, but also, once the continents are placed back together, mountain chains and stratagraphic layers on the now-separated continents line up, as do major fault zones. Other evidences could be cited. It does appear that major continental movements, in some form, did happen in the past, and if they did, we have to include them in the biblical model.

Continental separation was most likely part of the overall restructuring of the earth's surface at the time of Noah's flood, a tectonic event with no equal. The continents probably separated in the later stages of the Flood, after a great deal of sediment had already been deposited as mud (which quickly hardened into sedimentary rock) and after mountain chains and fault systems had developed. In all likelihood, this separation was instrumental in bringing about an end to the Flood itself.

There is plenty of water available to cover the earth. If the earth were completely smooth, with no high mountains and no deep oceans, the water would stand over a mile and a half deep. The Bible records that on one particular day, after Noah, his family, and the animals had safely boarded the ark, "All the fountains of the great deep were broken up, and the windows of heaven were opened. And the rain was on the earth forty days and forty nights" (Gen. 7:11–12; NKJV). A large amount of water rushed to the surface from below ground, while additional water fell from above. Tsunamies pushed ocean water onto the land. Before long, the entire continent was submerged.

Evidently, before the Flood and during the early stages of the Flood, the world's topography was much less pronounced — the oceans were shallower and the mountains were lower, allowing the waters to cover the entire earth for a time. But how did the Flood end? Where is the water now? Obviously, the water is now in the ocean basins, which are much deeper than the continents are high and which cover over two-thirds of the globe. Such deep and wide ocean basins could not have existed during the Flood, because then it would have been impossible for water to cover the continents, as the Bible implies. Somehow, nearing the end of the Flood, the oceans must have been deepened and widened, allowing the water to drain into them, thus ending the Flood on the continents. Continental separation may have been one of the physical mechanisms involved. This partially explains why no oceanic crust dating from the early earth has been discovered in today's ocean basins. Today's oceanic crust formed late in the Flood.

Nevertheless, we should keep in mind that plate-tectonic theory has never been observed and thus not "proven" in any real sense. True enough: the earth's surface is divided up into plates whose boundaries are identified by plotting the observed epicenters of modern earthquakes. And there is evidence for some plates sinking below an adjacent plate

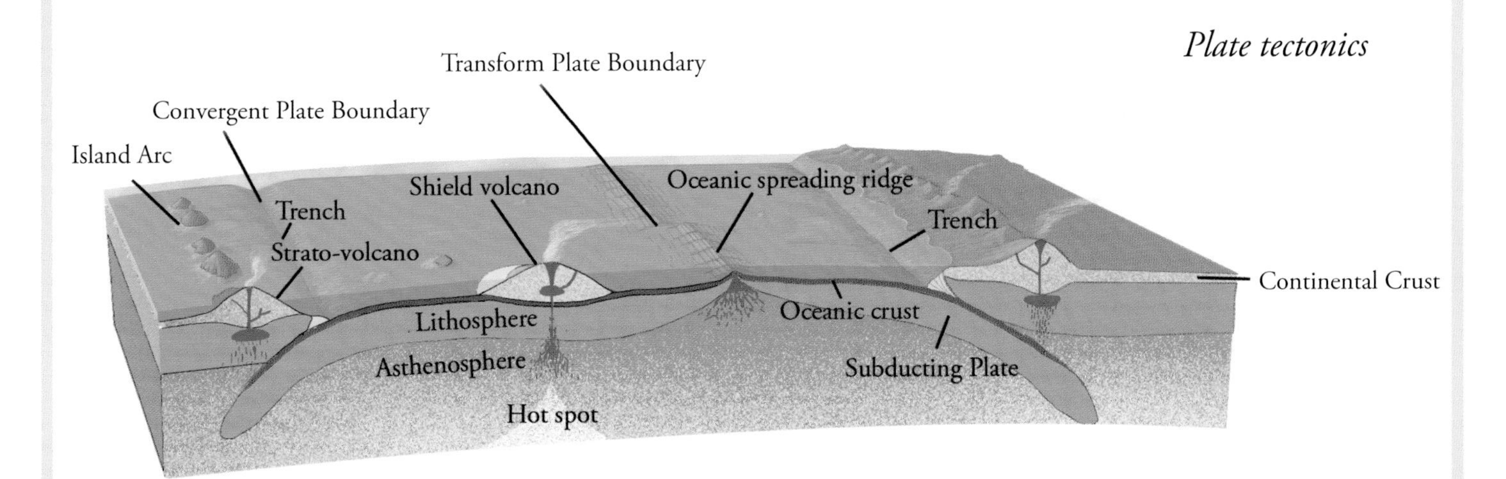

Plate tectonics

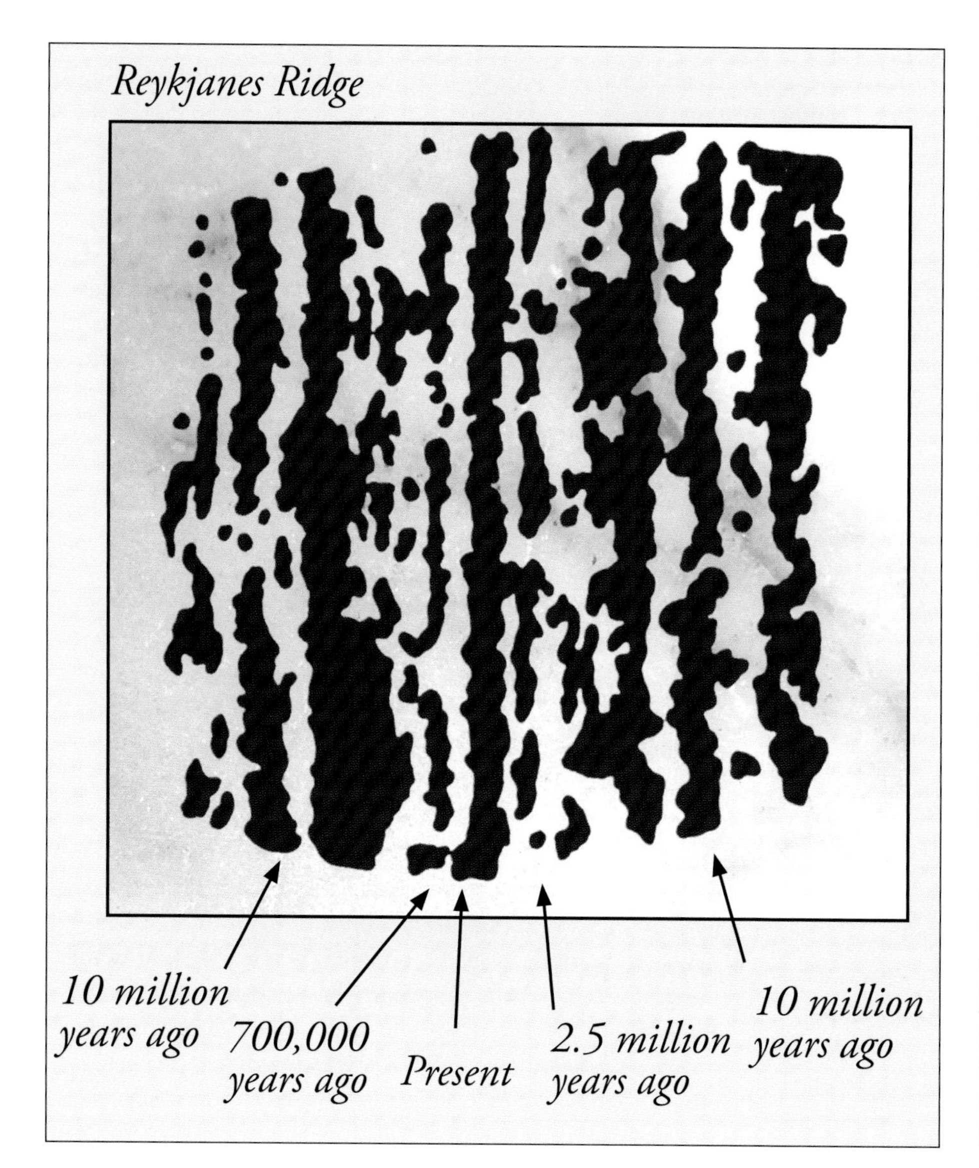

displayed this for years, but this fact is seldom mentioned by uniformitarians. These zones are probably best understood as resulting from rapid reversals coupled with rapid spreading and go hard against the slow-and-steady spreading hypothesis.[4]

There are yet other data that seem to contradict the standard theory. Precise measurements of distances across the Atlantic and at other places do not observe the predicted movement.[5] In some cases, there is no movement occurring today, and in others, the movement is opposite to that expected.[6] The main weakness of the theory of plate tectonics is that there is no way to move a continent without relying on unnatural conditions. It appears that major plate movements may have occurred in the past, but that this movement has come (or is coming) to a halt today.

Reconstructing history from partial evidence is risky business. We must reconstruct in submission to true history as given in Scripture, and even then the job is difficult, but Scripture does not give us all the details. Without Scripture, we have no chance. And, as a matter of fact, the only proposed scenario for continental separation that provides an adequate mechanism for plate movement is a young earth, creation-based idea which involves runaway subduction of oceanic crust, initiated by a cataclysmic event, such as an asteroid impact into the ocean. While there is admittedly no direct scriptural basis for this idea, it incorporates the geologic and geophysical evidence into the overall scriptural framework. This model, well received in both the creationist and non-creationist camps, was developed by creationist geophysicist and ICR professor Dr. John Baumgardner, with the flood of Noah's day in mind.[7] Formerly a researcher at Los Alamos National Laboratory, he feels that this cataclysmic event commenced some days or weeks after the Flood had laid down vast layers of sediment. The event destroyed all pre-Flood oceanic crust, subducting

and others moving laterally relative to the adjacent plate. But the idea that the continents were once connected and have moved to their present separate locations is a subjective reconstruction of history, although fairly well supported by a lot of data.

The discovery of the paleomagnetic striping patterns parallel to the spreading mid-ocean ridges has been recognized as an important proof of the theory of continental separation. Almost every textbook on geology reflects this, and most reproduce the same paleomagnetic trace as measured on the Reykjanes Ridge near Iceland. These paleomagnetic striping patterns look convincing, but they are hardly typical. Almost nowhere else does such a clear mirror-image pattern exist. In some places, the striping is perpendicular to the ridge, not parallel, and in others there is no clear pattern at all. The data are extremely complex.

Problems in the theory of spreading along the rift zones are compounded by studies showing that reversals are found not only perpendicular to the mid-ocean rifts in parallel zones, but also vertically in each rock zone. Drill cores have

4. J.M. Hall and P.T. Robinson, "Deep Crustal Drilling in the North Atlantic Ocean," *Science* 204 (May 11, 1979): p. 573–586.

5. D.E. Thomsen, "Mark III Interferometer Measures Earth, Sky, and Gravity's Lens," *Science News* 123 (January 8, 1983): p. 20–21.

6. W.E. Carter and D.S. Robertson, "Studying the Earth by Very-long Baseline Interferometry," *Scientific American* 255, no. 5 (1986): p. 44–52.

7. Dr. Baumgardner's model is best developed in a series of technical papers presented at the International Conference on Creationism, 1986, 1990, 1994, 2003. His two papers in 1994, "Runaway Subduction as the Driving Mechanism for the Genesis Flood" and "Computer Modeling of the Large-Scale Tectonics Associated with the Genesis Flood," are well worth the study.

it beneath the continents, moving the continents, and forming new oceanic crust between them. While contributing to the horror of the Flood, these movements eventually led to its end.

To sum up, plate tectonics is an observable fact. The plates do exist and some do move with respect to one another. Furthermore, the idea of the separation of a prior supercontinent in the past is well supported by the evidence. But large-scale movements are most likely made possible only by the rapid and dynamic events surrounding the Flood. At the very least, the Flood provides us with the energies and circumstances capable of moving a continent. Certainly, more research must be done, but imagine the depth of frustration experienced by uniformitarians who are trying to move the continents around with only present-day energy levels and process rates.

Rapid Reversals Coupled with Decay

Back to magnetic-field decay. If the magnetic stripes formed slowly, over long periods of slow separation as proposed by evolutionists, what do we make of the fact that the most recent reversal is dated at 700,000 years ago? (Some have proposed possible reversal events 20,000 years ago and greater, but these are not well accepted.) Earth's magnetic field would have been so strong, life would have been impossible had the field decayed along its present trend for 700,000 years, or even 20,000 years. Furthermore, during a slow reversal event, the magnetic field would be quite weak for long periods of time, with deadly effects on life. On the other hand, how do young-earth advocates handle the fact that the earth's crust does contain rocks with reversed magnetic orientation, particularly those along the active mid-ocean ridges?

Dr. Russell Humphreys,[8] long a physicist at the Sandia National Laboratories in New Mexico, and now an ICR physicist, has attempted to solve this problem. He has adopted as fact that the flood of Noah's day did occur only a few thousand years ago. With this as his starting point, he has proposed a very ingenious solution, one that explains the true data, including reversals, in an elegant and straightforward theory.

In the early years following publication of Barnes's original concept of freely decaying electrical currents, creationists had few ways to handle the fact that many data support the idea of field reversals. As we have seen, these reversals, and the data indicating them, are very complex. But the reversals did occur. Literally thousands of reversely polarized crustal rock specimens have been studied, both from land and sea.

Another category of specimens comes from archaeological sites — from bricks, kilns, campfire stones, pottery, etc., the dates of which can be discerned. Iron minerals in these artifacts were able to orient themselves with the earth's field when originally heated. This orientation was preserved when the object cooled and, if the specimen's original position is ascertained, its original magnetic orientation can be inferred. Archaeomagnetic measurements indicate that the earth's magnetic field was about 40 percent greater in A.D. 1000. It has declined ever since and is still declining today. Thus, both paleomagnetic and archaeomagnetic measurements contradict the concept of a magnetic field whose intensity is freely decaying due to simple electrical resistance. Briefly listed below are several lines of reasoning and discoveries. Weaving them together, Humphreys has been able to develop his model.

It has been recently shown that our sun's magnetic field regularly reverses itself, in connection with its sunspot cycle, every 11 years. Evolutionists had believed the sun's field was generated by a dynamo in some regards similar to earth's, but now they recognize a big problem. How can the field frequently reverse, each time using up significant energy, yet maintain itself for billions of years? The dynamo concept is on shakier ground than ever.

The nature of earth's field seems to be due to electrical currents in the rather motionless core, not slow fluid currents maintained by a dynamo. The presently observed decay is quite consistent with that predicted by a simple model of electrical resistance. The original field dates from the creation of the earth, which was complete with a "very good" magnetic field caused by electrical currents that are now decaying. It makes sense that God would furnish the earth with such a protective shield. The decay probably commenced with the curse on the earth in Genesis 3:17, due to Adam's rebellion.

Dr. Humphreys has developed a corollary theory for the likely strength of other planetary magnetic fields at creation. The predictions of this theory have now been supported by space-probe measurements.[9] This concept, when applied to earth, provides an original strength for the earth's field.

Another startling discovery involved firm evidence of a very rapid reversal event on earth, taking only about 15 days,[10] the time estimated for a pool of molten lava to cool. Evidence of this reversal was found within a now-hardened basalt rock. Evidently, a complete reversal occurred during the short time the lava pool was cooling (a maximum of 15 days for this volume of lava).

Still another discovery involves fluid motions in the outer core, gentle eddy currents thought to be dragging the

8. Dr. Humphreys has published his ideas in numerous papers. Two summary papers have appeared in *Acts & Facts, Impact* articles Numbers 188 and 242. These contain many references for further study, and a synopsis of the theory is included. Other papers include "The Creation of the Earth's Magnetic Field," *Creation Research Society Quarterly (CRSQ)*, Vol. 20 (2), 1983, p. 89–94; "The Creation of Planetary Magnetic Fields," *CRSQ*, 1984, Vol. 21 (3), p. 140–149; "Reversals of the Earth's Magnetic Field during the Genesis Flood," *International Conference on Creationism (ICC)*, 1986, Vol. 2, p. 113–126; "Has the Earth's Magnetic Field Ever Flipped," *CRSQ*, 1988, Vol. 25 (3), p. 130–137; and "Physical Mechanism for Reversals of the Earth's Magnetic Field During the Flood," *ICC*, 1990, Vol. 2, p. 129–142.

9. See Humphreys' article "Beyond Neptune: Voyager II Supports Creation," *Impact*, no. 203 (May 1990).

10. R.S. Coe and M. Prevot, "Evidence Suggesting Extremely Rapid Field Variation during a Geomagnetic Reversal," *Earth and Planetary Science Letters* 92, (1989): p. 292–298.

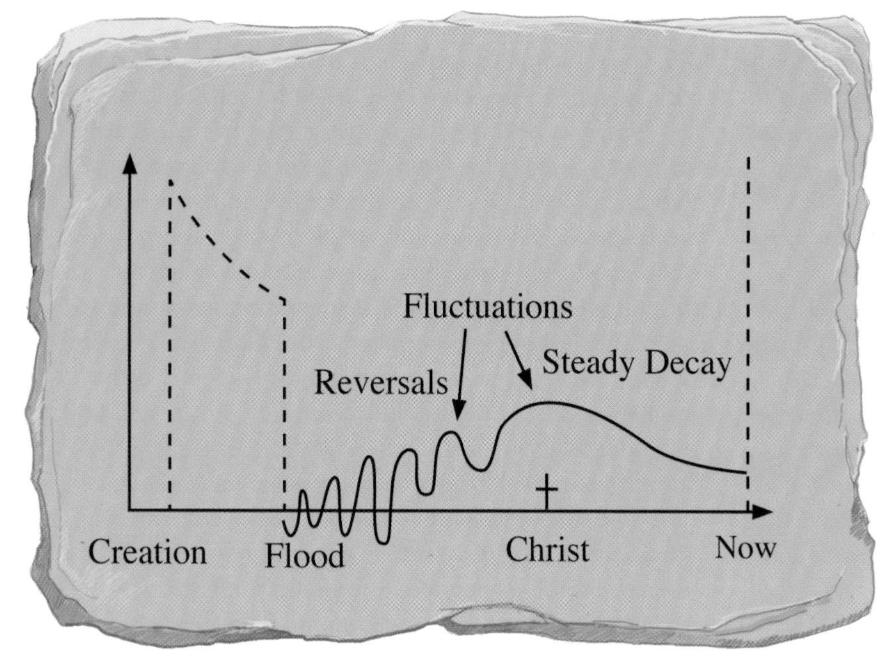

Magnetic field intensity at the earth's surface, from creation to now

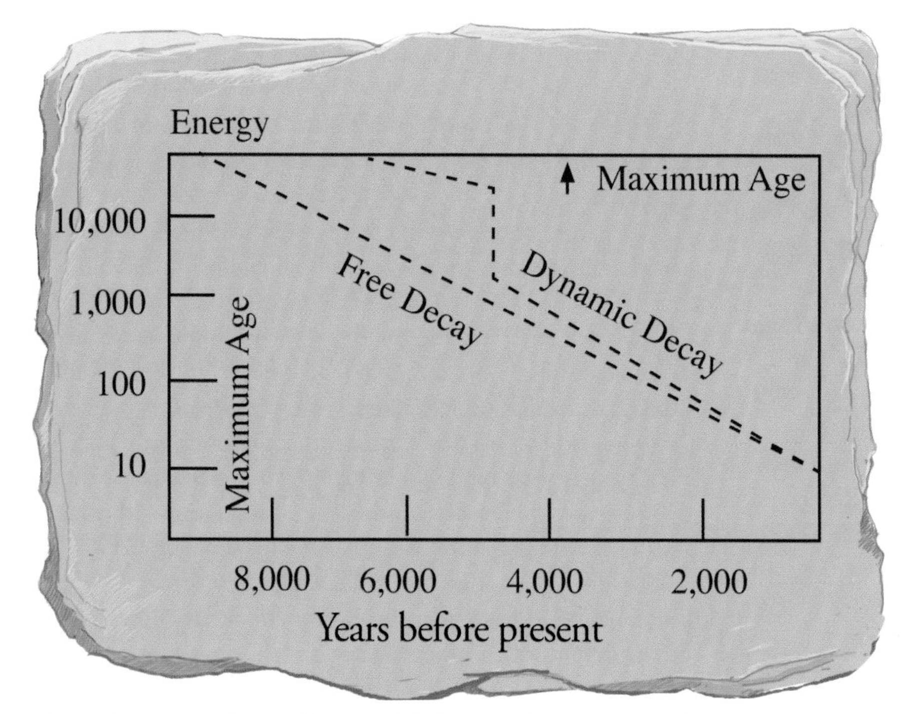

Total energy (in trillions of kilowatt hours) stored in the earth's magnetic field. Free decay theory gives maximum age of 8,700 years.

Dr. Humphreys proposes that at the onset of the Flood, a powerful event associated with plate movements and the breaking up of the "fountains of the great deep" (Gen. 7:11), fluid convection was initiated in the outer core. The movement of molten metallic material in the presence of the existing magnetic field would produce a magnetic flux. A strong enough flux of magnetic energy would cause the entire earth's magnetic field to eventually reverse — a natural consequence of rapid convection flows. Continuing movement would cause continual rapid field reversals, which would be recorded in rocks being continually extruded and deposited on the earth's surface. Note that these reversals do not add to the field's energy. Instead, rapid reversals within a decaying field use up its energy even more rapidly, contributing to and hastening its overall decay.

As the Flood year ended, the energy for massive fluid movements was no longer present, and the magnetic flux waned. Today, we measure only a relic convection current. The earth's field gradually returned to its original configuration and decay rate.

A look at the field's total change in energy is more enlightening, at this point, than examining its change in intensity. The intensity reflects the effect of the field on the earth, from orienting a compass needle to polarizing the magnetic particles in molten lava. The intensity can go to zero and reverse in the complex scenario above. But the total energy in the system cannot increase unless outside energy is added to it. If the energy level drops to zero, there is nothing left to start it up again. It can only decay, as does every energy system, and the more it is perturbed, the faster it decays.

Based on the measured intensity of the earth's field, scientists can calculate its total energy. As the intensity declines, so does the total energy. The half-life of the intensity is 1,400 years, but the half-life of the field energy is only 700 years! The types of trauma experienced by the field during the Flood, as briefly outlined in the preceding paragraphs, would serve to temporarily increase the decay of the field. Instead of a free decay of the magnetic field, we should, instead, consider a dynamic decay model.

huge plates along. These currents do exist and have now been measured by geophysical techniques, but they are not at all what were expected from the hypothesized dynamo.[11] They are, however, compatible with the revised free-decay model.

11. L.J. Lanzerott et al., "Measurements of the Large-scale Direct-current Earth Potential and Possible Implications for the Geomagnetic Dynamo," *Science* 229 (July 5, 1985): p. 47–49.

Dr. Humphreys has produced two graphs that illustrate his theory. The first graph, which is qualitative only, portraying the general idea, shows how the field's surface intensity varies with time, and demonstrates the measured decay at present. This is preceded by a series of numerous rapid reversals at the time of the Flood, followed by a lengthy period of fluctuation during which the earth's field settled back down. Before the Flood, the field was presumably much stronger than today but was still decaying at the present half-life.

The second graph, which is numerically accurate, plots the field's total energy versus time. Again, it shows the measured decay rate, but also a time of almost instantaneous energy loss due to the rapid reversals during the Flood. The half-life before the Flood would be the same as now, but with the rapid one-time decrease of energy due to the Flood.

Humphreys postulates a maximum possible energy for the earth's magnetic field at creation, consistent with his now substantially verified planetary model. He finds that the known decay would project back to this maximum in a time remarkably consistent with the biblical date for creation.

Old-earth advocates maintain hope that somehow the dynamo theory can still be salvaged. At present, it conflicts with observations of rapid reversals in modern lava flows, sunspot cycles, minor convection currents in the core, and it has no support in physical theory. The only existing model for the magnetic field that handles all the data specifies a young earth and a recent creation. It is based on sound physics, and its predictions have been proven by observation.

To summarize, unless the earth's magnetic field has been altered or energized by an unusual magnetic event in the past, about which we know nothing, the present decay rate yields an upper limit of 20,000 years or so for the age of the earth.

However, the earth's age is not necessarily that high, because this number was derived using uniformitarian assumptions of decay (which, in this case, have a better chance of being valid than those assumptions applied elsewhere). But even using the standard dating assumptions, the age calculated is young, not old. Furthermore, the evidence of magnetic reversals is quite compatible with predictions based on the biblical Flood.

Since this chronometer is based on worldwide measurements, monitored for a long time, and showing a dramatic trend, it perhaps represents the very best application of uniformitarian principles. The weight of the evidence is on the side of the young earth, not on the side of an old earth.

Helium in the Atmosphere

A powerful young-earth argument involves the helium found in our atmosphere. Helium, of course, is a very lightweight gas because the helium atom contains less mass than any other atom except hydrogen. Helium is found in the atmosphere in measurable quantities, and based on the volume of the atmosphere and the percentage of helium, the actual number of helium atoms in the atmosphere can be estimated.

Helium is produced beneath the earth's surface by the process of radioactive decay. When certain of the radioactive isotopes undergo an alpha decay episode, they give off an alpha particle. This particle consists of two protons and two neutrons. It quickly attracts two free electrons, thus becoming equivalent to a helium atom, which because of its extremely small size, lightweight, and mobility migrates through the pores in rock and eventually makes its way to the surface of the earth where it joins the other gases in the atmosphere. Obviously, if we know how fast the helium is being added to the atmosphere and how much helium is in the atmosphere, then we can estimate how long it would have taken for all the helium to accumulate, providing us with a maximum age of the atmosphere.

Dr. Larry Vardiman, chairman of the physics department at ICR, has done a great deal of work through the years on this very important chronometer. He continues to refine his and our understanding of it. His work presents an "airtight" argument.[12]

Sensors have measured the rate of introduction of helium into the atmosphere. Believe it or not, the measured rate stands at 13 million helium atoms per square inch each second! This phenomenal rate compares to the theoretical rate of helium escape into outer space of a maximum of about 0.3 million helium atoms per square inch each second. Therefore, helium in the atmosphere is accumulating at a very rapid rate. Dividing the known amount of helium in the atmosphere by the rate of accumulation shows that all of the helium in the atmosphere today would have accumulated in no more than two million years!

Please do not conclude that the atmosphere is two million years old. Instead, this measurement shows that, using the uniformitarian assumptions inherent in every dating process, the atmosphere could not possibly be any older than two million years. Many are convinced it is much younger.

These uniformitarian assumptions include the notion that the rate of accumulation has never been any different throughout the past. But during Noah's flood, the rate may have been much more rapid, because the earth's crust was in such turmoil that the helium would have been able to escape crustal rocks more easily. Accelerated nuclear decay would further increase the rate. Both these factors would reduce the maximum age.

Another fact presents itself, however: that of the recent discovery of large volumes of helium in the earth's crust which do not appear to be of radiogenic origin.[13] If non-radiogenic helium (identical to radiogenic helium) is added

12. See Dr. Larry Vardiman's monograph *The Age of the Earth's Atmosphere*, Institute for Creation Research, 1990.

13. See, for example, H. Craig and J.E. Lupton, "Primordial Neon, Helium, and Hydrogen in Oceanic Basalts," *Earth and Planetary Science Letters* 31 (1976): p. 369–385.

to the earth's atmosphere from time to time, then the age decreases even more.

This argument from helium build-up also assumes that at the time the atmosphere formed, there were absolutely no helium atoms present, and that all of the helium atoms present now have come about by this process. But at the time of creation there most likely were some helium atoms in the atmosphere, once again making the age of the earth much lower. Helium is a very useful, "very good" element, and the wise Creator would probably have included some in the original atmosphere.

Many scientists have, over the years, tried to propose mechanisms by which helium might more readily escape into outer space, overcoming the earth's gravitational pull, but none has been fully successful.

A recent understanding of solar flux, which proposes that lightweight helium would be differentially swept away from the atmosphere, has possible merit but has not yet been endorsed by all scientists. The problem for old-earth thinking is huge and not yet solved.

There is another point we can make here. We have seen that helium is lightweight, inert, and mobile, and rises in any fluid medium. This includes both gas and liquid. The rocks of the earth's crust contain both gas and liquid in the tiny spaces between grains and in cracks. They must be filled with some fluid, and if any helium were present, it would rise, eventually reaching the surface where it enters the atmosphere.

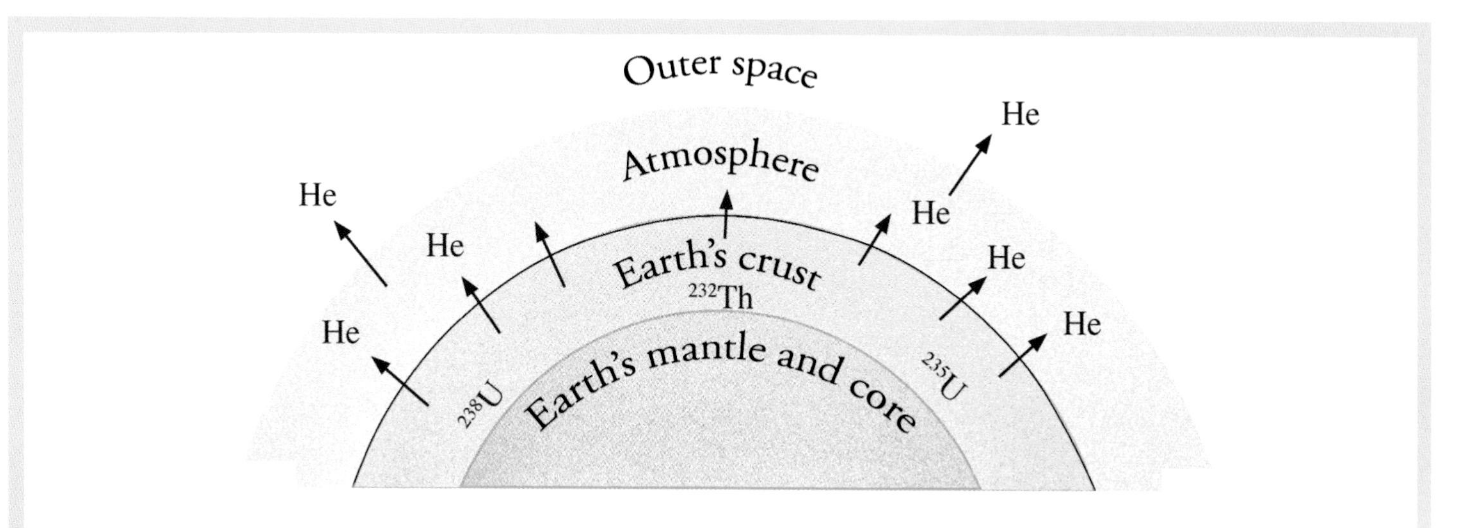

All of the helium now in the atmosphere would accumulate in a maximum of two million years!

This also assumes that nothing has happened to add or take away any helium from the atmosphere. Can we assume that no comet has come by and sucked all the helium off? Probably. Can we assume that no asteroid has blasted into the earth bringing helium with it? Perhaps. Can we assume that since helium does have some finite weight, it does not continue to rise and escape the earth's gravitational pull? Again, probably. In order for the helium to escape, it has to overcome earth's gravitational pull by achieving "escape velocity," as does any object. Escape velocity is many times faster than the speed of sound. Certainly, some atoms would reach such outwardly directed velocities when in an excited state in the outer atmosphere, but this would be, at best, a relatively rare occurrence. As we have seen, the maximum loss is significantly lower than the rate of helium influx from the crust. If the atmosphere is as old as evolutionists say, there ought to be a lot more helium here!

We can conclude from all this that the earth's atmosphere is quite young, much too young to have allowed evolution to take place. But keep in mind that with this method or any method, we cannot accurately date things. The only thing we can do is put a maximum age on them.

You might ask how the evolutionists answer this problem, and the fact is, they do not have an adequate answer.

But the fact is, crustal rocks presently contain a large amount of helium! How long would it take for a helium atom at any depth to percolate through the rocks and reach the surface? Gas movement through a rock is a function of the rock's permeability, a measure of the ease with which fluids can migrate through it, and the driving force, in this case the difference in density between the helium and the other fluids (usually a saltwater brine). Different rock types have different permeabilities, but no rock provides a helium-proof seal, especially over long periods of time. Helium would move through and exit the rocks faster than any element other than hydrogen. And yet it is still found in rocks.

Radioactive decay in the rocks continually replenishes the helium, so the presence of it there is no surprise. But if this production has continued throughout billions of years, and the helium rushes to the surface, there should be much more in the atmosphere! The fact that helium is in the rocks in abundance but not in the atmosphere is a puzzle.

QUESTIONS

1. Summarize the argument for a young age for the earth from magnetic field decay.
2. Give the uniformitarian explanation for alternatively polarized basaltic rocks along the mid-ocean rift.
3. Give a young-earth/Flood explanation for these same rocks. Compare the two ideas and discuss which is most likely.
4. Does plate tectonics fit in with the biblical model? In what way?
5. Summarize the "helium build-up in the atmosphere" age indicator and identify how the three necessary dating assumptions apply to this method.
6. Compare the magnetic-field-decay chronometer with the salt-in-the-ocean chronometer. Which do you think is more precise, and why?

Chapter Eight

GEOLOGIC EVIDENCE FOR A YOUNG EARTH

The publication of the book *The Genesis Flood,* by Whitcomb and Morris in 1961, is generally recognized as the catalyst for beginning the modern creation movement. Not that it discussed creation very much; rather, it explained the nature and power of the Flood. And the Flood is the key. Such a Flood could account for the fossils and the strata that have traditionally been misinterpreted as evidence of long ages of uniformity. For the first time, biblical inerrancy could be considered a credible, scholarly position. On the authority of Scripture, the catastrophic Flood really occurred on a wide scale, and the evidence for extensive catastrophism in geology abounds. The young-earth position directly follows from the global Flood doctrine, just as belief in an old earth by otherwise Bible-believing Christians necessitates holding to the local-Flood concept.

Destruction left by tsunami

But things have changed in the years since. The creation movement has even caused a revolution in secular geologic thinking. At the very least, secular geology has adopted many of the "radical" positions espoused in *The Genesis Flood,* for now we find the entire discipline of geology moving back toward catastrophism. Many leading geologists now even identify themselves as "neo-catastrophists" and have begun to invoke large-scale, dynamic processes for the production of geologic layers and earth features. These geologists freely speak of continents moving about, of large meteorites impacting earth and causing the dinosaurs to go extinct, of volcanic events dwarfing anything in human history, etc. These ideas were routinely scoffed at in the days before *The Genesis Flood.*

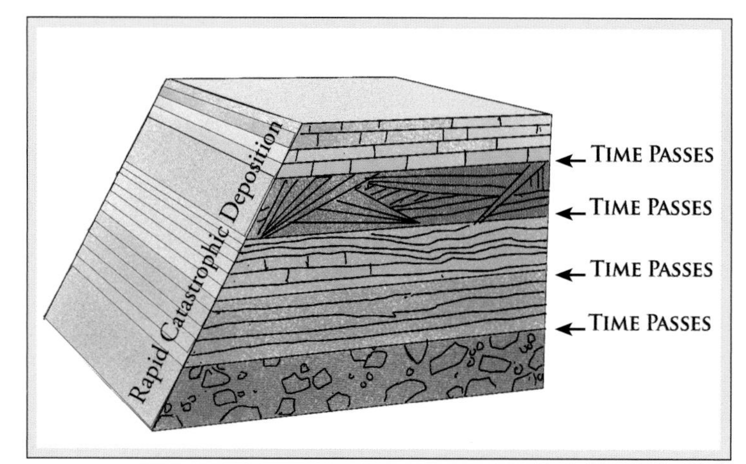

Consider for a moment the perspective of the late Dr. Derek Ager, former president of the British Geologists Association. While attempting to distance himself from creationist geologists who believe in Noah's flood, he spearheaded a revival in geology back toward dynamic processes. "The hurricane, the flood or tsunami may do more in an hour or a day than the ordinary processes of nature have achieved in a thousand years. . . . In other words, the history of any one part of the earth, like the life of a soldier, consists of long periods of boredom and short periods of terror."[1]

Ager insists, as do numerous leading geologists of today, that many (and perhaps nearly all) of the geologic deposits are actually the result of a series of rapid catastrophic events, usually water related. For instance, it is no longer considered laughable to argue that each horizontally bedded layer of fossil-bearing strata in the Grand Canyon was laid down by a catastrophe of one sort or

1. Derek Ager, *The Nature of the Stratigraphical Record* (New York: John Wiley and Sons, 1981), p. 54, 106.

another. The growing number of "neo-catastrophist" geologists who advocate this position feel that the catastrophes that laid down the Tapeats Sandstone were not part of the same catastrophe or catastrophes that laid down the overlying layers up to the rim of the canyon. The geologists would claim that millions and millions of years separated each sequence of catastrophes. By doing so, they recognize catastrophism in geology but still hang on to the concept of the old earth and retain the time necessary for evolution to occur.

Please grasp clearly what these scientists are advocating. They would say that nearly all of the rock material was laid down rapidly, as sediments, by catastrophic events. These events were separated by great lengths of time. But while the real evidence points toward rapid catastrophic deposition which took very little time, great amounts of time supposedly passed between the layers where no evidence is found! The evidence for time is the *lack* of physical evidence. Virtually all of the actual evidence in the rocks points toward catastrophic flood processes lasting only a short period of time.

Back in the early days of modern creationism, particularly with the publication of *The Genesis Flood* in 1961, the duty of the creationist geologist was to demonstrate catastrophism as opposed to strict uniformitarianism (the idea that each geological layer accumulated slowly and gradually by processes and process rates similar to those occurring today).[2] Now, with the acceptance of rapid, catastrophic processes by many leading geologists, the creationist's duty has somewhat changed. Now we must also strive to tie these layers together into one catastrophe and show that the length of time that passed between the deposition of any two adjacent layers, and thus much of the entire series, was not long at all.

Discussed below are several ways that demonstrate how the layers can be tied together into a rather short period of time. Dating the earth by use of these methods will not be advocated. Rather, what will be shown is that the evidence speaks of a single, rapid geologic event, which was responsible for the majority of the world's fossiliferous sedimentary rocks and which continued through the geologic column, leaving no time for evolution.

Surface Features

One way to show that only a short time elapsed between the deposition of one bed and the deposition of an overlying bed is to show that the various surface features present on the top surface of each bed would not last very long if exposed. Therefore, these features had to be covered rather quickly, before they had a chance to erode or be destroyed.

One very common feature, seen in many rock layers in many locations, is the presence of ripple marks, formed as water moves over a surface. These can frequently be seen on a beach after the tide has receded, and can also be seen on the ocean bottom where a particular current direction dominates. In many other situations we see what have been called raindrop impressions, although these fragile raindrop marks may actually be blisters formed as air bubbles escaped from rapidly deposited sediments under water. Animal tracks are also common. In any case, these features, which had to be formed in soft sediment or they would not have formed at all, are very fragile, and if present on any surface, soft unconsolidated material or hard rock, will not last very long.

Keep in mind that almost every sedimentary rock layer was deposited under water. Every geologist agrees with this.

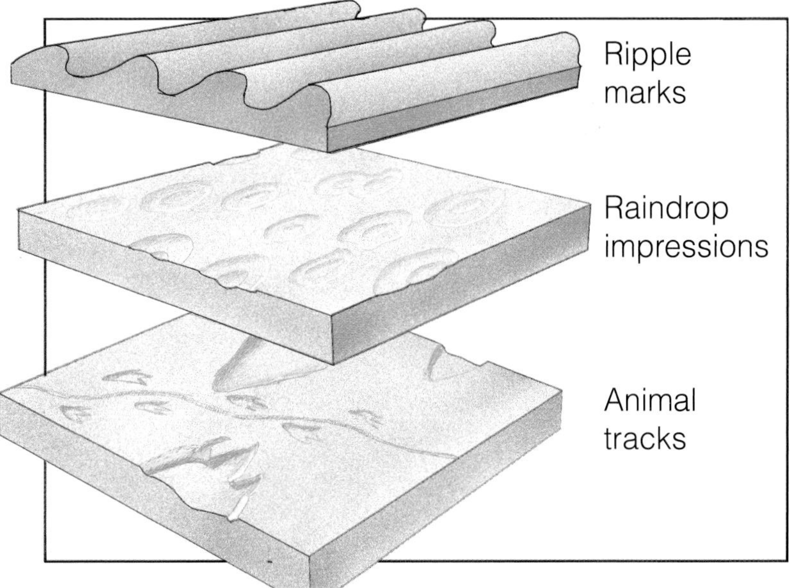

Surface features are easily destroyed. They must be quickly protected in order to be preserved.

Unless erosion dominates locally, sediments normally accumulate on an ocean bottom, lakebed, delta, beach, lagoon, stream bank, etc., in the presence of water currents. If subsequent events lift the deposit up out of the water, erosion and/or non-deposition will result. But if a zone stays under water, it will continue to be subjected to water action and will likely receive more sediment. In such an active environment, ripple marks can be preserved only if they are quickly buried by overlying materials, so that they are protected and have time to harden into rock.

In many places around the world, these ocean-floor sediments have been solidified into rock and are now uplifted onto continental surfaces. Ripple marks and similar features

2. The book *The Genesis Flood*, by John Whitcomb and Henry Morris, is considered the catalyst for the modern creation movement. For the first time, a systematic and scientifically credible defense of biblical world history was possible. It is still a highly valuable work.

Dinosaur tracks of various sizes in central Texas.

are readily seen in many locations, "frozen" in solid rock. Many examples come readily to mind. In a streambed I once hiked down in Oklahoma, numerous limestone layers could be seen, each only a few inches thick. Each one displayed obvious ripple marks about one inch high. Interestingly, the ripple marks in different layers were in different directions, indicating the water current responsible for deposition shifted rapidly and erratically while deposition continued. How could all the ripple marks be preserved?

If such a mark is exposed on any surface, under water or above water, it will soon erode and be washed away. Even on a hard rock surface, markings will erode in a few decades. There is no possibility that fragile features will last unprotected for millions of years, waiting to be re-submerged and buried, and thus protected from destructive forces. We cannot determine exactly how much time passed between the deposition of two layers simply by looking at ripple marks, raindrop impressions, animal footprints, etc., but we can conclude that much less time passed than it takes for surface features to be eroded and disappear.

Since almost every layer gives demonstrable evidence of having been laid down rapidly and catastrophically, and since nearly all such catastrophic layers have surface features that were not eroded, one can reasonably conclude that the whole sequence of rocks was deposited by different episodes in a rapid, possibly continuous, event.

Bioturbation

A similar line of reasoning can be used by observing the deficiency of preserved evidence of living communities within a layer of rock. Obviously on and below nearly every surface, whether on land or in the sea, abundant life is present which will leave its mark. In the ocean bottom or near the shore, worms, clams, fish, and all sorts of plants and animals live and disturb the sediments. Many actually ingest the mud, utilizing the nutrients present.

On land, tree roots, gophers, and numerous other animals will alter the surface soil layers in fairly short order. Weathering will further hasten deterioration.

Consider the example of Hurricane Carla in 1961, which devastated the central Texas coast. As the hurricane retreated, it laid down a recognizable layer of sediments on the shore and far out into the Gulf of Mexico. These graded and well-layered sediments contained within them many sedimentary structures such as buried ripple marks and cross bedding. These internal markings were well studied in the years after Hurricane Carla and were recognized as rapid deposition features.[3]

About 20 years later, others went back to study what had happened to the stratum. Due to bioturbation, the disturbance of the geologic zone by biologic activity, the layer could hardly be found, and once located, it retained almost no evidence of sedimentary structure. Within just a couple of decades (and probably much more quickly), life at the surface of this bed, both on shore and off, had destroyed the internal character that had been formed by catastrophic processes.[4] Indeed, in any environment, from a desert sand dune to the shallow marine, life is abundant and continually

Ripple marks left by water action on surface of formerly horizontal Hakatai shale, Grand Canyon.

3. Miles O. Hayes, "Hurricanes As Geological Agents: Case Studies of Hurricanes Carla, 1961, and Cindy, 1963," *Report of Investigation, University of Texas Bureau of Economic Geology*, No. 61 (Austin: University of Texas, 1967): p. 56.

4. As reported in Robert H. Dott, "1982 SEPM Presidential Address: Episodic Sedimentation — How Normal Is Average? How Rare Is Rare? Does It Matter?" *Journal of Sedimentary Petrology* 53, no. 1 (March 1983): p. 12.

agitates the sediments within several feet of the surface. Particularly in shallow water, where most of the sedimentation occurs, living communities of plants and animals are especially active.

Compare the layer from Hurricane Carla to sedimentary layers of rock around the world, almost all of which are full of sedimentary structure. While individual exceptions could be cited, they are exceptions. The broad trend is for each stratum to contain abundant internal structure. Evidently, the sediments were not exposed to an environment of biologic activity for any length of time before they were buried out of reach of plant and animal activity and subsequently hardened. Perhaps the sediments continued to build up so rapidly that the structure was out of reach of burrowing animals, but this implies continual catastrophic deposition. Where fossilized bioturbation does exist, it usually looks quite different from modern habitats. It better resembles that left by burrowing animals as they escape from deepening sediments, having been buried there against their will. These escape burrows are frequently oriented upward only, not in the variety of directions employed in living communities. It is as if the organisms were digging out of a continually growing supply of sediments.

Again, we cannot tell how long the lower layer existed before the overlying layer was deposited, but we can say that it was less than the time for bioturbation to destroy sedimentary structures within the lower zone.

In this manner we can march up the geologic column, tying the layers together, and conclude a relatively short time for the entire sequence.

Several cycles of graded bedding are shown as formerly vertical rock face lies horizontally. Such sedimentary structure is quickly destroyed by bioturbation.

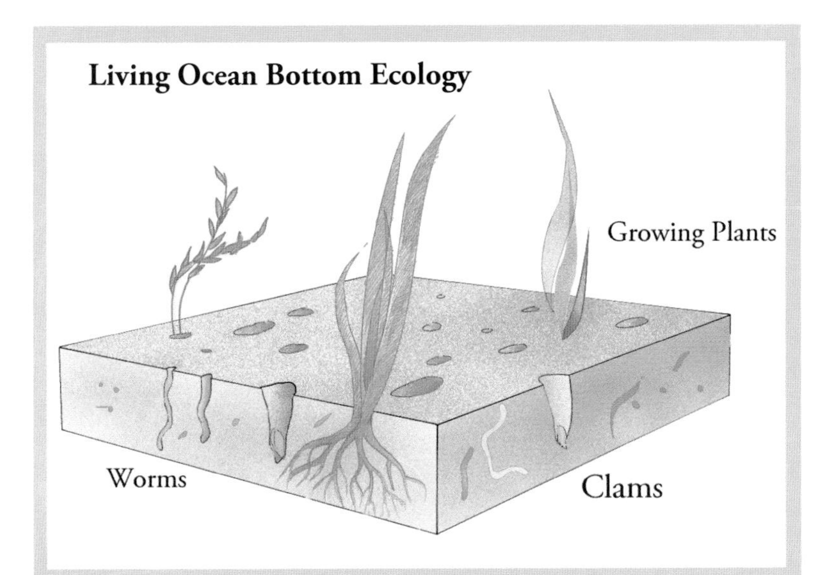

Lack of Soil Layers

Exactly the same logic can be applied to another feature, the almost complete lack of recognizable soil layers anywhere in the geologic column.

Within standard, old-earth thinking, the continents now exposed have on numerous occasions been underwater, as evidenced by the fact that nearly all of the rocks themselves were deposited by ocean water, perhaps by offshore wave action, in the deep ocean, in deltas, in lagoons, or by major storms or mud slides. When uplifted and exposed as land, they presumably were covered with soil, wherein plants and animals could live. Even in near shore environments, underwater "soils" are needed.

Soils today consist primarily of weathered rock, broken up by the cycle of freezing and thawing water, by chemical deterioration of rock minerals, by wind and water erosion, and by the action of rooting plants and burrowing animals. To this is added organic debris — mostly decaying plants and animal carcasses and droppings. Without soil, abundant life is impossible, but we know from the fossil record that abundant life has existed throughout much of this planet's history. It takes a while for soil to form, but once present, it tends to remain, barring erosion, often held in place by roots.

What happens to the soil as the land surface submerges beneath the sea? Whether the land is covered rapidly by a catastrophic process, or slowly by transgression of the sea, certainly some of the soil would be covered by ensuing sedimentation and preserved.

So what do we make of the fact that convincing soil layers, or even soil materials, are seldom found in the geologic record? Geologists ruled by their uniformitarian paradigm claim to have discovered soil layers, but the underconsolidated layers are not "soils" in any true sense. Classification systems categorize modern soils well, but ancient candidates are markedly different. In a discussion of soil types it was said that "many paleosols do not possess adequate characteristics to allow for proper classification by the order level following Soil Taxonomy. This is a fact."[5]

A possible soil sometimes mentioned is underclays, often found beneath coal seams and thought by some to represent leached soil layers; but the make-up of underclay is not what one would expect of a soil layer capable of supporting a lush swamp. The thick growth necessarily present in a swamp is missing in an underclay. The little rootlets present hardly speak of saturated conditions, swarming life, and intertwined trees and shrubs.

There is no evidence of much time needed for sediment accumulation of series of layers, including coal.

This attempt at identifying a fossil soil is rare. The geologic record is one of rocks, with few exceptions, not soils or paleosols. Typically, poorly consolidated rocks are not thought to consist of materials that have ever been soils.

Standard evolutionary geology tells us that land surfaces supporting abundant life have been here continuously for hundreds of millions of years. Where, then, are the soils?

A better explanation is that only one soil existed before the depositional episode that resulted in the majority of the geologic record. The soils that are missing never existed. The time to produce many soils never happened.

Undisturbed Bedding Planes

Much the same logic can be brought to bear on the nature of the bedding contacts themselves. Frequently, one will find two formations of totally different rock types, lying one on top of the other, with a "knife-edge" bedding plane between them.

Note the picture of a contact seen in the Grand Canyon between two such rock units. Here the brown-colored Hermit Shale lies below the whitish Coconino Sandstone, as it does throughout much of the region.

The Hermit Shale is thought to have accumulated as silt and mud in an offshore environment. It is found in a marine geologic context and contains index fossils by which evolutionists date it at about 280 million years of age.

The overlying Coconino Sandstone, dated at about 270 million years, tells a different story, although its history is in dispute. Most uniformitarian geologists interpret it as a desert sand dune deposit, now solidified into hard rock. They base this interpretation on the presence throughout the rock of inclined planes, called cross bedding (i.e., sedimentary structure), found at an angle to the general horizontal bedding of the rock unit as a whole. These are thought to be the undulating sand dune surfaces in an otherwise flat desert.

Other geologists interpret these giant features as an underwater sand dune deposit. They base their contention on certain features more representative of wet sand than dry sand, such as the angle of the cross-beds, presence of amphibian tracks fossilized in the sand (what are amphibians doing in the desert and how could their little footprints be preserved in loose, dry, sand?), source of the original sand, features of the sand grains, etc.[6] The underwater case would probably be convincing to all, if it were not for certain implications which necessarily follow.

We know that moving water can transport sand grains, with more rapid water required to move larger grains for a given water depth. We can measure the average sand grain size present in the Coconino and determine the velocity needed. It turns out that the Coconino is made of fine sand grains ranging in size from 1/8 mm to 1/4 mm in diameter.

5. W.C. James, G.H. Mack, and H.C. Monger, "Classification of Paleosols: Discussion," *Geological Society of America Bulletin* 105 (1993): p. 1637. See also Peter Klevberg and Richard Bandy, "Postdiluvial Soil Formation and the Question of Time, Parts I and II," *Creation Research Society Quarterly* 39 and 40 (March 2003 and Sept. 2003): p. 252–268, 99–116.

6. W.E. Freeman and G.S. Visher, "Stratigraphic Analysis of the Navajo Sandstone," *Journal of Sedimentary Research* 45, no. 3 (1975): p. 651–668.

Obviously, a measurable velocity of water at the sand-water interface is required to move fine sand grains. As it turns out, a velocity of three to five feet per second in deep water is necessary.

Measurements of the sand dune geometry coupled with experimental results show that those giant sand dunes (or in this case, long, underwater undulates) were made in a water depth of over 100 feet.[7]

Now we know from observation that water generally moves much more rapidly on the surface than it does at depth. In order for water at a 100-foot depth to move at three to five feet per second, it must be moving at a much greater velocity on the surface.

The Coconino Sandstone, thought to be fossilized sand dunes, conformably overlies the Hermit Shale, an offshore deposit.

Actually, at a depth of 100 feet in the open ocean, sustained water velocities of three feet per second have never been observed. Clearly, it would take a storm of unprecedented magnitude. Such a catastrophe is far beyond that which most uniformitarians dare to consider. Of course, most creationists favor the underwater model, since they are not intimidated by the thought of catastrophic water events, and also, since virtually all rock units are best understood as having been deposited during the height of the flood of Noah's day. It is hard to imagine how a desert deposit would develop during the Flood. But it is more than just an interpretation of necessity. The evidence clearly favors the underwater model. Those who advocate the desert interpretation illustrate the maxim, "I wouldn't have seen it if I hadn't believed it."

Crossbedding in Coconino Sandstone. Note person for scale.

But let us return to the bedding plane between the Hermit Shale and the Coconino Sandstone. Regardless of how the Coconino Sandstone was deposited, it originated in a completely different environment than the Hermit Shale and, according to evolution, was separated in time by about 10 million years. If the Coconino Sandstone represents a desert (one which covered over 100,000 square miles, by the way), then the deltaic environment that accumulated the Hermit Shale material had to be uplifted, out of water, to an elevation high enough and dry enough to be a desert. Can you imagine the erosion that would take place over this gigantic area, particularly as it was near sea level, both above and below? And yet, the upper surface of the Hermit is exceptionally flat, with no evidence of normal erosion. It is not possible, as far as has been observed, for the kinds of erosional processes associated with regional uplift to scour off all possible overlying sediment and leave behind a completely flat Hermit surface on which the Coconino desert could form. Or if no other sediments were ever present, how could it remain stagnant with no erosion, leaving a flat, featureless Hermit surface

7. For an explanation of this, see Steven A. Austin, *Grand Canyon: Monument to Catastrophe* (El Cajon, CA: ICR, 1994).

on which sand began to collect 10 million years later? No surface on earth remains stagnant, with no erosion and no deposition. It certainly would not sit there with nothing at all happening for 10 million years! Especially for this 10 million years! According to the evolutionary old-earth scenario, the earth was, at that time, enjoying an extended period of wet climate. A huge desert with little rainfall near a warm ocean is a contradiction in terms. Even if the Coconino was formed underwater, no surface such as the top of the Hermit would remain there for a long time without any change.

The point is, the existence of the sharp, knife-edge contact between those two formations argues against the passage of long periods of time between their depositions, regardless of their index fossils. If it were not for the assumption of evolution, these two beds would speak either of continuous, rapid deposition with perhaps a near-instantaneous shift in current direction and sediment load, or of rapid deposition of the Coconino after an episode of "sheet erosion" due to massive volumes of water flowing rapidly at equal depth over a wide area and equally eroding the sediment in all locations. In both cases, we are talking about a flood on the scale of the Genesis flood.

Contacts between rock units in nearly every area exhibit the same knife-edge contact, not between every two consecutive layers at all locations but between at least some layers in each locality and between "all" consecutive layers in some locations. The rocks simply do not support vast ages passing between the deposition of successive layers.

Missing Time between Layers

The lack of evidence for time passing between the layers is compounded by the immensity of the supposed time gaps between layers. Considering the Grand Canyon, conventional thought has dated each layer and identified the supposed environment in which it was deposited. The change of sediment type necessitates a change in depositional environment, and for each change, uplift or submersion must occur. Large-scale, vertical continental movements obviously require significant time and energy. Uniformitarian thinking stresses that this happens quite slowly, but consider the changes to the land that would ensue. Wouldn't there be a gradual change in sediment type and a mixing of both for a while? If this happened suddenly, there would be no mistaking the change in conditions. Given the abrupt change in strata between the two successive layers, isn't this exactly what we see? If standard time classifications are correct, much time elapsed between successive layers — a time of either erosion of intervening strata or non-deposition of strata, all while the continent was being uplifted or submerged, with land, desert or sea life thriving or being driven to extinction. The time for deposition needed and depositional environments for the layers reveal the impossibility of all this happening slowly and leaving little evidence. Remember, while deposition continues, there is no time gap.

Polystrate Fossils

Underground coal mines have always been extremely dangerous places to work, particularly in times past, before mechanization revised coal-mining methods. Miners are continually in danger. One of the most dangerous aspects of a coal mine is the presence of features known as kettles. Seen as rather circular shapes in the mine's roof, kettles are actually the bottoms of cylindrical bodies of rock which can easily detach and fall, crushing the miners beneath.

As it turns out, these circular features are the bottoms of fossilized, upright tree trunks. The lower portions, including the roots, are frequently mined away along with the rest of the coal, leaving only the trunk penetrating up through the roof into the strata above. If not stabilized and secured by bracing, roof

The Coconino Sandstone immediately underlies the Toroweap Limestone, again with no evidence of erosion.

bolts, or some other device, these cylindrical tree trunks can prove deadly.

The popular explanation for the origin of coal suggests that peat (an organic deposit thought to be the precursor of coal) accumulated in a swamp. As the swamp trees and bushes lived and died, organic material would accumulate as peat in the stagnant water of the swamp. Great thicknesses of peat are thought to have accumulated over the years as the swamp slowly submerged beneath the sea.

Once the peat swamp was completely submerged by the ocean, it was buried by slowly accumulating mud on the ocean floor. This overlying mud is thought to have slowly hardened into rock (usually shale or limestone), while the peat, deeply buried for millions of years, gradually was compressed, and metamorphosed into coal through the action of heat and pressure. This process involves driving the water and other volatile materials out of the peat, leaving behind mostly carbon.

Furthermore, ocean-bottom mud accumulates very slowly, usually at about one millimeter to one inch per year near the continental margins or in a shallow sea. In the deep ocean, sediments accumulate at about one millimeter per 1,000 years. At this rate, deep burial and alteration of peat into coal, and mud into rock, would require millions of years. In some eastern U.S. coal regions, up to 50 different coal seams are stacked on top of each other, separated by even more slowly accumulating limestone and shale layers. Theoretically, in evolutionary terms, each layer took a vast time for accumulation, making the total time for deposition lengthy indeed, as the entire region slowly bobbed up and down like a yo-yo — under the ocean and out of the ocean.

But fossil trees, such as mentioned above, give us additional information that helps us date the entire sequence and tie at least some of the layers together. If the trees grew in the place in which they are now found (in other words, trees growing in the swamp), then after the peat had accumulated and the whole area eventually slowly submerged, their dead trunks would have extended up into the ocean water overhead, sometimes as much as 30 to 40 feet, while slowly being buried by accumulating mud.

Grand Canyon, Arizona

Consider an exposed tree trunk extending 30 feet up from the bottom of an ocean. Of course, the tree would now be dead. No woody tree can long survive the action of seawater and marine animals. Some may grow with their roots in salt water, but when any tree is covered by seawater, it will die. How long would it take that dead tree trunk to rot and fall over? Could it remain upright for millions or for even hundreds of years, while the mud slowly accumulated around it? Obviously not. Penetrating completely through overlying layers, some fossilized trees even intersect more than one coal layer! These trees have come to be called polystrate fossils because they penetrate many *[poly]* strata. Did such trees ride the strata down and up again and then down again for millions of years? From studying these fossilized trees, we can conclude that the length of time for accumulation of the peat (which later turned into coal) and the overlying sediments was shorter than the time it takes for wood to decay. Obviously, wood decays in only a few decades at most, whether in an active ocean environment, standing in air, or buried in sediments.

Polystrate fossilized trees which extend through more than one layer in effect tie the entire series of layers together into a short period of time. This period of time cannot be explicitly determined from the data, but it is wholly incompatible with the long-age model normally taught.

One polystrate fossilized tree might be understood as having been deposited in a freakish scenario, but the fact is, the world contains many polystrate fossilized trees. In coal mines, they are quite common. Dramatic examples are sometimes found in areas where the coal cross section is exposed by erosion or by open pit mining.

Certain geologic sites have been especially crucial in shaping current thought. Thus it is with the amazing sequence of beds and fossils exposed along the Bay of Fundy, Nova Scotia, Canada, near the town of Joggins.

Sir Charles Lyell, friend and colleague of Charles Darwin, and principal architect of the principle of geologic uniformity, published his classic book *Principles of Geology* in 1830. In it, he proposed that slow and gradual processes, operating on a local scale much as are seen today, had sculptured the earth's surface over vast eons of time.

Arguments for Rapid Sedimentation at Joggins

1. A distinctive soil level is missing. Only a few of the trees arise from the organic coal layers. Often the trees rest on top of a coal seam, but roots seldom penetrate into it as they would if the tree grew in a peat bog. Those stumps arising from non-organic layers have no obvious soil present.

2. The vertical stumps often penetrate two or more strata, including thin seams of coal. Often they overlap other trees, arising from overlying layers. A dead, hollow, and submerged stump could not persist for the long period of time necessitated for a second forest to grow and collect as peat.

3. Segments of roots are often found inside the once-hollow trunks, while other fossil roots are normally detached and buried in the surrounding sediment. This seems to be a very unlikely scenario for any growth *in situ* hypothesis.

4. Leaves seldom remain on a forest or swamp floor for long periods without decay, yet well-preserved fossil leaves are abundant, thus indicating rapid burial.

5. Some of the fossilized trees are inclined, not directly in vertical growth positions. A few are found upside-down. None of the tree root systems are complete; all have been truncated.

6. The marine tubeworm *Spirorbis*, frequently found in fossilized association with the fossil trees, implies that all were exposed to seawater.

7. The surrounding sandstones are crossbedded, implying rapidly moving water.

8. The hollow vertical trees are typically filled with different sediments than the surrounding matrix. The internal sediments are themselves crossbedded.

9. The long axis of both the partial roots and the rootlets have a preferred orientation as would result from movement, not growth in place. The direction parallels current direction as discerned from ripple marks and crossbedding.

While a fuller understanding awaits more research, we can say with confidence that the "just-so story" told by Lyell and his modern-day disciples simply doesn't fit the facts. His story was unfortunately sufficient in his day to convince many scientists and theologians to abandon the doctrines of recent creation and global Flood, but it is insufficient today, now that more is known.

Excerpted from John D. Morris, "The Polystrate Trees and Coal Seams of Joggins Fossil Cliffs," *Impact*, no. 316 (October 1, 1999).

Lyell traveled far and wide, searching for evidence to support his model. One such site was at Joggins, where, he claimed, upright fossil trees rose from several successive layers of coal. It could hardly be imagined, he argued, that tree trunks could maintain their upright posture during transportation in a watery catastrophe.

The Geologic Setting at Joggins

Two schools of thought exist within uniformitarian geologists, who variously interpret these beds as: (1) a flood plain in which a river occasionally overflowed its banks, burying the surrounding marsh in mud; and as (2) a coastal plain occasionally inundated by rising oceans. In both cases, sediments are assumed to have been building up as the underlying basin subsided, with deposition keeping up with sinking. The coal beds are thought to record a recurring swampy bog, where organic materials collected for hundreds of years, only to be buried either by river flooding or sea level rises. Over time, thick layers of mud and sand would collect, later to be uplifted and returned to a swamp condition. Could it be instead that the abundant polystrate trees, which always

Tree fossil extending through several layers of rock

intersect numerous thin coal layers, interspersed with other rock types, were deposited by successive Flood events, and not over vast eons of successive uplifts?

The argument is not limited to large fossilized tree trunks. Once, on a field trip in Oklahoma, I observed thinly bedded limestones present in a hillside, scores of three-inch-thick limestone layers, stacked on top of one another like pancakes. Evolutionists interpreted the limestone layers as the result of lengthy, slow accumulation processes. But throughout the entire outcrop, evidence of rapid, continuous accumulation can be seen. Multiple polystrate fossils are found protruding up through several limestone layers each. These were not large trees but fossilized reed-like creatures called Calamities, in some cases up to six inches in diameter but usually just an inch or so. These segmented "stems" were evidently quite fragile once dead, for they are usually found in tiny fragments. Obviously, the limestones could not have accumulated slowly and gradually around a still-growing organism, but must have been quite rapidly deposited in a series of underwater events.

Most fossils are formed by rapid burial. This fish was so rapidly buried he didn't have time to swallow lunch.

Many fossils are buried in pristine condition, before scavenging or decay could take place. Here, even the fish scales are preserved.

Other types of fossils likewise testify to the same conclusion. Sometimes, an animal's fossilized body will intersect more than one layer or lamination within a rock, and the same argument applies.

One of the standard examples cited for long ages involves the Green River Formation in Wyoming. Here, extensive shale deposits consist of millions of millimeter-thick laminae, interpreted by uniformitarians as representing winter/summer sequences of sedimentation in calm lake environments. Yet fossils exist here in abundance!

By the way, how do fossils form? Do dead animals or plants sink to the bottom of a lake or an ocean and remain, while minuscule yearly amounts of sediment cover them up and fossilize them? No, of course not. They either float to the surface or sink to the bottom, where, in either case, they are eaten by scavengers or decomposed by bacterial or mechanical action. In no case do they remain for long. But here in the Green River Formation, fossils are often found in "fresh" condition, sometimes giving evidence of having been buried alive. While specific mechanisms vary, suffice it to say that in order to be preserved, they must be buried quickly, out of the reach of destructive agents.

And this is how it is at the Green River Formation. Fossilized catfish are found in abundance, some up to ten inches long, having the skin and soft parts preserved in some cases, obviously buried rapidly. The catfish fossils are found in many orientations, transgressing numerous millimeter-thick laminations. They did not die and lie for hundreds of years on the lake bottom while being slowly covered.[8] Other types of fossils, including "enormous concentrations" of bird fossils[9] are found in these "lake-bottom" sediments. Surely the time has come to recognize that this formation, often used as proof that the Bible is wrong, actually supports rapid catastrophism instead.

8. J.H. Whitmore, L. Brand, and H.P. Buchheim, "Implications of Modern Fish Taphonomy for the Preservation States and Depositional Environments of Fossil Fish, Fossil Butte Member, Green River Formation, Southwestern Wyoming," *Geological Society of America Abstracts with Programs* 35, no. 6 (2003): p. 105.
9. Alan Feduccia,"Presbyornis and the Evolution of Ducks and Flamingos," *American Scientist* 66 (May/June 1978): p. 298.

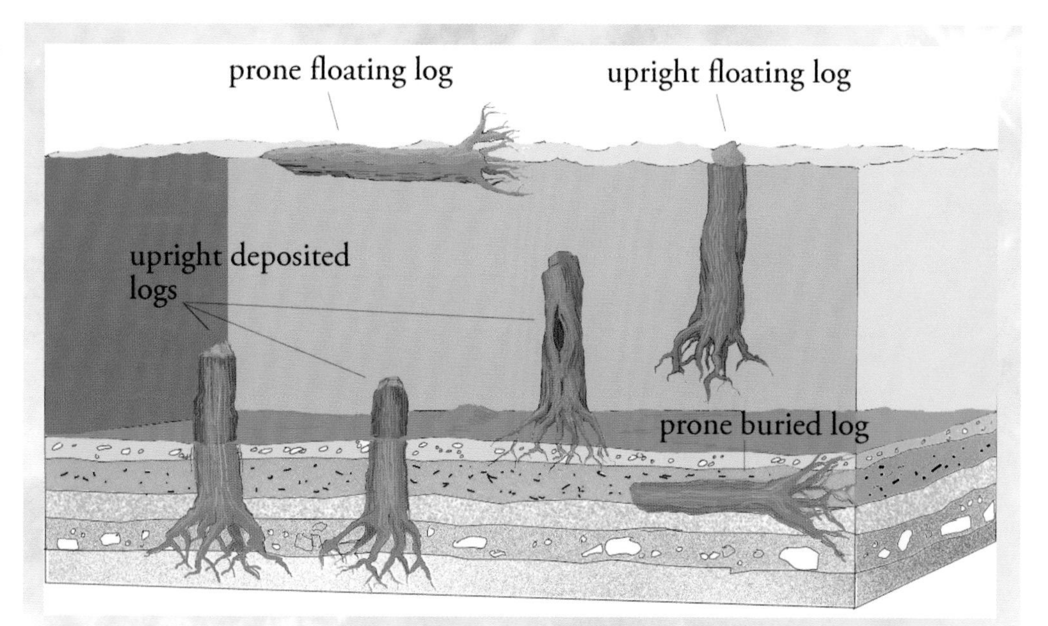

Trees floating in Spirit Lake at Mount St. Helens frequently sink with an upright orientation as they waterlog.

Coal

Regarding the origin of coal, it is noteworthy that the metamorphosis of peat into coal has never been observed under normal conditions. All grades of coal, lignite, and peat can be seen, but any changes seem to have ceased. Perhaps the old peat-bog theory should be abandoned. Research has shown that coal does not take millions and millions of years of heat and pressure to form as is commonly asserted. In recent years, several laboratory schemes have been devised whereby coal or coal-like substances can be made rapidly, in hours or, at the most, days.[10] It does not even require pressure, but mainly higher temperature (ideally, perhaps, very hot water[11]). It must be heated in a way in which the organic material is isolated from oxygen so that it cannot ignite. The process needs heat to get it started, but produces its own heat and pressure once it starts.

A catalyst, the presence of which causes the reaction to occur relatively rapidly, aids this chemical reaction. That catalyst is a certain type of clay, montmorillonite, a derivative of volcanic ash. Interestingly enough, many clay layers, usually called the underclay, often underlie coal beds. These layers are quite unsuitable as a soil and typically give scant evidence of biological activity. Thin, volcanic clay layers, called partings, are also found throughout the many coal layers, and frequently volcanically derived material is disbursed throughout the organic material itself and forms clinkers when the coal is burned.

The clay partings themselves are quite interesting. Many times these thin, flat layers cover hundreds of square miles in area.[12] In contrast, extensive, flat layers do not exist in modern peat swamps, where the surface is quite undulating, with many stream channels and local high places throughout. There is no such thing as one flat plane in a peat bog. It appears that peat must accumulate rather rapidly under the right conditions, and that the right conditions do not occur in peat swamps. Likewise, it appears that the clay partings require a flat depositional plane, not an active, growing peat swamp. Some other model of coal formation is obviously needed.

The May 18, 1980, eruption of Mount St. Helens devastated 150 square miles of forest north of the mountain. Within minutes, about four million logs were floating on Spirit Lake, surrounded by great volumes of organic material and volcanic ash. Within just a few years, an organic deposit consisting mostly of tree bark and decayed woody materials and containing volcanic ash had accumulated at the bottom of the lake. This peat has much the same make-up and geometry as coal. Many sheets of bark are piled on top of each other, having been abraded off the floating trees and sunk to the bottom. Since it is known that the hard, black shiny bands (vitrain layers) in coal are actually mummified bark, the Spirit Lake peat looks very much as if it would make good coal if buried and cooked.

To make matters more interesting, many of the floating tree trunks are becoming waterlogged and, as they do, they typically sink to the bottom, root end first, and ground themselves in the organic muck and bark sheets already at the bottom of the lake. As the organic material continues to accumulate, and as volcanic and erosive activity continues, adding volcanic ash and other sediments to the lake, these upright trees are being buried on the lake bottom. If further sediment accumulation occurs, these tree trunks will be buried in an upright "polystrate" position.[13]

10. See, for example, A. Davis and W. Spackman, "The Role of Cellulosic and Lignitic Components in Articulate Coalification," *Fuel* 43 (1964): p. 215–224; George R. Hill, *Chemical Technology* (May 1972), p. 296 and John Larson, "From Lignin to Coal in a Year," *Nature* 31 (March 28, 1985): p. 16; R. Hayatsu et al., "Artificial Coalification Study: Preparation and Characterization of Synthetic Macerals," *Organic Geochemistry* 6 (1984): p. 463–471.
11. E. Pennisi, "Water, Water Everywhere: Surreptitiously Converting Dead Matter into Oil and Coal," *Science News* (Feb. 20, 1993): p. 121–125.

12. Steven A. Austin, "Evidence for Marine Origin of Widespread Carbonaceous Shale Partings in the Kentucky No. 12 Coal," *Geological Society of America Abstracts* 11 (1979): p. 381–382.
13. See Steven A. Austin and John D. Morris, *Footprints in the Ash* (Green Forest, AR: Master Books, 2004). The Institute for Creation Research has begun leading tours to Mount St. Helens every other August for several years.

The peat not only resembles modern coal beds in character and geometry, but volcanically derived clay abounds throughout. If the mountain were to erupt again, depositing a layer of hot material on top of the peat deposit, it would likely be quickly turned into coal, probably looking just like the bituminous coal beds found today. And polystrate trees would penetrate this coal layer.

The sequences of sediment can accumulate rapidly, such as this series of beds at Mount St. Helens.

Regional Evidence for Continual Deposition

So far in this chapter, we have discussed evidence that local sets of strata were deposited rather continuously, with no significant time gap between any two consecutive layers. A similar line of reasoning can be applied to geologic layers on a regional scale.[14]

We have already noted that many leading geologists have become committed to neo-catastrophism, claiming that catastrophic processes laid down nearly all deposits rapidly, but that the catastrophes were episodic, separated in time by perhaps millions of years.

With few exceptions, the environment of deposition is underwater — that is where deposition takes place. When a deposit is uplifted out of water, and exposed to rainfall, wind, and river action, that is when erosion — not deposition — takes place. To modern old-earth advocates, an erosional event marks the passage of time, a hiatus in the overall (rapid) depositional sequence. We are interested in just how much time did elapse.

In the young-earth/Flood model, nearly the entire sequence of fossil-bearing rocks was deposited in short bursts of activity during the Flood, with rapid deposition interspersed with rapid erosional episodes. In this model, erosion was as rapid and catastrophic as deposition, neither taking much time. But in the old-earth model, while deposition can be considered as either rapid or slow, erosion usually takes long periods of time. (Rapid erosion requires a catastrophe.)

Erosion episodes are normally easy to recognize in the rock record. In general, they are represented by a zone where the adjacent rocks are not in a conformable sequence, which is the term applied when one layer overlies the other in a parallel, undisturbed manner. Conformity indicates continual deposition, with no erosional break. If strata are not in conformity, the contact is termed an unconformity or a disconformity. The cross sections shown pictorially define those concepts and identify the various types of erosional expressions.

In a conformity, each rock layer (itself laid down rapidly) is parallel with those above and below it. As discussed earlier in this chapter, reasoning from the presence of surface features, lack of bioturbation, lack of soil layers, or presence of polystrate fossils, we can conclude that, as a rule, no significant time passed between the deposition of any two conformable layers, and thus the entire sequence accumulated rather rapidly.

Individual layers (or beds, members, etc.) are many times combined into a group of similar layers called a formation. A formation would typically contain the same index fossils (i.e., groupings of fossils arranged by evolutionary ideas and believed to have lived at the same time). Usually, each layer within a formation is of the same basic rock type (for example, limestone), although an individual layer might vary from the norm. Geologists will seldom call for an erosional episode within a formation, which is considered to be a period of continual deposition, fast or slow, over a short or long time period.

The change from one formation to another might be represented by a change in rock type (perhaps from limestone to sandstone) or a change in fossil content, and a corresponding change in the age assigned. Between these two formations, erosion may have occurred, as represented by a lack of conformity between formations.

In a disconformity, the rock layers remained parallel after deposition — no tilting or faulting occurred. But as seen in illustration B, an erosional sequence (which reminds one of river or stream erosion, forming an uneven land surface) has developed. Obviously, this takes time, but how much time?

In an unconformity, the lower rock layers have been tilted and then eroded, as seen in illustration A, and at a later time, the upper layers were deposited horizontally on top of the tilted eroded surface. The upper edges of the tilted beds

14. For a fuller discussion of this concept, see Henry Morris and Gary Parker, *What Is Creation Science?* (Green Forest, AR: Master Books, 1982).

of the lower formation would even have been exposed on the erosional surface for a while. Again, how much time elapsed?

The answer cannot always be obtained in the local setting. But the erosional episode, either the disconformity or the unconformity, can usually be traced laterally through the use of subsurface information from oil wells or other outcrops. This may take a lot of work, but as the layers and formations, which themselves may cover vast areas, are traced laterally, they will either pinch out into a zone where they were not deposited at all, or to an area where they were not tilted or eroded. In such cases, an erosional sequence can eventually be resolved into a conformable, continuous depositional sequence.

This might be more easily understood, and certainly more easily demonstrated, by considering the various geologic periods in a hypothetical sense. For example, the Devonian Period is thought to have extended from about 417 million years ago to 354 million years ago. The next older period, the Silurian, extended from 417 million years back to 443 million years ago. One might not be surprised to discover that formations designated as within the Devonian and Silurian periods were each deposited as continuous series. Frequently, the Devonian rests conformably on top of the Silurian, and by application of the principles discussed above, one might conclude that no great time gap occurred between the end of the Silurian and the beginning of the Devonian.

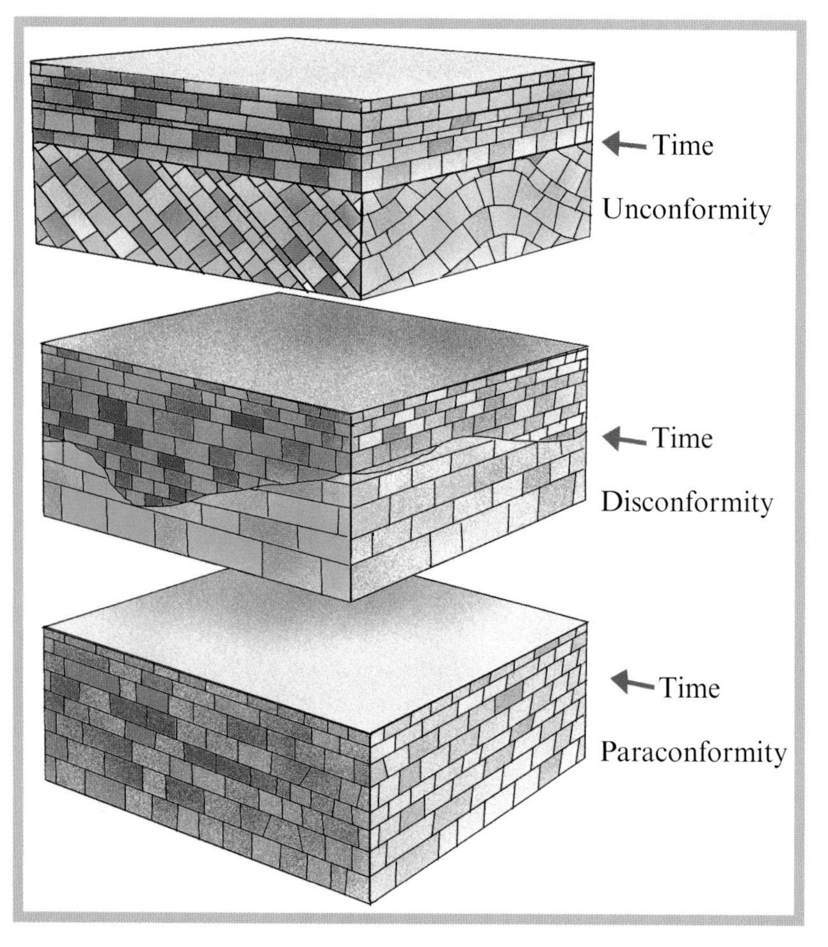

But sometimes an erosional sequence can be found between the two, indicating a time gap. The question is, how long? Even though the question might not be answered locally, and resolving it regionally might be difficult or impossible, the fact remains that in numerous other locations, no time gap is observed between the two systems. In fact, many locations can be cited where an entire series of layers, including the Ordovician (resting beneath the Silurian) and the Mississippian (lying above the Devonian), lie conformably, one on top of the other. Thus, the majority of the fossiliferous column can be resolved into a single, continuous depositional sequence.

Therefore, any local erosional episode, while it may represent more time than a normal conformable surface, still does not represent a significant time lapse. The entire column of Flood formations represents a single series of depositional episodes, interrupted locally by limited erosion, but continuing elsewhere.

In many cases, an individual formation may be overlain conformably by another formation, but the fossil content of the two demands (to evolutionists) that the formations' times of deposition be separated by many millions of years! This is called a paraconformity (illustration C) or pseudoconformity. A "surface of non-deposition and non-erosion" is implied — a surface that remained absolutely stagnant for millions of years. Obviously, there is no such stagnant surface on land today, with nothing happening on it, no erosion, no rooting by plants or burrowing by animals, anywhere on earth. Nor can a surface be stagnant underwater, with no bioturbation or deposition. This is a totally hypothetical concept illustrating the lengths to which old-earth advocates will go to salvage their millions-of-years theory.

Soft Sediment Deformation

One way of "tying the layers together" is to consider soft-sediment deformation. Evidently, many sediments were deformed (that is, bent or broken) while they were still in a soft, unconsolidated condition (i.e., soft, muddy sediments as opposed to hard rock).

In old-earth thinking, conformable layers of sediments were deposited consecutively, but separated in time, perhaps by millions of years. Subsequent to deposition, the strata sequence was deformed (i.e., bent or broken). This may have occurred at a time much later than the time of deposition. If already quite old, one would suppose that the sediments would have already hardened into solid rock, and should give evidence of having been in a hard, "brittle" condition when deformed.

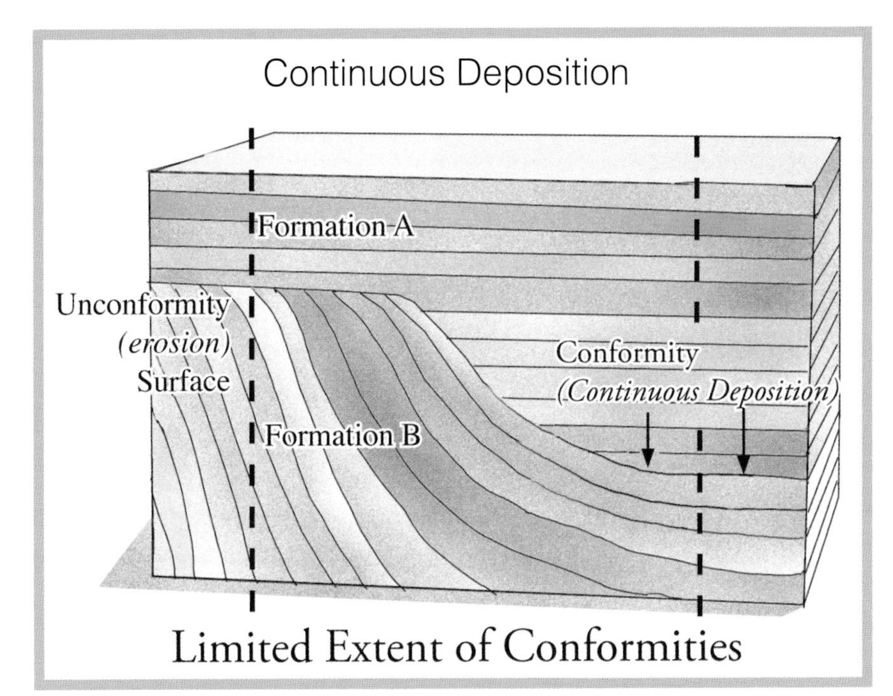

The young-earth model, however, predicts a much different situation. If creation/Flood thinking is correct, then great thicknesses of sediments were laid down during the year of the Flood and perhaps the first few centuries following. The lowest of these Flood sediments were laid down early in the Flood, and those nearer the top were laid down late in the Flood, only months later. Much deformation would have taken place late in the Flood as the oceans were deepened and widened, and the continents were uplifted. In many cases, these uplifts and the concurrent deformation would have taken place when the sediments were less than a few years old. We would expect that some of them would give evidence of having been deformed when still in a soft, muddy condition, not hard rock as they are today.

The first question that must be answered is this: How long does it take for soft, saturated sediments to harden into solid rock? Unfortunately, there can be no specific answer to this question, for each situation is different. In general, the presence of elevated temperature, the presence of an adequate cement to bind the grains or minerals together, and deep burial, forcing the pore water out and bringing the individual grains into contact with one another, all speed up the hardening process.

It must be recognized that even now, some of the sedimentary layers in the geologic column are softer than others. Some have not yet turned into solid rock. The conditions for hardening just weren't satisfied in all areas, usually the lack of adequate cement. But most of the layers have become, of course, solid rock.

Under normal conditions, sediments harden into rock in a matter of years, at the most perhaps as much as a

Paraconformities in the Grand Canyon — layers rest comfortably on each other. Only an evolutionary view of fossils would call for a time gap in between.

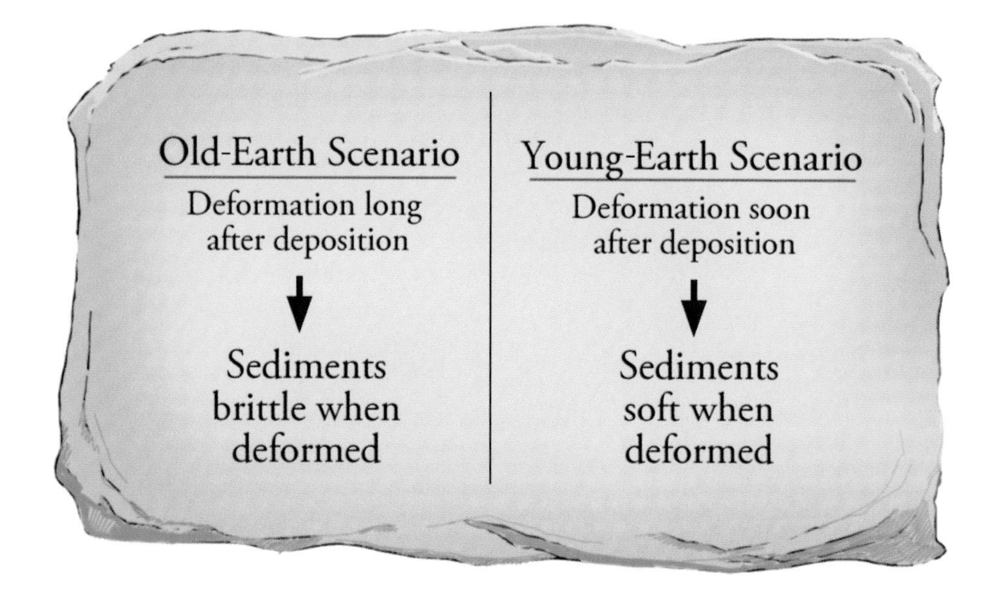

trees, and animals along the way. One mudslide after another covered the area like a stack of pancakes, resulting in a sediment pile up to 600 feet thick in places. These units, deposited by catastrophic water action, look essentially the same as rock layers frequently seen elsewhere. Even though these materials were not subjected to optimum conditions for hardening, within five years the sediments were hard enough to stand in a near-vertical slope. It does not take long to form rock from sediments; it just takes the right conditions.

Once a rock does become hard, it is extremely difficult to bend it without breaking it. Rocks would be expected to behave in what engineers call a hard, brittle fashion, and not in a soft, plastic, or pliable fashion. Usually, the rock's state when it deformed can be determined by examination, especially under a microscope.

Many times a rock will appear to have deformed while in a soft, unconsolidated condition, and yet the timing of deposition and bending raises concern. According to the old-earth scenario, rocks would often have been laid down millions of years before they were deformed. Since they had plenty of time during which to harden, they should have behaved in a brittle fashion, and yet, frequently, they seem to have deformed as would an unconsolidated mud.

hundred years. It does not take millions and millions of years to form rock from sediments. Under ideal conditions, it can happen within days.

For instance, modern-day concrete is very much analogous to a rock, albeit a man-made rock. Cementing chemicals are present which bind the grains together, and as the water in the mixture is incorporated into the mineral structure, or squeezed out and evaporated, the concrete turns quite hard. This happens in hours to days. Many rocks are formed in much the same rapid fashion.

Consider the sediments deposited by mudslides caused by the eruption of Mount St. Helens as the mountain's glacier rapidly melted and descended, incorporating mud, boulders,

This concept is illustrated in the Grand Canyon. When you stand on the 7,000-feet-above-sea-level south rim of the Grand Canyon and look over the edge, you will see horizontally bedded sedimentary layers totaling thousands of feet thick. The canyon is carved through an elevated plateau called the Kaibab Upwarp. The very same rocks which can be seen at Grand Canyon Village are also present 250 miles away in eastern Arizona,

Tightly folded strata at Split Mountain, California, must have been soft when bent, not hard as it is now.

(Above) At hinge point of monocline, the once soft sediment (now hard rock) flexes 90 degrees. Note two climbers for scale.

(Right) The normally horizontal Tapeats sandstone stands vertically in center of monocline.

but there they are a mile or so lower in elevation. The plateau was pushed up into its current elevated position some 70 million years ago, according to uniformitarian geologists, at the time the Rocky Mountains were being formed, and the canyon was later carved through this uplifted plateau.

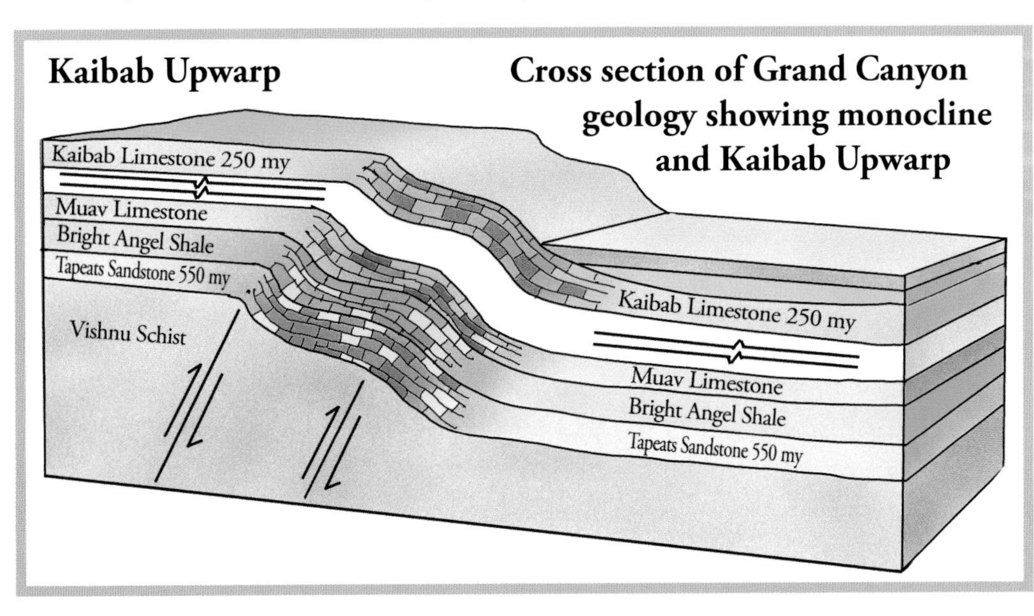

The strata are flat at Grand Canyon Village and are also flat but lower in eastern Arizona, 250 miles away. Most people do not know that on the edge of the plateau, where a monocline has draped the strata over a buried fault with a 5,000-feet displacement, the rocks are, in places, standing in a near-vertical orientation.

As can be seen in the accompanying cross section, the lowest sedimentary layer, in most locations the Tapeats sandstone, is thought by uniformatarian geologists to be on the order of 550 million years old. The Kaibab limestone on the rim is thought to be 250 million years old. But upwarp occurred only 70 million years ago. This means that the Tapeats sandstone was already about 480 million years old at the time of upwarp!

As we study the nature of bending at the hinge point, we will see that the sandstone appears to have been in a soft, unconsolidated condition when bending occurred. Scientists have not found elongated sand grains or the cement that bound the grains together in a broken and recrystallized state. It appears that the rocks, while having somewhat hardened due to the weight of the overlying sediments, were still rather soft and "fresh." They were not in a rock-hard, brittle condition at the time of bending. Evidently, they had not been there very long.[15]

15. For a similar study, see Steven A. Austin and John D. Morris, "Tight Folds and Clastic Dikes as Evidence for Rapid Deposition of Two Very Thick Stratigraphic Sequences," *Proceedings of the First International Conference on Creationism* (1986): p. 3–15.

Evolutionists will say, however, that if a rock is deeply buried and confined on all sides by surrounding pressure, bending can occur on an otherwise brittle rock. This is, of course, quite true, especially for certain rocks that can "flow," like rock salt. But in a hard rock like the Tapeats sandstone, that sort of bending always results in elongated sand grains or broken cement crystals, neither of which have been found in these deformed Grand Canyon rocks.

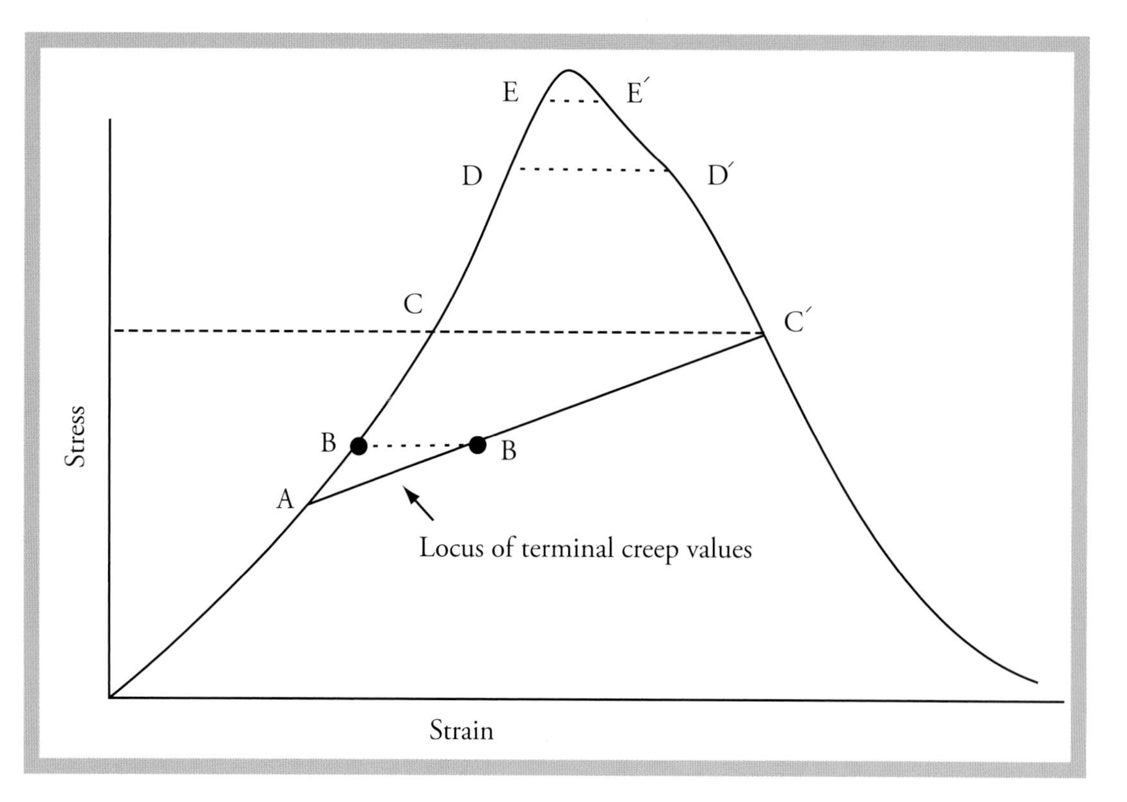

As can be seen on the accompanying stress-strain diagram, there is a limit to how far any substance can strain (or deform) under a given stress condition. Deformation will occur with the application of stress, and if the stress is maintained at a constant level, the material will continue to deform, or "creep."

Any rock can be incrementally loaded up to the failure point by the addition of stress. If the stress is maintained at a constant level below the rupture point, deformation will continue in most rocks to a terminal value, at which time the rock will either become stable, or it will fracture. Most rock types will not continue to undergo unlimited deformation. There is a limit to the amount of creep that will occur over time, as shown on the graph. Rock is not at all like a homogeneous material such as steel. Any tiny irregularity in the rock, either due to deposition or the increasing stress, would quickly propagate, causing failure of the whole.

As can be seen from the photographs of the point of greatest bending, these rocks bent at a 90-degree angle within a distance of 100 feet or so. This would place the rock in the outer half of the fold in tension. Hard rock is notoriously weak in tension, and yet this material stretched quite a bit. At places along the monocline, the entire layer visibly thinned as it bent. It's hard to imagine how hard rock could have withstood that much stretching, even if confined. Hard rock simply does not behave this way! From all we can gather, both visually and under the microscope, the rocks were still in a soft, unconsolidated condition at the time of bending.

The 5,000 feet of uplift produced different reactions in different rocks. The Tapeats sandstone and overlying sedimentary rocks merely draped over the fold. They bent and stretched and accommodated the movement. More recent (post-Flood) faulting, such as along the Bright Angel fault, broke the same sedimentary layers that had by then hardened into solid rock, even though movement along the fault was much less.

Beneath the Tapeats in most locations lies the Vishnu Shist, an extremely hard metamorphic rock. This formation is the basement rock in this area and is correlated laterally with rocks across the continent. In the creationist model, it normally is assumed to date from creation itself, part of God's original creation of the earth. Perhaps it was metamorphosed and altered by the Flood, but it was already hard and brittle by the time of the Flood. Uniformitarians date it as over a billion years old.

The Vishnu behaved as brittle rocks should behave during the uplift of the plateau. It broke! Seismic studies have located the faults, and have concluded that one side moved upward at least 5,000 feet relative to the other side.

Thus, the hard, deeply buried metamorphic rocks broke, while the sedimentary rocks, almost as deeply buried, which are now quite hard and break when faulted, merely draped over the fault at the time of the uplift. It appears that at the time they were recently deposited muds, and had not yet hardened into stone, as they have since the Flood.

This does not prove the young earth or the Flood or any other biblical doctrine. All we can say from this observation is that the Tapeats sandstone had not yet had enough time to harden into solid rock at the time it was deformed. The currently accepted dates of the deposition and deformation are incompatible with the nature of the rocks themselves. This observation, in effect, wipes out 480 million years of supposed earth history.

The situation at the Grand Canyon is far from unique. There are many, many other places where rocks have

Clastic sandstone dike squeezed up from below before sand hardened.

deformed while in a soft, unconsolidated condition. The Rocky Mountains are full of such occurrences. The Appalachian Mountains are as well. One such occurrence might be passed off as an anomaly, but the world is full of examples of soft sediment deformation, just as it should be if the earth is young and the Flood really is responsible for most of the world's geologic features.

Clastic Dikes

A similar argument can be made from the observance of features called clastic dikes. A clastic rock is made up of pieces of a previously existing rock. Sandstone, for instance, is made up of sand grains, and sand grains are usually pieces of quartz, most often derived from the erosion of previously existing granite and other rocks. Thus, sandstone is a clastic rock. A dike is a vertical, wall-like feature, buried underground. Many igneous dikes can be seen surrounding volcanoes, but our interest turns to clastic dikes.

Once I was asked to investigate some very interesting sandstone dikes in central Texas. These dikes were found in Rockwall County, east of Dallas. The county seat of Rockwall is Rockwall. Both are named after some very unusual "rock walls" which are found throughout the county. Farmers frequently curse these dikes because their plows are broken as they encounter stone "walls" hidden just below the ground surface.

On occasion, the rock walls have been excavated to see what they look like. From the side, they appear to be man-made rock walls consisting of broken flagstone, almost like bricks. The "bricks" sometimes appear to be beveled, with a mortar in between. Many of the local citizens are absolutely certain that a prehistoric race of giants built these rock walls as a fortress. However, every geologic study has concluded that they are clastic dikes and not a fortress after all.

Some of the local real estate agents, hoping to use interest in the ancient "fortress" as a means to increase property values, asked geologists from the University of Texas at Austin, and others from Baylor University, to come and see evidence they had gathered. But much to their dismay, the geologists again called the rock walls clastic dikes, and gave them a purely natural cause.

Next, the real estate agents called the Institute for Creation Research for help. Since they wanted to promote their area as the site of a prehistoric race of giants, and knew the Institute for Creation Research didn't agree with the commonly held geologic time table, they thought ICR might be sympathetic. I was on the faculty at the University of Oklahoma at the time, and since I had long been affiliated with ICR, I was asked to go down and investigate.

After days of studying, as much as I might have liked to conclude that these walls were made by a pre-Flood race of giants, I had to inform my frustrated hosts that the walls were in reality clastic dikes. There is a perfectly good geologic explanation for them. But there is also a wonderful young-earth lesson to be learned from these clastic dikes.

Most of the dikes are sandstone and are of significant size, varying from 1/4 inch to 18 inches in thickness, getting slightly thicker with depth. Dimensions vary, but some stretch for several miles, and are up to 150 feet in height. There is no discernible change in sand-grain size or lithology, either vertically or horizontally. Sometimes a smaller dike branches off a larger one, occasionally to rejoin it. A few other dikes consist of limestone or marcasite.

Apparently, the swarm of dikes stems from a series of related events, but all are found in cracks within limestone layers, common in central Texas, which, according to the standard dating scales, are on the order of 80 million years old. Some geologists have interpreted the dikes to be due to infilling of submarine cracks by material from above,[16] but this is not likely, at least not for the larger dikes made of sandstone. No horizontal layer of sandstone more than a few inches thick is present stratigraphically above the dikes that could serve as a source, and in no case would pure sand settle out in cracks in the sea bottom without abundant impurities present. Only the limestone dikes show a hint of horizontal deposition, as would be expected if they settled out from above, but this would also occur if injection took place laterally. The sandstone dikes show no compelling evidence of being formed by shallow or deep marine sand settling out from above.

Examination of the sandstone dike material indicates that it is essentially the same as that of a sandstone bed

16. John Napier Monroe, "The Origin of the Clastic Dikes of Northern Texas" (master's thesis, Southern Methodist University, 1949).

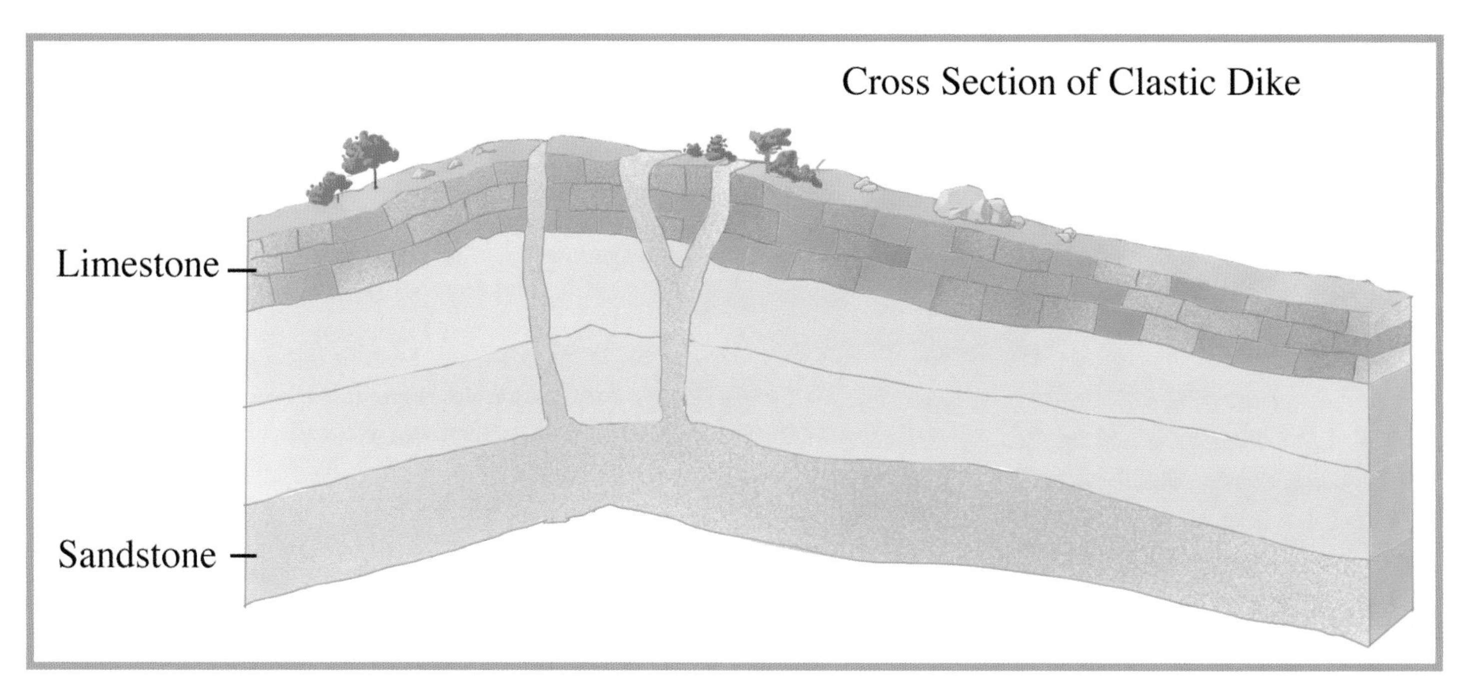

buried beneath the dikes.[17] They are made of the same chemical constituents, and exhibit the same array of sand grain sizes. The only difference between the dikes and the mother sandstone bed is that the sand grains in the dike appear to be similarly oriented, with their long axes tending to point in the same direction. This would result if the material were squeezed upward from below (as with grit in a toothpaste), but would not result from deposition or settling out of moving water. No deformed sand grains are seen, and there is no hint of broken and recrystallized cement. The material in the dikes appears to have still been a saturated and unconsolidated sandy mud at the time it was squeezed up into the overlying limestone.

Old-earth advocates tell us that the source sandstone bed was already millions of years old at the time of squeezing. Something is wrong here. Evidently, the source bed had not yet had time to harden before injection occurred. Again, this does not prove the young earth, but it does cast doubt on supposed earth history.

As with the case of soft sediment bending, the clastic-dike argument can be applied in many places around the world. For instance, the mountain-building episode that formed the Rocky Mountains uplifted sediments over 20,000 feet in some places. The time of uplift, as we have already mentioned, was approximately 70 million years ago, so they say. Thus, many of the underlying rocks were already hundreds of millions of years old at the time of uplift, and should have been quite hard. But it appears that this uplift episode injected soft material that has now hardened into clastic dikes. These dikes, the make-up of which is identical to the Sawatch sandstone (dated at 470 million years old), were injected as soft sandy mud into the much older Pike's Peak granite. If, as is apparently true, the uplift is the same as the Laramide Orogeny that formed the Rocky Mountains 70

17. Martin Kelsey and Harold Denton, "Sandstone Dikes Near Rockwall, Texas," *University of Texas Bulletin*, no. 3201 (1932): p. 138–148. Very little interest has been shown in the dikes in recent decades. Dr. T.J. Gholy, geologist at East Texas State University, has, however, investigated them over the years. His conclusion, which agrees with the article and with my conclusion based on my own field work, is that the main dikes were injected from below (personal communication).

Sandstone "pipes" injected from below while source sand was still soft

million years ago, then this scenario wipes out 400 million years of earth history.[18]

Another fascinating study could be cited from Kodachrome Basin State Park in Utah.[19] Here, dikes are found in association with giant sandstone "pipes," rather cylindrical features sometimes reaching 170 feet in height and 50 feet in diameter.[20] The same problem crops up again. The time of deposition of the source bed is thought to be about 25 million years before the time of injection.

These are not isolated examples. The world contains quite a few examples of clastic dikes (and pipes), just as it should if the biblical account of the Flood and the young earth are correct.

Reevaluation of a Classic Old-Earth Argument

Many people have the mistaken impression that geology has proved that the earth is billions of years old. As we have seen, nothing could be further from the truth!

One of the classic arguments used in favor of the old earth comes from the Petrified Forest of Yellowstone Park, where beautifully preserved petrified tree stumps are found in great numbers. At Specimen Ridge, a hillside now gouged by erosion reveals some 27 or more horizontal layers of consolidated volcanic material, each of which contains abundant petrified wood, including many tree trunks in a vertical position with the root ends down and the trunk up. Many other trunks are horizontal. Similar exposures at nearby Specimen Creek consist of over 50 layers.

The upright trees have traditionally been interpreted as having been buried and petrified in their place of growth, as explained on the geologic marker present there. The series of pancake-like layers are interpreted as containing in petrified form, successive, in-place forests, each of which was buried by volcanic ash. It is claimed that after each volcanic eruption the upper surface of the volcanic-ash layer slowly weathered into suitable topsoil in which seeds and sprouts could take root. Within a few hundred years, a second forest grew to maturity, which in turn was also buried by a second volcanic-ash eruption. This repeating pattern occurred at least 27 times, so it is thought. Each forest required at least several hundred years to develop, because petrified trees containing up to 400 or so tree rings are typically present in each layer. The whole sequence of events is assumed to have taken many thousands of years at a minimum, perhaps much longer. At any rate, more time elapsed than can be easily fit into biblical chronology.

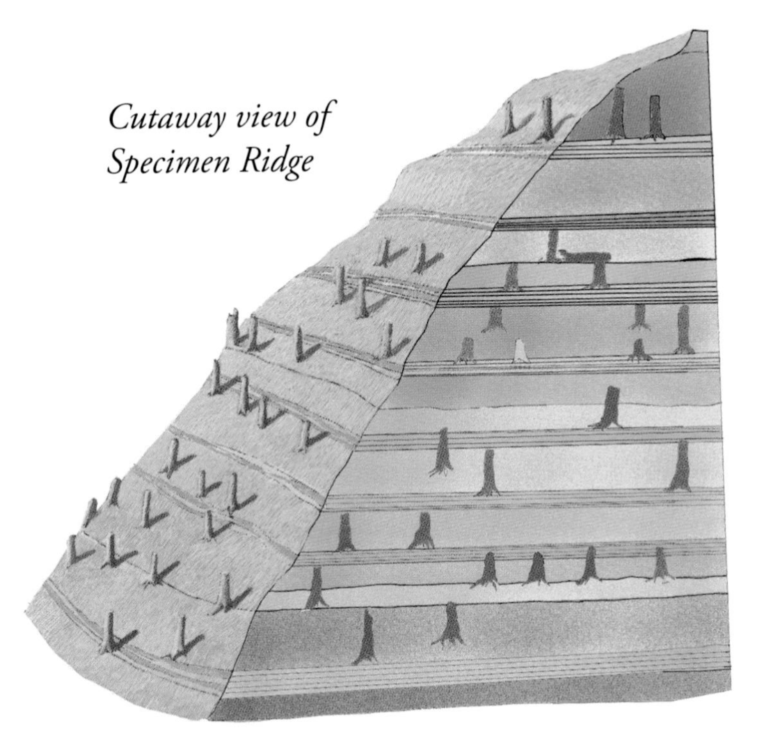
Cutaway view of Specimen Ridge

This might be a good time to point out that petrified wood does not take millions of years to form. Wood can, under certain conditions, be petrified rapidly, as several laboratory experiments have shown.[21] During one field experiment, researchers fastened a block of wood on the end of a rope and dangled it down into an alkaline spring in Yellowstone Park. They submerged it in the silica-rich, hot waters to see if such an environment would petrify the wood. When they came back one year later and pulled the log out of the hole, they found that substantial petrifaction had occurred.[22] There are many examples of man-made wooden objects petrifying within a few years. Furthermore, artificially petrified wood is even being produced commercially these days for true hardwood floors. It does not take long to petrify wood; it just takes the right conditions.

Geologic Evidence for the Young Earth

1. Surface features
2. Deficiency of bioturbation
3. Lack of soil layers
4. Undisturbed bedding planes
5. Polystrate fossils
6. Limited extent of unconformities
7. Soft-sediment deformation

18. One of our graduate students at ICR, Mr. Bill Hoesch, conducted a comprehensive field study of this area — his thesis, "The Timing of Clastic Dike Emplacement along Red Creek Fault, Fremont County, Colorado," was published in 1994; Ariel A. Roth, "Clastic Pipes and Dikes in Kodachrome Basin," *Origins* 19, no. 1 (1992): p. 44–48.
19. M. Huuse et. al., "Giant Sandstone Pipes Record Basin-scale Liquefaction of Buried Dune Sands in the Middle Jurassic in SE Utah," *Terra Nova* 17, no. 1 (2005): p. 80–85.
20. Apparently they were injected from below by unprecedented regional shaking, liquefying and melting sediment and forcing it into overlying cracks.
21. Refer to Steven A. Austin, "Catastrophes in Earth History," *ICR Technical Monograph*, no. 13 (1984).
22. A. C. Sigleo, "Organic Geochemistry of Solidified Wood," *Geochimica et Cosmochimica Acta* 42 (1978): p. 1397–1405.

Petrified trees in growth position, but not growth location.

Creationists, over the years, have studied the Petrified Forest in Yellowstone to see whether the evidence allowed any other interpretation. I was first there in the mid-70s and observed the many upright trees petrified with their roots down, trunks up. The question was, did they grow there? If so, then the earth is older than a straightforward reading of Scripture would indicate. Or, could they have been moved into this location from another location, somehow maintaining an upright posture?

We noticed several things about the trees. In each case, they were only stumps; no complete trees were present. Furthermore, the stumps typically were of a common length, usually 10 to 12 feet tall.

Likewise, the roots, while often oriented in a downward direction, did not have fully developed root systems. In living trees, the roots are much wider than the trunk of the tree, even extending out farther than the branches. The roots of these petrified trees appear to have been broken off near the base of the tree. Only root balls are present, not the fully developed root system. Thus, the trees are much different from living trees, and we suspected, as had other creationists before us,[24] that they did not grow where they are now found.

Each layer of trees, embedded as they are in volcanic ash, exhibits other evidence of having grown somewhere else and having been transported to this location. Each of the

Ground water percolating through hot volcanic ash, which typically is full of silica, is thought to be the most suitable natural environment for the rapid petrifaction of wood.

The series of ash layers containing petrified trees, some upright, was once considered by many to be the most convincing argument against the Bible. This classic and dramatic site certainly has much to tell us. Consider the following quote from former Bible-believer turned skeptic Dr. Ron Numbers. He has become a widely published chronicler of "errors" in creation thinking, convincingly writing from an enlightened insider perspective. His progression in thinking for rejecting creation and Christianity follow.

> I vividly remember the evening I attended an illustrated lecture on the famous sequence of fossil forests in Yellowstone National Park . . . first agonizing over, then finally accepting, the disturbing likelihood that the earth was at least thirty thousand years old. Having thus decided to follow science rather than the Scripture on the subject of origins, I quickly, though not painlessly, slid down the proverbial slippery slope toward unbelief. . . . The [agnostic] tag still feels foreign and uncomfortable, but it accurately reflects my theological uncertainty.[23]

Even though upright, this tree has no roots. It did not grow here.

23. Ronald L. Numbers, *The Creationists* (New York: Alfred A. Knopf, 1992), p. xvi.

24. John C. Whitcomb and Henry M. Morris, *The Genesis Flood* (Phillipsburg, NJ: Presbyterian and Reformed, 1961): p. 418–421. This position was advocated in this groundbreaking book.

layers gives evidence of having flowed as a water-saturated mud primarily consisting of volcanic ash. The consistency of the layers of volcanic mud and the common height of the stumps suggest that they may have come from a common source.

Other investigators have noted features about this area that likewise support a "rafting-in" model. Dr. Harold Coffin found that the twigs and branches, as well as horizontal tree trunks, are oriented in a preferred direction. This would be the case if they had been rafted in by moving mud. He also noted a great variety of plant material, seemingly too much variety to have all been growing in one location when covered by volcanic ash. It appeared, then, that the trees may have come from some distant source in a mudflow that picked up a variety of materials along the way.[25]

Upright floating logs in Spirit Lake

In 1975, I predicted a way to solve the problem. I suggested that the tree rings in petrified trees from several layers should be compared. I predicted that if the layers had come from a common source and the trees had lived at the same time, then tree-ring patterns in different layers would match. But if they had grown in successive forests, at totally different times, their tree-ring patterns would show no correspondence whatsoever.

This is indeed a wonderful time to be a young-earth creationist, because so much information is now available that confirms our understanding of Scripture. A friend of mine, Dr. Mike Arct, recently performed such a study on the nearby Specimen Creek area. In his study, he discovered a "signature" ring pattern in several different layers, demonstrating that the various "forests" grew at the same time and must have been transported to this location in successive mud flows,[26] thus disproving the consecutive-forest model.

The recent eruption of Mount St. Helens further reinforces this rafted-in interpretation. As a result of the eruption on May 18, 1980, an energetic blast cloud raced from the upper mountain and devastated 150 square miles of forest. Likewise, a concurrent avalanche sped from the summit into Spirit Lake, causing a wave almost 900 feet high, which scoured slopes adjacent to the lake.

Many trees from the "blow-down zone" found their way into Spirit Lake, but others sloshed into rivers draining Mount St. Helens and were carried along in mud flows for scores of miles downstream. As this mud moved along, many of the trees were observed to be floating upright, roots down, moving along at a high rate of speed. Perhaps this was due to the fact that boulders may have been trapped in the truncated roots, or because the wood in the roots is more dense than that in the trunk. For whatever reason, they were floating in moving mud, still in an upright position. When the mud finally came to a halt, they were still upright, and are still upright today.

Likewise, today on Spirit Lake, as many of the trunks become waterlogged, they turn to an upright position and sink. They bury themselves in the ash and peat deposit at the bottom of the lake, a fact that we confirmed both by scuba investigation and side-scanning sonar. Since Mount St. Helens continues to be active, depositing more material in the lake as time goes on, these upright trees will be buried in separate geologic layers, even though they came from the same forest. If the lake were to fill up and be excavated by geologists centuries from now, the (by then petrified) trees might look as if they represented several separate forests. But, of course, they don't, and, furthermore, their tree-ring patterns would certainly match.[27]

So we can see that on Mount St. Helens, two completely separate mechanisms resulted in upright trees being deposited where petrification can take place. They are deposited in

25. Harold Coffin, *Origin by Design* (Hagerstown, MD: Review and Herald Publishers, 2005). For a good discussion of this and other subjects, see this book.

26. M.J. Arct, "Dendroecology in the Fossil Forests of the Specimen Creek Area, Yellowstone National Park," Ph.D diss., Loma Linda University, 1991. See also his master's thesis, "Dendrochronology in Yellowstone Fossil Forests" (1985).

27. John Morris and Steve Austin, *Footprints in the Ash* (Green Forest, AR: Master Books, 2004).

Forest devastated by Mount St. Helens eruption

growth position, but not in growth location. We suspect that similar events occurred at Yellowstone Park.

Interestingly enough, several recent interpretations of the Yellowstone Petrified Forest have included references to the events at Mount St. Helens. Many geologists are now agreeing that the Yellowstone petrified trees were, indeed, from the same standing forest, transported on a series of mud flows. And, wonder of wonders, the evolution lesson along the roadside has been removed. The classic argument that the Bible is wrong has been shown to be wrong. The Bible stands. Dr. Ron Numbers was misled!

Parenthetically, Dr. Arct also found some other intriguing features in the Yellowstone petrified tree rings. Within many of the layers, trees were present with up to 900 tree rings. The rings were large, and showed almost monotonous regularity, indicating excellent growing conditions year after year. No frost patterns were found at all. These older trees were of the same family as the various redwood species that today grow to great ages, even in hostile environments, and are essentially immune to fire, insects, and disease. Furthermore, these large trees typically had their bark removed, as do the floating trees in Mount St. Helens' Spirit Lake. Did abrasion during transportation scour the bark from the trees in Yellowstone as it did on the trees in Spirit Lake?

Couple these findings with the fact that in the same layers, many other stumps were found equally well petrified, but with only 30–50 tree rings. Many of these still retained their bark (sometimes even in "woody" condition), athough their branches had been stripped off. Furthermore, their tree rings showed great variation from year to year.

Next, consider the fact that the time period before the Flood was probably less than 2,000 years. No tree could have grown to the ages of present redwoods, some of which are over 4,000 years old and still growing.

Can this series of deposits represent a time of volcanism in the centuries following the Flood? Could the older trees be pre-Flood trees, which had floated through the Flood year in a floating mat, finally to be grounded as the Flood waters receded? Perhaps they remained on the ground while other trees sprouted from their cones and grew around them. Both would then have been removed by dynamic mud flows associated with post-Flood volcanism, of which there was much.[28]

Conclusion

Thus we have seen, from a variety of different measurements and techniques, that the geologic and physical evidence of the world is quite compatible with the biblical doctrine of the young earth. We cannot prove the Bible from looking at geology, nor do we try to. We accept Scripture by faith, but insist that if the Bible is really true, then the geologic evidence must support it — and indeed it does! The evidence not only supports the Bible, but a great deal of geologic evidence is quite incompatible with an old-earth scenario.

28. For a thorough study of this and related subjects, see Greg J. Beasley, "Long-Lived Trees: Their Possible Testimony to a Global Flood and Recent Creation," *Creation Ex Nihilo Technical Journal* 7, part 1 (1993): p. 43–67.

QUESTIONS

1. Virtually every sedimentary rock is now understood as the result of rapid catastrophic deposition requiring only a short period of time. Where do old-earth advocates put the great amounts of time required for evolution?

2. List several ways to "tie the layers together" into a short period of time, thus minimizing the time for the whole series of strata.

3. What is meant by "bioturbation" and how does this argue for a young earth?

4. Under what circumstances could a "polystrate tree" be preserved today?

5. Investigation of the recent Mount St. Helens eruption and its aftereffects has been used throughout the book. Summarize its young-earth implications.

Chapter Nine

WHAT DO THE ROCKS MEAN?

Recently I was invited to make a short appearance on a radio talk show hosted, as it turned out, by a Christian-hating, Christian-baiting skeptic. The general subject was creation/evolution, and he characterized all creationists as ignorant, bigoted fundamentalists, and stated that "he had one on the phone." He bragged to show the error of creation by demanding of me "one proof" that the rocks are only 6,000 years old.

I began by pointing out that rocks are rather generic with respect to age, and that there is no hard evidence that they are of any particular age. Each rock must be understood within a world view, using certain assumptions about the past. But he would have none of it. Again he demanded "one proof" of young age. All appeals to allow his listeners to be informed fell on deaf ears. His was on a bully pulpit or "bully mike." He refused to be educated on how rocks are dated, wrongly thinking that rocks speak. His listeners perpetuate his bigotry, which he wrongly received from others before him, to this day, just as students repeat their classroom instruction and scientists parrot the expert. We should be able to do better.

While I have not in this book, and (as I have maintained) indeed could not have, proved scientifically that the earth is young, I have given significant evidence that fits much more easily in the young-earth model than in the old-earth model. In fact, some of the evidence does not seem to be at all compatible with old-earth ideas. The weight of the evidence comes down on the side of the young earth.

More important, however, is the way of thinking about the unobserved past that is presented here. My contention throughout has been that only Scripture gives specific information about the age of the earth and the timing of its unobserved events. Rocks, fossils, isotope arrays, and physical systems do not speak with the same clarity as Scripture. The truth is there in nature, but can we find it? Such systems in many ways are rather generic with respect to age: they can be adequately interpreted within more than one model, depending on one's presuppositions.

In order to properly interpret the data, we must first go back to Genesis and develop our overall model, get our thinking straight. Then we interpret the physical evidence within that model. In the biblical model derived from a straightforward reading of Scripture, fossiliferous rocks were by and large deposited by Noah's flood. Fossils are the remains of organisms that descended from those created during creation week and died in the Flood (with some exceptions). Radioisotope dating methods suffer from wrong assumptions about the past, mainly because all physical systems were drastically altered by the global and destructive nature of the Flood, and also because the assumptions used deny the possibility of creation. Scripture does not give us all the details, but only as we place our interpretations in agreement with the teachings of Scripture do we have a chance to rightly understand the past.

Evolutionists follow exactly the same method of thinking, only they bow before a different philosophy — that of naturalism, evolution, and uniformitarianism. These doctrines about the past are, at best, based on unprovable assumptions, and are not well-supported by the data. By definition, they deny the great worldwide events of Genesis. But if creation and the Flood are facts of history, they must be included in one's view of the past. To deny historical truth before attempting to reconstruct history is forever to embrace error.

Does It Matter?

The questions then arise: "Why are we concerned with something so elusive?" "Shouldn't we concern ourselves only with knowing the Rock of Ages, and forget about the ages of rocks?" Followed by the statement, "Let's talk about where we're going, not about where we've been."

Comments and questions like these may seem very spiritual, but they are little more than cop-outs. All too many Christians have chosen not to see or become involved in the battle around us, in effect surrendering to the enemy, and in so doing, abandoning all those who come under the influence of the enemy.

Battlefronts captured by those with views adversarial to Christianity include the news media, television, politics, academia, the judicial system, public education, and, in this case, much of science, with resulting havoc everywhere. Each of these battles was winnable, and some of them still are! The Christian's resources far surpass those of the humanist, and the evidence is very clearly on our side. Losses are avoidable.

The evidence is especially on our side in real science. Creation far excels evolution as a scientific model. Evolution survives only by suppression of alternatives. The tactics of evolutionists include ridicule, personal attacks, bureaucratic policies, and court rulings. Mostly, evolution survives because so few people have ever been allowed to hear a credible case for creation. All that most people know is what they have been taught.

Few advocates of either creation or evolution even recognize the philosophical nature of the question. The discussions usually sink to a "my evidence versus your evidence" level, while in reality all evidence must be interpreted, and nearly all evidence can be included in either model. The discussions should be "my interpretations based on my assumptions versus your interpretations based on your assumptions" and the reasonableness of each set of assumptions and interpretations. And, of course, we must never confuse circumstantial evidence with direct evidence.

Please do not think I am claiming that a proper presentation of creation and young-earth thinking guarantees victory in every legislative committee, school administration, radio talk show, and think tank. Many of these arenas have been infiltrated by assertive secularists and are now dominated by persons who know they are in a battle, and know which side they are on. Often, the rules are set up so that creationists are not even allowed in the discussion, let alone taken seriously.

But the battle is winnable, at least on a local and individual level, and the battle is worth fighting! The following pages give several reasons why a follower of Christ must join the battle, for the battle is for the minds and hearts of men and women, boys and girls, scientists and laypersons, Christians and non-Christians. The fight must be carried to several battlefronts, and all soldiers of the King can play a vital role. Eternal matters are at stake!

The Scientific Battlefront

Few people, especially Christians, ever stop to think that God has ordained science, and that each human has been commanded to take part in this enterprise. As God's week of creating came to an end, He placed Adam in charge of all creation. Adam was told to "subdue" the earth, and "have dominion" over it and all of the creatures in it (Gen. 1:28). Theologians call this the Dominion Mandate, and recognize that it passed through Adam to all his descendants.

> And God blessed them, and God said unto them, Be fruitful, and multiply, and replenish the earth, and subdue it: and have dominion over the fish of the sea, and over the fowl of the air, and over every living thing that moveth upon the earth.

The two verbs are significant. *Subdue* implies the serious study of the earth and its processes, as well as of all living things. We have come to call this understanding process "science." Mankind must fully understand the creation in order to carry out the next part of the mandate.

To *have dominion over* creation would fall into our modern category of technology, that of the utilization of our knowledge. God has placed mankind in the position of stewards over creation. We are to care for it, manage it, protect it, and utilize it for our good and God's glory.

Frequently, humanists claim that Christians, if allowed, would spoil the environment and ruin the ecological balance between species. Although some Christians are insensitive, no support can be found in Scripture for abusing the environment.

Actually, the Christian should lead the way in environmental concerns. In recent years, the humanist has laid exclusive claim to this God-commanded activity, and is using it to capture the hearts of young people. Along the way, they have twisted environmentalism into pantheism, with a host of attendant New Age evils. A good deal of illegitimate baggage has thus been added to proper, God-commanded concern for the creation. To modern environmentalists, man is the enemy, not the steward. Evolution is the creator, through Mother Nature and Father Time. A Christian must not participate in the pantheistic aspects of the modern environmental movement, but God expects all of us, not just environmentalists, to care wisely for His creation.

Another reason creation understanding is so important is that God deserves praise for His creative majesty, just as He does for His redemptive work. Christians' prayer lives suffer dramatically if we do not spend time praising Him for His creative acts and His sovereign care for the creation. His Word to us includes many references of praise to the God of creation. How dare we ignore them, and it!

> Thou art worthy, O Lord, to receive glory and honor and power: for thou hast created all things, and for thy pleasure they are and were created (Rev. 4:11).

Furthermore, God validates His Word in time and space, relating many prophecies and historical references in Scripture to specific times and places, things that are in principle, verifiable.

Jesus asked Nicodemus:

> If I have told you earthly things, and ye believe not, how shall ye believe if I tell you of heavenly things? (John 3:12).

If we do not believe Him when He teaches about "earthly things," how can we trust Him when He tells us of "heavenly things"? We can check the things of science and history, and when we do, we find His Word reliable.

On the other hand, if He is wrong about science and history, He is wrong, and by His own Word, the wrong prophet is a false prophet (see Deut. 18:20–22).

In order to fully appreciate God's creative power and majesty, we must first rightly understand His creation. This means we must study and comprehend it fully and rightly. Then we can praise Him from knowledge, and bring Him glory as we properly care for creation and obey His mandate.

This command to understand includes more than creation; it extends to the young-earth issue as well. The enemy uses evolution as a major weapon in his battle, and the old-earth idea undergirds all of evolutionary thinking. In witnessing to others about Christianity, many times you will encounter an unsaved person who will use the young-earth teaching of Scripture to reject Christ as revealed in Scripture, because if one is an untruth, the other must be, too. Creationists are tempted to stop with the creation versus evolution issue and ignore the age of the earth, but to many people, the old earth proves evolution. It certainly disproves Scripture, and, therefore, the scriptural doctrine of creation. Many on both sides consider the age of the earth as the weakest doctrine in Scripture. We must strengthen and defend it.

Intelligent Design

Here is an issue we can agree on, that of the intricate complexity of all things, especially in the biosphere. The design of living things is too great to deny. Every observer, from creationist to secularist, sees the intricate design in life and must ascribe it to something. Biblical creationists attribute this complexity to the creator God of the Bible, and claim things are exactly the way they should be if Scripture is correct, especially when you consider the information in the DNA molecule. No undirected process produces intelligent information that can be read and understood. Its coded information surpasses our own ability to understand it. Today's molecular biologists cannot write such a code or even devise a way to do the things a cell can do. Certainly a level of intelligence beyond our own was behind the writing of the DNA or the functions of a cell. Creationists recognize the source: the Creator God of Genesis.

Naturalistic evolutionists have no belief in a God, and thus no recourse to a supernatural mind behind it all. As did Darwin, they generally attribute the amazing design to natural selection. Unthinking random mutations have produced a written encyclopedia with intelligent information contained within. Surely some things cannot be.

Now there is a new alternative on the market. Called the Intelligent Design (ID) movement, it acknowledges the complexity and order, insists it proceeds from intelligence, but refuses to speculate on the identity of the intelligence and designer. It also rightly brands naturalistic evolution as the religion of naturalism.

Thus we have three options: unintelligent design by random causes, intelligent design by an unknown cause, or intelligent design by the intelligent God of the Bible. Origins views like these are at their core unprovable, but which is most credible? If God exists, creation thinking handles all the data. Naturalism only makes sense if there is no God and if natural forces are all there is. Reliance on blind natural forces stretches credibility, but that is the evolutionists' faith. Any view of origins is "religious," since it attempts to reconstruct the unobserved past. The best we can do is to determine which historical view is most satisfying scientifically, historically, and personally.

Creation and New Age

On the other hand, many secularists today have abandoned strict naturalism in favor of hazy New Age thinking. Even scientists are leaving Darwinian evolution in droves, recognizing that strictly natural processes, operating at random on inorganic chemicals, could never have produced complex information-loaded living cells. They have grown weary of arguing that random mutations in a highly complex genetic code provide improvements in it.

To avoid the implications of impotent nature, New Age disciples have chosen to believe that nature is alive and well and doing these things on purpose. Thus, they worship nature (some more openly than others), ascribing to nature qualities and characteristics formerly ascribed to God. They recognize the marvelous design in living things and know that an overriding mind must be behind it. That mind to them is Gaia, or Mother Earth. They would be nearly as critical of Darwinian evolution as creationists. How can you reach these New Age disciples?

Logical reasoning with one who has chosen absurdity as his faith is never easy. Arguing creation versus evolution with a New Age advocate seldom works. But sometimes discussing the age of the earth can provide an opening. To supply firm evidence that the earth may not be so old might just weaken his commitment to his anti-God philosophy.

The Biblical Battlefront

When I came to work at ICR in 1984, having left my faculty position at the University of Oklahoma, ICR had far outgrown its facility. The only office space left was an overflow room for the ICR library, in which were kept thousands of theological books dating from the 1700s and 1800s. A collector who had been interested in the history of modern creation and evolution had donated them to ICR. The books represented the thinking of Christian leaders through the decades during which naturalistic evolution replaced creation as the norm. Being a confirmed bookworm, I read many of these books, and skimmed nearly all of them.

During the 1700s, while exceptions could be cited, most theologians and scientists in western countries were Bible-believing Christians and creationists. But by the late 1800s, most scientists and theologians had abandoned the creation, Flood, and young-earth doctrines, and had accepted the position that the Bible contains errors and cannot be trusted, particularly as it relates to science and history.

Having studied geology in secular settings, I knew that in the late 1700s, James Hutton, and in the early 1800s, Charles Lyell, had proposed the principle of uniformity and, thus, an old earth. They are canonized by secularists for opening the door for Darwin in 1859 to completely discredit the Bible! Many leading scientists resisted these ideas, and defended Scripture as both true and scientific. But by the late 1800s, almost all such voices had been silenced. What could have brought such a turnaround?

My office reading provided the answer. In many cases, it was Christians who led the charge against Scripture. Beginning in the early 1800s, theologians readily adopted the old-earth ideas, then uniformitarianism instead of the Flood. They even toyed with evolutionary ideas long before Darwin. The Bible-believing scientists of the day were thus in the difficult position of trying to defend Scripture when theologians were against them.

Gradually, belief in a historical view of Genesis waned, and a generation later, when Darwin proposed his mechanism for evolution, even scientists fell into his trap, and few academics, either scientists or theologians, any longer accepted creation.

Parenthetically, things have not changed much. Scientists and laymen, not theologians, lead the modern creation revival. By and large, seminary-trained theologians oppose or are indifferent to biblical and scientific creationism. But it does not take a seminary degree to know that the Bible teaches creation and a young earth. In fact, it probably takes seminary training to accept the various perversions of Scripture, such as the day-age concept, the framework hypothesis, theistic evolution, and the local-Flood theory. Modern evangelicals are hard-pressed to find a major seminary that unequivocally holds to a historical, grammatical view of Genesis. Most prefer to allegorize it and welcome evolution and/or old-earth thinking into their theology.

Recently, a group of professors from a major, conservative evangelical seminary met with scientists from ICR. Every one of them had abandoned the recent creation position, usually in favor of the framework hypothesis. At the end of the meeting, each participant was asked to identify what it would take to change his position. Each scientist insisted he would change to belief in the old earth only if he was convinced Scripture taught long ages, even though each was certain science was in favor of the young-earth position. Conversely, the theologians admitted they held to an old earth in spite of the obvious sense of Scripture and would adopt a young-earth belief only if the consensus view of secular scientists shifted to recent creation. No wonder the church is so weak, if its leaders have adopted what formerly they would have considered heresy.

Today, the hardest pill for liberal and neo-evangelical theologians to swallow may be the young-earth doctrine. Even many "fundamental" theologians hold the so-called gap theory to accommodate the geologic ages, while moderate "evangelicals" espouse the day-age concept, while elite seminarians have adopted the framework hypothesis. All cling to the old-earth idea.

Historically, it was the issue of the age of the earth that was the first doctrine of Scripture to be abandoned by compromisers, then the Flood, then the creation. Today, the cycle has reversed. With evolution now exposed as not credible, many Christians are re-adopting creation, but still hold on to the old-earth and local Flood. How much better it would be to come all the way back to a biblical world view (one which employs better science, by the way).

Much is at stake, even the issue of biblical inerrancy. Can God's Word be trusted? When it gives times and places and genealogies, does it contain meaningful information? To Christian old-earth advocates, many Scripture passages must be ignored or allegorized.

Let's look at the biblical flood, as a primary example. The Bible teaches that the Flood was a global event, which destroyed the pre-Flood world and all its land-dwelling inhabitants not on Noah's ark.

Consider the following passage:

> And the flood was forty days upon the earth; and the waters increased, and bare up the ark, and it was lifted up above the earth. And the waters prevailed, and were increased greatly upon the earth; and the ark went upon the face of the waters. And the waters prevailed exceedingly upon the earth; and all the high hills, that were under the whole heaven, were covered. Fifteen cubits upward did the waters prevail; and the mountains were covered. And all flesh died that moved upon the earth, both of fowl, and of cattle, and of beast, and of every creeping thing that creepeth upon the earth, and every man: All in whose nostrils was the breath of life, of all that was in the dry land, died. And every living substance was destroyed which was upon the face of the ground, both man, and cattle, and the creeping things, and the fowl of the heaven; and they were destroyed from the earth: and Noah only remained alive, and they that were with him in the ark. And the waters prevailed upon the earth an hundred and fifty days (Gen. 7:17–24).

How could words more clearly state the global nature of the Flood? But in spite of the obvious intent of Scripture, many Christians have followed evolutionary leads and claim that the Flood, if it occurred at all, was only local, limited perhaps to the Mesopotamian valley, but not global in extent, and certainly not responsible for the rock and fossil records.

It is true that the Hebrew word translated *all* in this passage can sometimes be taken in a limited sense, just as in English. Such a word must be understood, then, in light of its context, and here, it can only mean "all" in a global sense: "All flesh. . . . All in whose nostrils was the breath of life . . . all that was in the dry land. . . . every living substance . . . upon the face of the ground . . . the fowl of the heaven . . . destroyed from the earth." It is just not sufficient to say that *all* is sometimes to be understood as limited. To defend the local Flood, it must be demonstrated that *all* is limited to *some* in this case in spite of the fact that the all-inclusive nature of the Flood is repeated over and over.

Some other phrases could only mean a global flood: "all flesh . . . I will destroy them with the earth" (Gen. 6:13). (Note that "the earth" means planet Earth, not just the local area.) "I do bring a flood of waters upon the earth to destroy all flesh, wherein is the breath of life, from under heaven; and every thing that is in the earth shall die" (Gen. 6:17). (Note that the phrase *under heaven* refers to the atmosphere, which is worldwide.) The animals "of every sort" were to be brought in by twos "to keep them alive" (Gen. 6:20), a capricious command if the Flood were only local. The list could go on and on. Noah's flood covered the globe! The entire earth!

Both Christ and Peter in the New Testament echoed this same teaching.

> But as the days of [Noah] were, so shall also the coming of the Son of man be. For as in the days that were before the flood they were eating and drinking, marrying and giving in marriage, until the

day that [Noah] entered into the ark, and knew not until the flood came, and took them all away; so shall also the coming of the Son of man be (Matt. 24:37–39).

The world that then was, being overflowed with water, perished: But the heavens and the earth, which are now, by the same word are kept in store, reserved unto fire against the day of judgment and perdition of ungodly men (2 Pet. 3:6–7).

Note that both Christ and Peter based their doctrines of the coming judgment of the whole world on the fact of the past judgment of the whole world in Noah's day. If the Flood had been only local, and much of the earth and at least some people had survived it, what kind of judgment is to come? Will it also be local? Will some sinners be excluded? The local Flood idea produces theological chaos!

Not only did the Flood cover the globe, this mountain-covering, year-long cataclysm accomplished a large amount of geologic work, operating at rates, scales, and intensities far in excess of modern floods. At the very least, it did what all floods do, eroding some areas and redepositing the eroded material elsewhere as sediments. The sediments would be full of plants and animals that died in the Flood. If Noah's flood happened the way the Bible says it happened, then modern day sedimentary rocks containing fossils are its result.

The Flood deposits would then give evidence of having been laid down catastrophically, not by calm, uniform processes. They would frequently be of vast regional extent, not local, as uniformitarians propose. Erosion, as well as deposition, would be of catastrophic proportions! Many evolutionists now call themselves neo-catastrophists because they recognize these features and admit they are dominant. Something radically different was going on in the past: something catastrophic, something global, something like the flood of Noah's day.

Yet many evolutionists still wrongly use rocks and fossils as evidence of evolution and the old earth, misinterpreting their true history. But if Noah's flood produced the rocks and fossils, there is hardly any evidence left for evolution and old-earth concepts.

Modern evangelicals who adopt the old-earth concept and/or evolution must deny the Flood as a global, geologically significant event, and all of them who have thought about it in a consistent manner do. Most claim the Flood was only a local flood. Others propose a nonsensical tranquil flood. Perhaps the majority just look the other way and ignore the whole issue. In each case, they deny a clear teaching of Scripture, one that forms the basis for much vital teaching in the New Testament. Christians desperately need to return to a consistent belief in all of God's Word if we are ever to be effective in reaching the world.

The Flood of Noah's Day
The Bottom Line

The worldwide, mountain-covering deluge would have deposited most of the world's fossil-bearing rock.

The naturalist — denying the fact of the Flood — misinterprets the rocks and fossils.

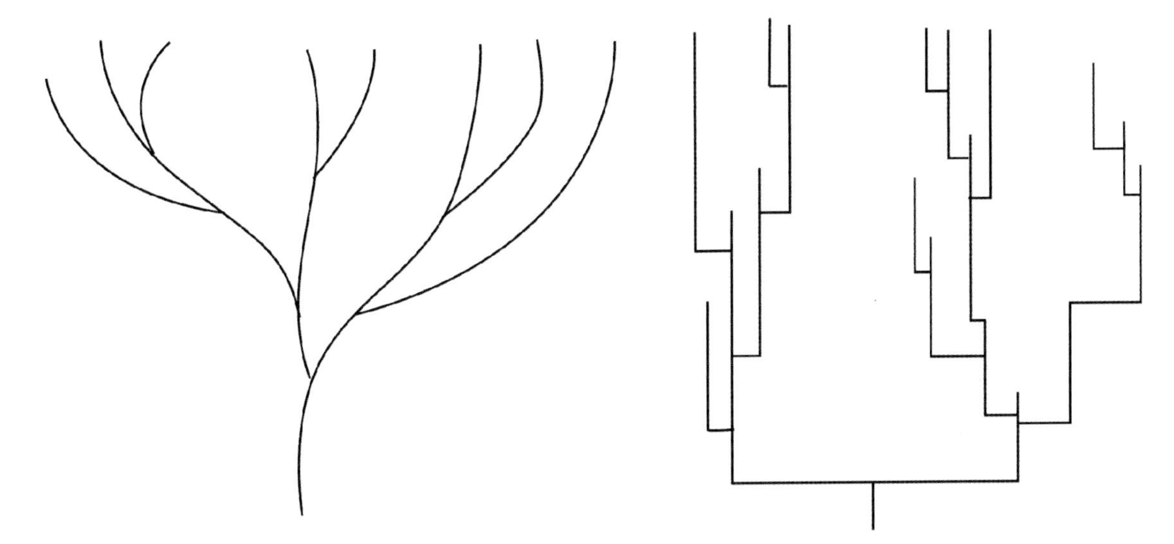

If the Flood was a global event, it laid down the rocks and fossils, and there is no evidence for evolution or for an old earth.

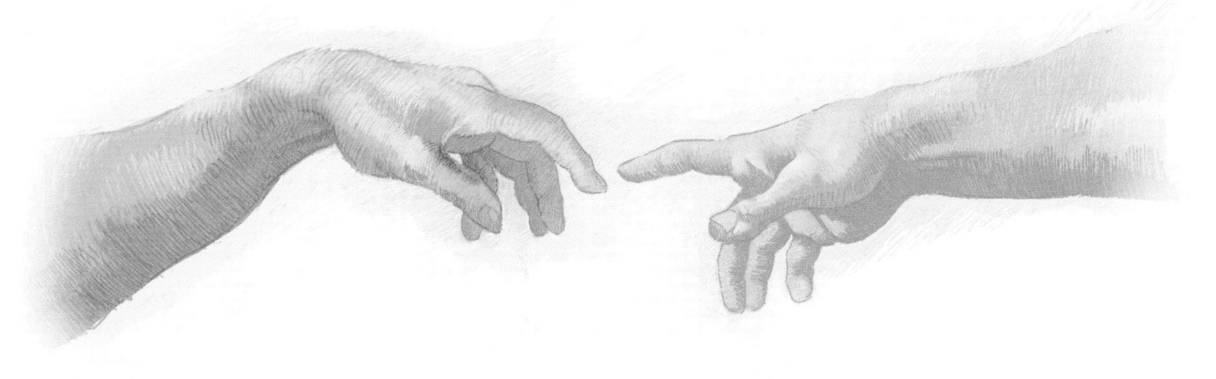

This situation was dramatically illustrated by an event that happened to ICR several years ago. At the time I was teaching a course in biblical and scientific apologetics to students at Christian Heritage College (now San Diego Christian College), ICR's sister school. I had been teaching about the Flood, and how those who desired to accommodate the old-earth view into their view of Scripture always had to modify the clear doctrine of the global Flood (that is, if they are knowledgeable and consistent in their understanding of old-earth thinking). I showed how both historically and logically, an old-earth advocate cannot hold to a global, geologically significant Flood, for the evidence for long ages is in the rocks and the fossils. But if Noah's flood happened, it deposited the great majority of the world's fossiliferous rocks. Thus, in order to hold to the old-earth idea, one must conclude that the flood of Noah's day was only local, or tranquil, but not responsible for the rocks and fossils.

One day after class I got word that two Christian scholars were coming to ICR a few days later to discuss our view of the young earth. One of them, astronomer and big bang/old-earth advocate Dr. Hugh Ross, had announced he was coming to ICR for a "biblical confrontation." He felt it was his Christian duty to confront us with our erroneous teaching of the young earth. The other scholar, philosopher/theologian Dr. Norman Geisler, also an advocate of the old earth, was coming in support of Ross, not so much to confront ICR with error, but to take part in the discussion.

Of course, this is serious business, and we took it so. We arranged for all of our scientists as well as interested SDCC faculty to be present for the dialogue. If we were in error, we wanted to know it and correct our thinking.

The day before they came, I predicted to my class that these scholars, if they were consistent in their old-earth thinking, would accept either the local Flood theory or the tranquil Flood theory, in order to maintain their belief in the old-earth as well as in Scripture.

The confrontation lasted two days. It consisted primarily of Dr. Ross trying to convince us of the validity of the big-bang theory, radioisotope dating, Einstein's theory of relativity (which many young-earth creationists hold), and plate tectonics (which many young-earth creationists also hold, albeit with a different time frame). Ross even claimed that to a great degree his salvation experience was connected to the big bang and old-universe concepts, for as a teenage science buff searching for religious truth, he found that the Genesis account of the Bible was the only religious writing which he could make fit with the big bang and old universe (which he already "knew" to be true).

Geisler was less committed to any of these specific positions, but adamantly held to the old earth. He even distanced himself from certain of Ross's positions, such as the idea that Neanderthal man was a human-like animal, although with a larger brain than modern man, with the ability to talk, conduct burials with religious significance, etc., but had no eternal spirit. Geisler held instead that Neanderthal was a descendant of Adam, but Ross insisted that the eternal spirit in man came later, when Adam was created, long after the Neanderthals, and based his position exclusively on old radioisotope dating of Neanderthal fossils.

But then came the question: What do you think about Noah's flood? Ross freely admitted that while it was a major flood, it covered only portions of the Middle East. It did not cover Europe, Asia, or Africa, and did not drown the inhabitants of these areas. It certainly could not have covered America, nor did it affect the Indians already living here, nor did it cause the Grand Canyon. The Grand Canyon was eroded millions of years ago, according to secular geologic interpretation and radioisotope dating. To Ross, the Flood must have only appeared to Noah to be global, for it covered as far as Noah could see, but certainly was just a local flood. He referred to it as a "universal" Flood, meaning as far as Noah could see. By all means, it did not deposit the rocks and fossils. Geology has proved they are millions and millions of years old!

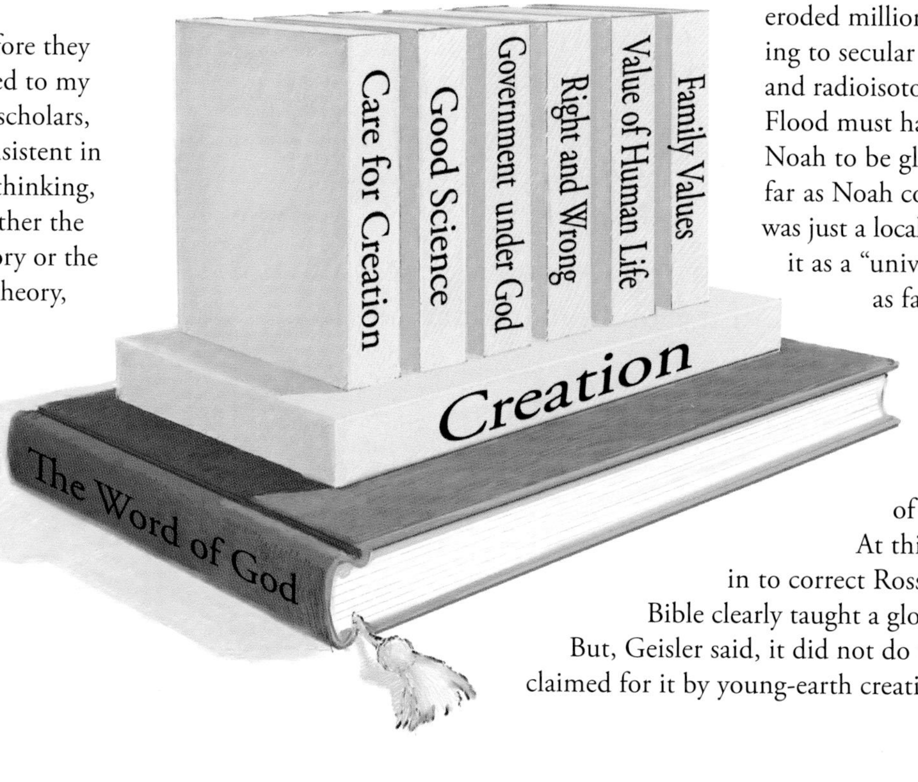

At this point, Geisler chimed in to correct Ross. He insisted that the Bible clearly taught a global, worldwide Flood. But, Geisler said, it did not do the geologic work claimed for it by young-earth creationists. He held that it must have destroyed all the pre-Flood human inhabitants, but left little geologic trace on the planet. It rose, covered the world, drowned all of life on land, and then simply drained off. No rocks, no fossils. I asked how he could hold such a position, since even the minor, local floods of today do tremendous geologic work. How could a flood, which he admitted was much larger and more dynamic than any observed flood, do no geologic work? Thus, he proposed a tranquil Flood.

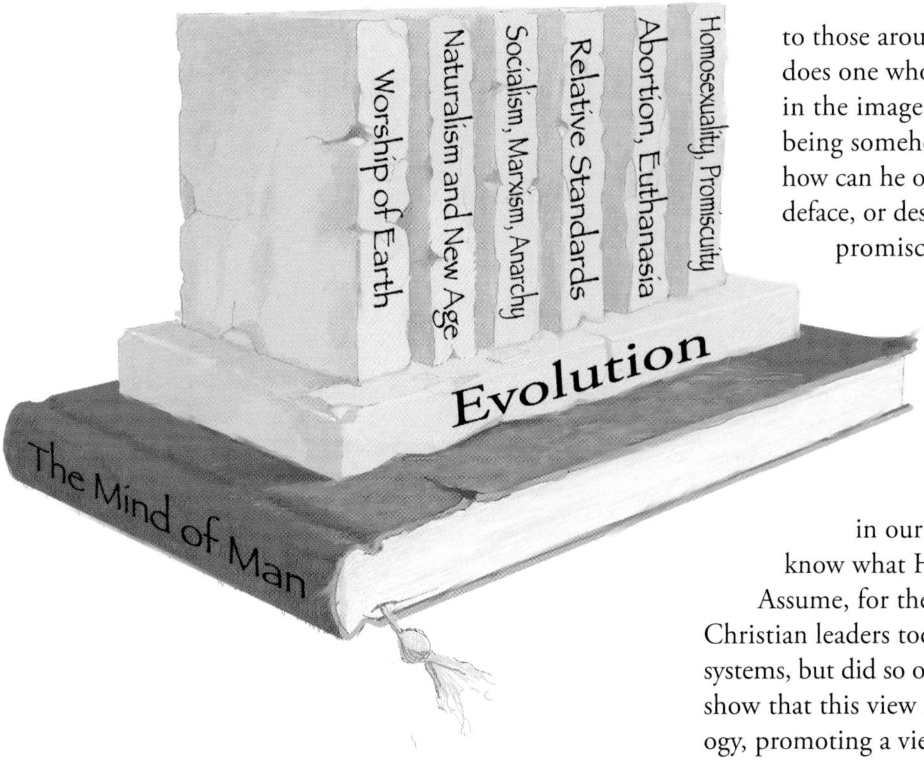

The proper way to approach this issue is to accept Scripture at face value, as the writer of Scripture, God, intended the reader to understand it, and to place our thinking, our research, our interpretation of data, all in submission to His truth. We must rethink our presuppositions, allowing God, not secular scientists, to set our historical world view. We must judge the opinions of all scientists (including our own opinions) by Scripture. The Bible commands, "Be not conformed to this world: but be ye transformed by the renewing of your mind" (Rom. 12:2). "Prove all things; hold fast that which is good" (1 Thess. 5:21). Once we succeed in allowing God and His Word to direct our study, we will do better science.

The Theological Battlefront

It has been rightly noted that ideas have consequences, ideas have power. The way a person thinks influences the way he or she relates to society, to self, and to God.

Obviously, evolutionary ideas have great impact on one's view of life and its meaning. One who considers mankind to be the random by-product of chance events operating on the primeval slime makes decisions and relates to those around him in a very different way than does one who believes men and women were created in the image and likeness of God. If each human being somehow bears God's image and likeness, how can he or she take any action that will harm, deface, or destroy that image? If man is an animal, promiscuity, homosexuality, racism, treachery, abortion, infanticide, euthanasia, and violence are all understandable as animal traits.

Young-earth ideas influence all our thinking. Do we think of God as long ago and far away, or nearby and intimately interested and involved in our lives and in earth history? Did He know what He was doing as He created?

Assume, for the moment, the stance taken by many Christian leaders today, that God created the earth and its systems, but did so over 4.5 billion years. I will attempt to show that this view is internally inconsistent in its theology, promoting a view of God totally unlike the God of the Bible.

First, consider God's omniscience. If He knows everything, including His purpose in creation, why did He take so long, as a seeming afterthought, to recreate His own image in a creature with whom He could communicate, on whom He could shower His love and grace, and from whom He could receive reciprocal love? What was His purpose in the billions of years of evolutionary blind alleys and extinctions? Is He powerless, able to accomplish His purpose only with trial and error, fits and starts? Was He testing various animals to see whether He could find one worthy of His special attention and image? What about the dinosaurs, those majestic beasts that supposedly went extinct long before man was created? Were they considered as possible candidates for God's image, only to be rejected? And why all the death, bloodshed, and violence over all these millions of years? Why did He set up this bizarre scenario to finally produce man? If God is omniscient, why does it appear that He did not know what He was doing? If He is omnipotent, surely He could have done it in a better way. And why, if evolution and long ages are correct, did the God of foreknowledge, the Alpha and Omega who knows the end from the beginning, produce so many types that ended up extinct?

Mutation and Natural Selection

The main mechanisms for evolution are touted as mutations and natural selection. Without mutations, evolution could not acquire new genetic information, and without natural selection, the survival of the fittest trend cannot

work. Both obviously occur today, yet they do not produce evolutionary change. As we showed in chapter 6, the trends are the opposite of evolution, leading to extinction, not innovation.

Consider how these mechanisms mesh with the character of God as revealed in Scripture. Are those the methods He would utilize to produce His image in man?

By definition, mutations involve random damage to the genetic information code. Never have mutations been observed to add useful information which was not there before. It might be conceptually possible, but the odds against adding new information by random alteration are astronomical. Would God use random damage to produce His very good creation, including His very image? Perhaps He could orchestrate good damage, but this damage would not be random or consistent with His wise and beneficent nature.

Similarly, natural selection occurs all around us, but it can only select from the variety produced by random mutation and genetic recombination. It has no mind; it does nothing on purpose. It conserves by natural processes the best variety present; it innovates nothing. But God is a supernatural God, with wisdom and power quite distinct from nature. Would such a supernatural God, who strictly forbids us to worship nature, accomplish His creative handiwork by natural processes?

Grace, Mercy, and Love

God's gracious, merciful, and loving nature is likewise incompatible with millions of years of evolution. Is not survival of the fittest, where the strong survive and the weak perish and might makes right, more in line with salvation by works than salvation by grace? God does not think that way. "Blessed are the meek," protect the poor and defenseless, and even children inherit the kingdom. Evolution, the bloodthirsty cult of tooth and claw, does not mesh with God's essence. He could not use evolution to produce His image and remain true to His character. Even evolutionists seem to understand this and recoil from the implications of evolution, yet hold this belief because they do not believe in God. Locked in naturalism, atheism, and anti-supernaturalism, they have no options, and wonder why a Christian would accept any form of evolution.

To an evolutionist or old-earth creationist, the world both before and after Adam's creation was essentially the same as the world today — animals killing one another and diseases ravaging plants and animals, all in the presence of poison ivy, thorn bushes, parasites, viruses, etc. Beneath Adam's feet in the Garden of Eden (thought by old-earth advocates to be in the Tigris-Euphrates valley) were probably thousands of feet of fossil-bearing rock, interpreted by old-earth advocates to be the result of a lengthy history of violence on earth: survival of the fittest in action. But all of this is so unlike God, the ever-living source of life and love. God "saw everything that he had made, and indeed it was very good" (Gen. 1:31).

God does not call our present world very good. He deems it so bad that He has promised it will "melt with fervent heat," and then He will create a "new earth, wherein dwelleth righteousness" (2 Pet. 3:13).

> Then God saw everything that He had made, and indeed it was very good. So the evening and the morning were the sixth day (Gen. 1:31; NKJV).

And I saw a new heaven and a new earth: for the first heaven and the first earth were passed away; and there was no more sea. . . . And I heard a great voice out of heaven saying, Behold, the tabernacle of God is with men, and he will dwell with them, and they shall be his people, and God himself shall be with them, and be their God. And God shall wipe away all tears from their eyes; and there shall be no more death, neither sorrow, nor crying, neither shall there be any more pain: for the former things are passed away. (Rev. 21:1–4).

Christians who advocate the old-earth idea typically feel that Satan was cast out of heaven long ago, long before Adam was created, and was present on earth throughout the ages. But if that is so, where were Satan and the myriads of demons when God pronounced everything very good? Was Satan lurking behind a tree just waiting for a chance at Eve? Was he already actively working to distort God's creation, causing extinction and death? That is not very good at all. How could the holy, perfect God of the Bible declare it to be so?

To make matters worse, God has promised a restoration of earth to what it was like before Adam sinned. To an old-earther, Adam lived just a few thousand years ago, at the end of 4.5 billion years of history. Adam's world was essentially no different from ours. So what will this world be restored to: billions of years of extinction and death? No, the Bible says it will be a time without bloodshed and carnivorous activity, when the wolf and the lamb will lie down together, where even the lion will be vegetarian, and where harmony will exist between man and the animal kingdom once again. To an old-earther, this has never happened. How can the earth be restored to such a state?

The wolf also shall dwell with the lamb, the leopard shall lie down with the young goat, the calf and the young lion and the fatling together; and a little child shall lead them. The cow and the bear shall graze; their young ones shall lie down together; and the lion shall eat straw like the ox. The nursing child shall play by the cobra's hole, and the weaned child shall put his hand in the viper's den (Isa. 11:6–8; NKJV).

The Curse

The root theological problem with old-earth thinking has to do with the curse on all creation due to Adam's sin, as described in Genesis 3, and the resulting "wages of sin," death. From observation, we know that all things are in the process of dying. People grow old and die. Animals die. Plants wither and fade. Machines wear out. Civilizations die. The moon's orbit decays. Stars burn out. "The whole creation groaneth and travaileth in pain together until now" (Rom. 8:22), and has done so since the very moment of Adam's fall:

For the earnest expectation of the creature waiteth for the manifestation of the sons of God. For the creature was made subject to vanity, not willingly, but by reason of him who hath subjected the same in hope, because the creature itself also shall be delivered from the bondage of corruption into the glorious liberty of the children of God. For we know that the whole creation groaneth and travaileth in pain together until now (Rom. 8:19–22).

The passage, Romans 8:19–26, strikes at the heart of the old-earth concept. Let us look at the words carefully. The words *creature* (v. 19, 20, 21) and *creation* (v. 22) are actually the same word in the Greek language. In each case the proper translation is "creation." The "whole creation" (v. 22) is groaning under the effects of the curse, awaiting deliverance such as has already been provided "the children of God" (v. 21) in the spiritual realm. Everything is under this "bondage of corruption," including animals, plants, and the very earth itself. The earth's human population (v. 23–26) likewise suffers physically, but God's children will

By way of explanation, plants are biologically alive, but have no "breath of life" (Gen. 2:7). Furthermore, "The life of the flesh is in the blood" (Lev. 17:11). Plants have no consciousness, no breath, and no blood, and thus are not living in the biblical sense of living. They were created specifically to nourish living things. Their biological death (and perhaps also that of many of the lesser forms of life technically classed as animals) does not constitute the death of a biblically living, breathing, blood-filled creature.

experience the "redemption of our body" (v. 23). Everything suffers under the curse!

The creation has been made "subject to vanity" (v. 20), a state implying failure to achieve the "very good" purpose for which it was created. Because of sin and the resultant curse, it stopped measuring up to God's design as it originally did.

The tense of the verb "was made subject," speaks of a past, completed event at which all of creation was affected. There are only two candidates for this event, Genesis 1:1 and Genesis 3:14–19. If the creation of all things in Genesis 1:1 included the making of all things "subject to vanity" (as Dr. Hugh Ross and other old-earth advocates claim), then God is the author of much pain and suffering and death. Did God create bloodthirsty animals, poisonous plants, infectious diseases, parasites, etc.? Did He call it all "very good"? Did God design conscious animals, capable of expressing emotions such as loyalty and care for one another, to suffer excruciating pain and horrid death?

The situation gets worse when humankind is considered. The world immediately after Adam's creation would suffer the same symptoms as our world, both being "subject to vanity." Is this world "very good"? What about miscarried babies, heartbroken widows, lepers, cancer victims, handicapped infants and adults? What about famine, natural disasters, and drought? What about birth defects and tragic mutations? Factor in human behavior patterns including genocide, human sacrifice, brutality on unimaginable scales, which (according to their view of carbon dating) archaeologists tell us have been going on for millennia, long before the biblical date for Adam. This world is not "very good." This world of ours could not be similar to God's created "very good" earth. If it is, God is responsible for all these painful and horrible things. Where is His holiness in all this? Where is His justice?

If, however, the event that ruined creation is the one recorded in Genesis 3, then the presence of pain, suffering, and death makes sense. Man's rebellion against God brought the curse and death, the "bondage of corruption." God's holy nature and justice shine as He faithfully pronounces the penalty for sin as He had promised (Gen. 2:17), but He also promises in His grace to send a solution to the problem of sin and death (Gen. 3:15), a solution we now recognize as God's only Son, Jesus Christ.

Adam and Eve were created to live forever in fellowship with God. They had access to the Tree of Life in the Garden. They and the animals were commanded to be vegetarian, and no carnivorous activity was to take place:

> And God said, Behold I have given you every herb bearing seed, which is upon the face of all the earth, and every tree, in the which is the fruit of a tree yielding seed; to you it shall be for meat. And to every beast of the earth, and to every fowl of the air, and to every thing that creepeth upon the earth, wherein there is

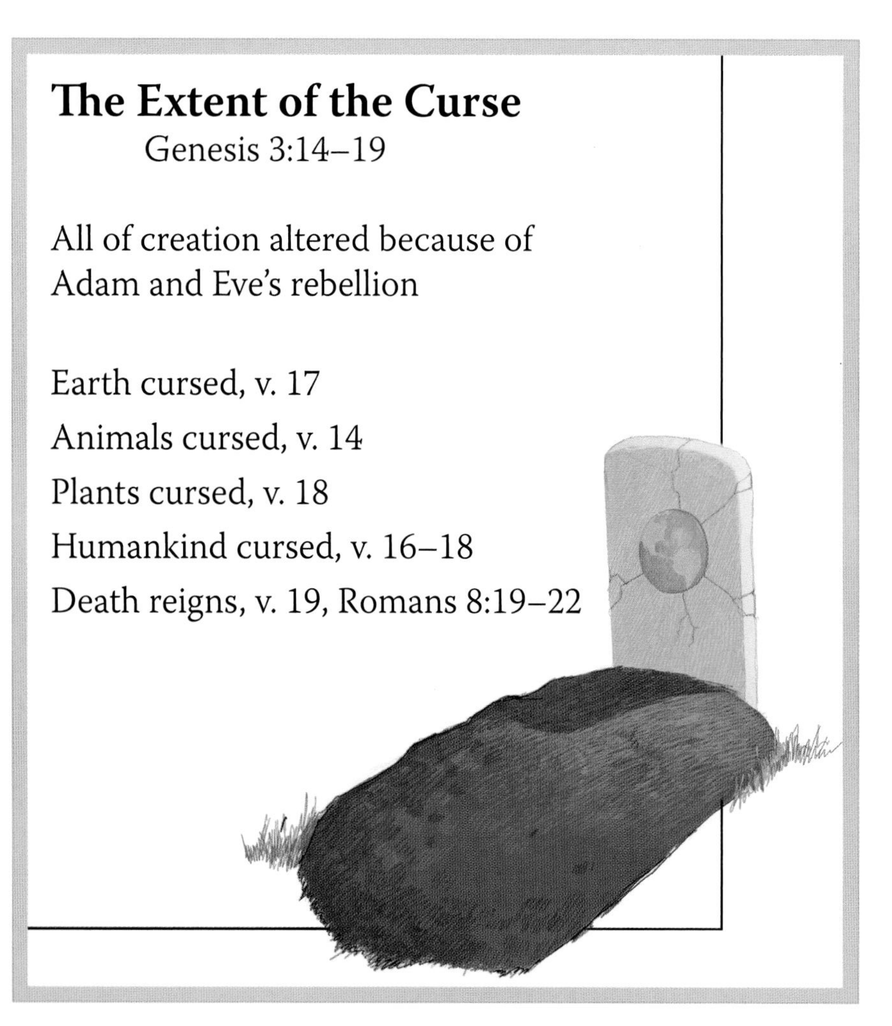

The effect of the Curse. The world was no longer "very good."

life, I have given every green herb for meat: and it was so (Gen. 1:29–30).

But sin distorts everything. Sin distorted God's original "very good" creation. God had promised that if man disobeyed and ate of the forbidden tree, "thou shalt surely die" (Gen. 2:17), or literally, "dying you shall die." Man would die spiritually and begin the process of dying physically: for "dust you are, and to dust you shall return" (Gen. 3:19; NKJV). Everything partook of this curse — the animals (v. 15), the plants (v. 18), the ground (v. 17), and Adam and Eve (v. 15–19). Everything is now under this "bondage of corruption" (Rom. 8:21).

The Extent of the Curse

The very first recorded death was that of an animal to provide a covering for Adam and Eve, painfully aware of their sin (Gen. 3:21). Throughout the Old Testament, we see blood sacrifices for sin commanded. "Without shedding of blood is no remission" of sin (Heb. 9:22). The biblical teaching of the entrance of death because of sin makes sense only if the earth is young.

> Wherefore, as by one man sin entered into the world, and death by sin; and so death passed upon all men, for that all have sinned (Rom. 5:12).

> But now Christ is risen from the dead, and has become the firstfruits of those who have fallen asleep. For since by man came death, by Man also came the resurrection of the dead. For as in Adam all die, even so in Christ all shall be made alive (1 Cor. 15:20–22; NKJV).

But what if the earth is old? The fossils must then be understood to show that the dying of living creatures had already been going on for hundreds of millions of years before Adam sinned. Death, extinction of the less-fit as the more-fit survive through the process of natural selection, has dominated history. Death is then normal; death is natural; death is just the way things are. If God created this kind of world, then what kind of God do we have? Is He sadistic, capricious, and cruel?

But it gets even worse! To an evolutionist, death is the central focus. Death fuels evolution. Death produced man. For instance, it was the extinction of the dinosaurs that gave rise to the mammals, and eventually to man. Carl Sagan, the late evolutionary spokesperson of the late 20th century, says it this way:

> The secrets of evolution are death and time — the deaths of enormous numbers of lifeforms that were imperfectly adapted to the environment; and time for a long succession of small mutations that were by accident adaptive, time for the slow accumulation of patterns of favorable mutations.[1]

Charles Darwin recognized the key role of death in evolution by natural selection. The final, climactic paragraph of *Origin of Species* points this out. After describing for several hundred pages the evidence for and effects of natural selection, he concludes: "Thus, from the war of nature, from famine and death, the most exalted object which we are capable of conceiving, namely, the production of the higher animals (i.e., man) directly follows."[2] In other words, from death comes man.

Actually, Charles Darwin credited the existence of pain and suffering and death for his commitment to natural selection. In response to a plea not to be so atheistic in his

1. Carl Sagan, *Cosmos* (New York: Random House, 1980), p. 30.
2. Charles Darwin, *The Origin of Species* (London: J.M. Dent, 1971), p. 463.

writings, Darwin responded: "I had no intention to write atheistically, but I own that I cannot see as plainly as others do, and as I should wish to do, evidence of design and beneficence on all sides of us. I cannot persuade myself that a beneficent and omnipotent God would have designedly created the *ichneumonidae* (a parasite, ed.) with the express intention of their feeding within the living bodies of caterpillars, or that a cat should play with mice. Not believing this, I see no necessity in the belief that the eye was expressly designed."[3]

Thus, to an evolutionist, death is the natural state of things, and death produced man. The death and extinction of the unfit is absolutely essential for evolutionary change to occur through survival of the fittest. Even to an old-earth creationist, death preceded man (even the death of human-like "animals"), and God used death to prepare the way for man. In either case, a world dominated by death, pain, and suffering was here before man and certainly before man sinned.

The Effect of the Curse

Next, notice that death is also the central focus of Christianity. First, death is the penalty for sin. "The wages of sin is death" (Rom. 6:23), for sin separates us from a Holy God. But that is not all.

What happened in the Garden of Eden after Adam and Eve sinned? What happened when God came down to fellowship with them that evening? Where were they? They were hiding — hiding in the bushes from God. Sin had erected an awful barrier between them and God. Sin does that, doesn't it? Sin had created a gulf between sinful man and his sinless God.

God acted from His character of justice as He pronounced the penalty for sin. His holy nature demanded that sin's wages be paid. He was fully just in establishing that penalty. As Creator, He had the authority to set the rules over His creation and the penalty for breaking the rules. Adam and Eve had chosen to rebel and had chosen sin and its penalty. It was God's holy and just nature that demanded the death penalty for sin. Not just physical death, but spiritual death, eternal separation from the living God.

But more was at work than God's justice. His grace was also on display.

Think about it. Adam and Eve were created to live forever. They had access to the Tree of Life. Their newly created bodies contained no genetic defects or diseases. They would have lived forever — hiding in the bushes — separated by their sin from a holy God. Can you think of anything more horrible? There is another name for eternal separation from God because of sin. The Bible calls it hell. Adam and Eve were not in the physical place called hell, but their situation was no less ultimate, tragic, and hopeless.

Furthermore, think what Adam and Eve would be like now, if nothing had changed. They had chosen to rebel, they had refused to repent and even refused to accept the blame for their actions. Their commitment to sin was now well established. They had no access to God, nor did they care to have any. Surely, Satan and their own sinful natures would have led them into ever-deeper debauchery. And, by now, thousands of years later — well, we would best not even try to imagine.

GOD

The death penalty for sin served several purposes. It put a limit on how long a sinner could live, putting a cap on how debased he could become.

It also placed an ever-present reminder before Adam and Eve of the fact that their choice to rebel had ruined

3. Charles Darwin in a letter to Harvard professor Asa Gray, May 22, 1860.

Al-aqsa Mosque, Old City of Jerusalem

God's perfect creation. Every time they saw one animal kill another, or when their oldest son killed his brother, they must have said, "Oh, this is awful! What have we done?" It would drive them back to God for His solution to the sin-and-death problem.

Most of all, the establishment of death as the penalty for sin made it possible for the penalty to be paid by someone else: someone who did not deserve the penalty. Now God himself could come to earth; take upon himself the form of man whom He had created; live a sinless life, a life for which no sin penalty was needed; and die in place of condemned man. "The wages of sin is death" (Rom. 6:23), but "Christ died for our sins" (1 Cor. 15:3). He died so that we would not have to die. And then He rose from the grave, victorious over death, offering eternal life to those who believe. Death provides an escape from an eternal sin-plagued life, and serves as the door to a new life, one free from sin and death, made possible by the death and resurrection of the Creator.

But what if evolution and the old earth are true? What if the fossils were deposited long before Adam lived? What if the dinosaurs had become extinct before sin entered creation? Obviously, if death was here before Adam's sin, then creation had already been spoiled, and death is not the penalty for sin. But if death is not the penalty for sin, what possible good would have been accomplished by Christ's death? In evolution, it is "survival of the fittest." In Christianity, it is "the death of the fit for the unfit."

Do you see how the two concepts are incompatible? If death was here before sin, then Christ's death was ineffective and meaningless. The central focus of Christianity fails. The old-earth concept undermines Christ's work of redemption!

One can be a Christian and believe in evolution. Many do. Most people who come to Christ for salvation come as evolutionists, for that is all they have ever been taught. They have recognized their sin and its consequences before a Holy God and turn to Him for forgiveness based on His full and final payment for their sin. They might not have even heard of the six days of creation. But while it is possible for an untaught Christian to believe in evolution, it is impossible that both evolution and Christianity can be true. They are opposite world views. If evolution is true, Christianity is wrong!

Recently, I had the distinct privilege of giving a lecture to 2,500 public school students, teachers, and university professors in Istanbul, Turkey, a predominantly Islamic country. My lecture was part of a conference sponsored by a quasi-governmental foundation advocating a return to the creationist world view in the Turkish education system.

This was my 14th trip to Turkey. All the others had been concerned with my expeditions to Turkey in search of Noah's ark.[4] Throughout the years, I had studied Islamic thought, to better prepare myself for the work in Turkey, and to be a fruitful ambassador for Christ among those lost in deep darkness, but before this trip, I seriously studied the Islamic teaching on creation and the Flood.

The Koran, the Islamic holy book, restates many Old Testament stories. It teaches creation in six days, Adam and Eve, the Garden, the original perfect state, eating the forbidden fruit, the expulsion from the Garden, the wicked pre-Flood world, and the world-wide Flood. A few differences occur, but the gist of the stories is the same.

Except, that is, for the Curse. Here the differences may at first seem slight, but they form the basis for the Islamic view of salvation, and their thinking has something very important to contribute to our discussion here.

In the Koran, when Adam and Eve ate of the forbidden fruit, they incurred Allah's severe displeasure. The Muslims acknowledge that the penalty for sin is death, and that Adam and Eve were expelled from the Garden to begin a life leading ultimately to physical death. Furthermore, they recognize that each member of the human race chooses to sin and deserves God's sentence of death.

The Wages of sin is DEATH . . .

Sounds familiar enough, but Muslims believe that man's sin caused the creation merely to fall "out of balance," no longer benefiting from its original perfection. They have no comprehension of the scriptural Curse on all of creation, nor that Adam's sin nature passed on to all of Adam's descendants. To them, each person's penalty for sin is due to his or her own personal sin, and, thus, it is also possible to regain Allah's favor by obedience to him. In fact, this is the only way of salvation. In the Islamic system, obedience involves praying toward Mecca five times a day, giving to the poor, participating in the fast during Ramadan, reciting the Muslim creed, making a pilgrimage to Mecca, i.e., the Five Pillars of Islam. Regular sins must be repented of, but it is up to Allah to grant forgiveness or not. There is no just basis on which Allah formally has chosen to forgive.

I submit that the Muslims' low view of the Curse, and their incomplete understanding of man's hopeless condition before God, both because of personal sin and the inherited sin nature from Adam, is the reason that they are today in such darkness. They choose, instead, to view sin and its punishment solely as a result of their own personal actions, and, thus, their own personal actions must save them. They have no need for a Savior. But the Bible teaches that Christ came to pay the penalty for our sin and for our sin nature, to do for us what we could not do for ourselves. The Curse on all of creation because of Adam's rebellion has only one remedy — the death of the sinless Son of God, himself the offended Creator! It may be that teaching this concept could provide the key to Islamic evangelism.

But what can we say to modern Christian evangelicals who hold the work of Christ on the cross as necessary for salvation, yet deny the foundational concepts of Genesis 1–3? Many modern evangelical seminaries give credence to the presence of a sin nature in each one of us, all the while

4. See my book for young people, *Noah's Ark and the Ararat Adventure*, for information on the expeditions, adventure, and discoveries on Mt. Ararat (Green Forest, AR: Master Books, 2006).

denying Adam as a historic person, denying the original "very good" creation, denying Adam's sin as a historic event, and denying the Curse as passing on to all creation (the animals, the plants, the earth, and all mankind) as a result of Adam's rebellious choice.

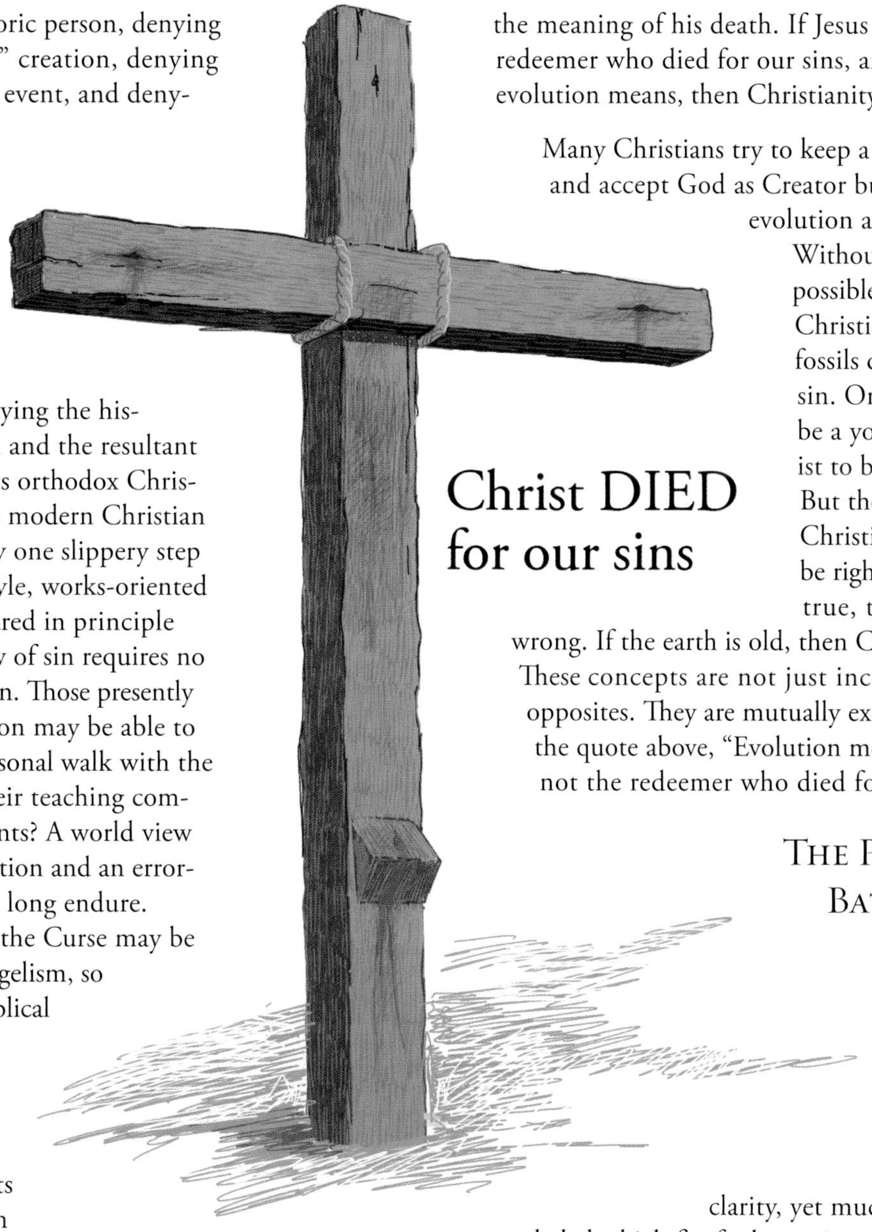

As you can see, denying the historic facts of Adam's sin and the resultant curse logically undercuts orthodox Christian doctrine and places modern Christian old-earth advocates only one slippery step away from a Muslim-style, works-oriented salvation, a position shared in principle by the cults. A low view of sin requires no Savior to save us from sin. Those presently advocating such a position may be able to maintain their own personal walk with the Lord, but what does their teaching communicate to their students? A world view with an illogical foundation and an error-filled revelation will not long endure.

Just as teaching on the Curse may be the key to Muslim evangelism, so clear teaching on the biblical Curse might provide the key to returning Christianity to a truly biblical world view.

This point and all its ramifications (i.e., death before sin, the problem of pain, the ever-present tendency for decay in all systems, etc.) occupy a major role in ICR's outreach. Perhaps there is no other single point besides this that better grabs the attention of sincere Christians who have been wrongly taught. We attribute much of the present revival of interest in creation on the part of Christians to the communication of no death before sin.

Often I think my evolutionary colleagues understand this issue better than my Christian brothers and sisters. Consider this quotation from an outspoken atheist:

> Christianity has fought, still fights, and will fight science [by this, he means naturalism] to the desperate end over evolution, because evolution destroys utterly and finally the very reason Jesus' earthly life was supposedly made necessary. Destroy Adam and Eve and the original sin, and in the rubble you will find the sorry remains of the son of god. Take away the meaning of his death. If Jesus was not the redeemer who died for our sins, and this is what evolution means, then Christianity is nothing![5]

Many Christians try to keep a foot in both camps and accept God as Creator but still accept evolution and/or the old earth. Without a doubt, it is possible to be a born-again Christian and believe that fossils date from before sin. One does not have to be a young-earth creationist to be a true Christian. But the old-earth idea and Christianity cannot both be right. If evolution is true, then Christianity is wrong. If the earth is old, then Christianity is wrong. These concepts are not just incompatible, they are opposites. They are mutually exclusive! As stated in the quote above, "Evolution means that Jesus was not the redeemer who died for our sins."

Christ DIED for our sins

The Personal Battlefront

As we have seen, the rocks and fossils, which are used as evidence for evolution and the old earth, do not speak with clarity, yet much evidence can be marshaled which fits far better into the young-earth scenario. The evidence, which can neither prove nor disprove, in a scientific sense, either idea about the past supports the young-earth view better. And, of course, the Bible clearly teaches the young-earth concept. In fact, Christianity makes no sense at all if the earth is old.

God is not a deceiver. He would not allow a world full of rocks and fossils to prove a view contrary to that specifically taught in Scripture. If scriptural history is correct and the earth is young, then the rocks must agree.

We have seen that some interpretations of the evidence are compatible with evolution and old-earth concepts. But these interpretations are not nearly the best interpretations. Only by adopting biblical history as fact and then interpreting the rocks can we hope to do so correctly.

The rocks, rather than speaking of long ages, speak of death and destruction. The rocks were formed from

5. G. Richard Bozarth, "The Meaning of Evolution," *American Atheist* (February 1978), p. 30.

sediments deposited by catastrophic water processes, operating at rates, scales, and intensities dwarfing those operating today. The fossils are dead things, things that died in the cataclysm (some in lesser catastrophes which followed the Flood).

This great watery upheaval was none other than the great flood of Noah's day. As Scripture teaches, it was a judgment on sin. God hates sin, and He saw the civilization in Noah's day as wholly wicked.

> And God saw that the wickedness of man was great in the earth, and that every imagination of the thoughts of his heart was only evil continually. And it repented the Lord that he had made man on the earth, and it grieved him at his heart. And the Lord said, I will destroy man whom I have created from the face of the earth; both man, and beast, and the creeping thing, and the fowls of the air; for it repenteth me that I have made them (Gen. 6:5–7).

The "wages of sin" has always been death. It was surely true in Noah's day, and God sent the Flood as a punishment for sin. Sin had so distorted God's once "very good" creation that God chose to annihilate it and start again. The rocks grimly remind us of the wages of sin and the wicked pre-Flood world.

But the rocks and fossils should also remind us that our present world exhibits exactly the same conditions that led God to judge the previous world.

> And as it was in the days of Noah, so it will be also in the days of the Son of Man: They ate, they drank, they married wives, they were given in marriage, until the day that Noah entered the ark, and the flood came and destroyed them all. . . . Even so will it be in the day when the Son of Man is revealed (Luke 17:26–30; NKJV).

The apt description of our world found here and its similarity to the world of Genesis 6 allows no other conclusion than that the coming judgment cannot be far away.

These rocks and fossils will not last forever either: they too will be annihilated. There will come a day when "the elements shall melt with fervent heat, the earth also and the works that are therein will be burned up" (2 Pet. 3:10). But "we, according to his promise, look for new heavens and a new earth, wherein dwelleth righteousness" (v. 13). In the new earth, we will not have fossils to remind us of death and sin.

Just as godly Noah accepted God's gracious provision of salvation during time of judgment, entrusting his life and safekeeping into God's hands, so we can escape the coming judgment. Our present-day ark of safety is not a wooden vessel. Rather, it is the eternal Son of God, Jesus Christ. Through His death on the cross, He paid the wages of our sin, and through Him we can avoid the death penalty for our sins, escape the judgment to come, and live forever with Him. "The wages of sin is death; but the gift of God is eternal life through Christ Jesus our Lord" (Rom. 6:23).

A Christian is one who recognizes that he has sinned and offended the holy Creator-God, thereby separating himself from God: "All have sinned, and come short of the glory of God" (Rom. 3:23). Each person's sin deserves the death penalty — eternal separation from anything good and holy.

Furthermore, a Christian is one who recognizes that nothing he can do will ever change the situation. But he also recognizes that Jesus Christ, God the Son, has already done all that is necessary. "Not by works of righteousness which we have done, but according to his mercy he saved us" (Titus 3:5). "For He made Him who knew no sin to be sin for us, that we might become the righteousness of God in Him" (2 Cor. 5:21; NKJV). "God demonstrates His own love toward us, in that while we were still sinners, Christ died for us" (Rom. 5:8; NKJV). But then He rose from the dead, in victory over sin and death, offering eternal life to all who believe. Jesus said, "I am the resurrection and the life. He who believes in Me, though he may die, he shall live" (John 11:25; NKJV).

A Christian is one who has gone to God the Father, repented of his sin, and asked God to apply the death of Christ to his own personal sin, to forgive him on that basis, since the penalty has already been paid. God responds with forgiveness, cleansing, victory over sin, and power to break sinful habits. Most of all, He gives us life — eternal life — where once there was only death. And then there will be long ages, not millions of years of death and suffering, but innumerable years of life with our Savior. He has done it all, "That in the ages to come He might show the exceeding riches of His grace in His kindness toward us in Christ Jesus" (Eph. 2:7; NKJV).

QUESTIONS

1. Why do we care about the age of the earth? What difference does it make?

2. How is the character of God called into question by the possibility of millions and billions of years?

3. What's "the bottom line issue" in age-of-the-earth discussions?

4. Did the curse of Genesis 3 affect only physical death, or spiritual death as well? How do we know?

5. How could discussion of the age of the earth point people to salvation through the work of Jesus Christ on the cross?

INDEX

accelerated decay, 52, 67
    summary, 67
alpha decay, 49, 87–88
anomalous artifacts, 74–76
assumptions in dating, 42–46, 50
biblical arguments for global Flood, 70
biblical creationism, 8, 31
biblical necessity of young earth, 124–131
biblical chronologies, 35–36
big bang, 37
carbon dating
    good for recent artifacts, 63
    useful in once-living specimens, 63–64
    in "ancient" rocks, 65–67
    in diamonds, 67–68
Cardenas Basalt, 49, 55, 56
catastrophism, 8
    neo-catastrophism, 9
civilization, dates of, 73
clastic dikes and pipes, 112–115
character of God and age, 129
coal formation, 106–107
Curse — necessary for full understanding, 131–137
dating
    comet, 20–21
    fossils, 10–13
    meterorites, 69–61
    Niagara Falls, 45–46
    recent volcano eruptions, 52
    rocks, 10–12, 48–70
    tree rings, 44–45
    wood, 52
"day" in Scripture, 28, 29
    "long" days, 30
    overlapping days, 31, 32
diabase sills and dikes, 50, 57
Dominion Mandate, 121–122
erosion of continents, 92–93
evolution, 8
    micro-evolution, 8
    macro-evolution, 8
    order, 31
evolutionism, 9
fossil record, 74
    rapid formation, 105

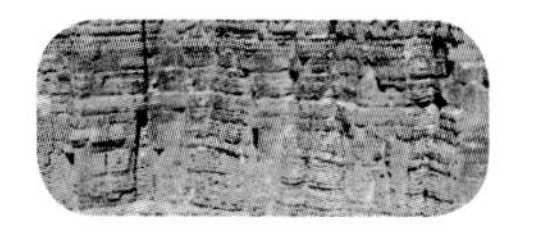

framework hypothesis, 9
geologic column, 9
geologic evidence for young earth, 96–115
    bioturbation, 98–99
    lack of soil layers, 99–100
    limited extent of unconformities, 107–109
    polystrate fossils, 102–105
    soft sediment deformation, 109–115
    summary, 115
    surface features, 97–98
    undisturbed bedding planes, 100–102
Grand Canyon
    plateau basalts, 55
    sills and dikes, 55
helium in the atmosphere, 87–89
human fossils, 75
human genome, 75–76
human population growth, 73
Ice Age, 65–70
image of God, 13–14
index fossils, 9
Intelligent Design movement, 123
interpretation of data, 19
isochrons, 12, 56
length of day, 28
magnetic field, 79–87
    causes, 81
    decay, 79–80
    reversals, 81–83, 85–87
maturity in creation (appearance of age), 40
meteoric dust on moon, 91
mutations, 8, 129
natural selection, 8
New Age thinking, 9, 123
old-earth creationists, 28, 29
petrified wood, 115–118
plate tectonics, 83–85
poetry in Scripture, 29
predictions of models, 22, 23
progressive creation, 9
punctuated equilibrium, 8
RATE initiative, 49, 53, 55–70
radiohalos, 61–63
regional evidence for continued deposition, 107–109
salt in oceans, 89–91
scientific creationism, 8
scientific theory, 14–16
sediments in ocean, 93–94

scientific benefit of young-earth thinking, 121–122
soft sediment deformation, 109–115
    brittle or soft, 110
    clastic dikes, 112–115
    clastic pipes, 113–115
    limit to creep, 112
    tight folding, 110–112
Specimen Ridge, 115–118
stasis, 8
theistic evolution, 9
thermodynamics, 39
uniformity, 9
uranium decay, 49
volume of rock on earth, 92
worldwide age indicators, 78–94
    dust on the moon, 91
    erosion of continents, 92–93
    helium in atmosphere, 87–88
    magnetic field, 79–87
    rocks on earth, 92
    salt in ocean, 89–91
    sediments in oceans, 93–94

Illustration / Photo Credits

Harold Coffin — 117

Istock — 17, 29, 45B, 64, 76, 96, 120, 135

Bryan Miller — 6, 7, 8, 9L, 24, 34, 38, 43, 44, 49, 54, 58, 60, 61L, 65, 66, 67, 72, 81, 83, 86, 88, 90, 92B, 93, 96B, 97, 99B, 106, 108, 109T, 110T, 124–134, 136, 137

NASA — 23, 91

Science Photo Library, Martin Bond / Photo Researchers — 10

Science Photo Library, Pascal Goetgheluck / Photo Researchers — 74T & 75T

Science Photo Library, David Hay Jones / Photo Researchers — 69

Science Photo Library — 56R, 127B

Snelling — 104

Swiche — 103

OTHER BOOKS BY JOHN MORRIS

Dinosaurs, The Lost World, & You

Where did dinosaurs come from? Where did they go? What were they like? Learn about dinosaurs, the Bible and the new theory of chaos and creation.

ISBN: 978-0-89051-256-2 • 48 pages • paperback • $3.99

Footprints in the Ash

John Morris & Steve Austin

How could the explosion of Mount St. Helens in 1980 give evidence crucial to the Genesis flood? Find out in this fascinating book that includes many photographs. Color interior.

ISBN: 978-0-89051-400-9 • 124 pages • hardcover • $16.99

The Geology Book

Dr. Morris takes the reader on a tour of the earth's crust, describing all of the components, explaining earthquakes, mountains, volcanoes, geysers, and so much more. Part of the Wonders of Creation series. Color interior.

ISBN: 978-0-89051-281-4 • 80 pages • hardcover • $13.99

How Firm a Foundation in Scripture and Song

This tribute to Christianity's great old hymns will release a refreshing shower of memories as the rich history and background of 28 hymns are related. This is a great gift for music lovers or a teaching tool for a study group. Includes free music CD.

ISBN: 978-0-89051-322-4 • 256 pages • paperback • $11.99

OTHER BOOKS BY JOHN MORRIS

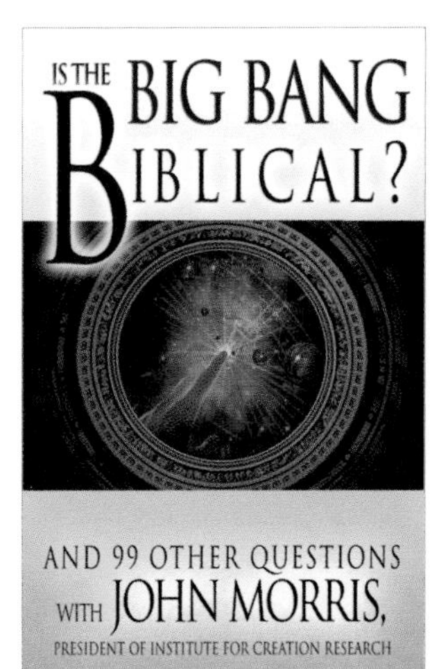

Is the Big Bang Biblical?

Dr. Morris tackles 100 questions relating to science and creation relevant to our time. He covers such topics as stem cell research, scientific dating methods, cloning, public education, and many others, including the big bang.

ISBN: 978-0-89051-391-0 • 224 pages • paperback • $12.99

The Modern Creation Trilogy

Henry M. Morris & John D. Morris

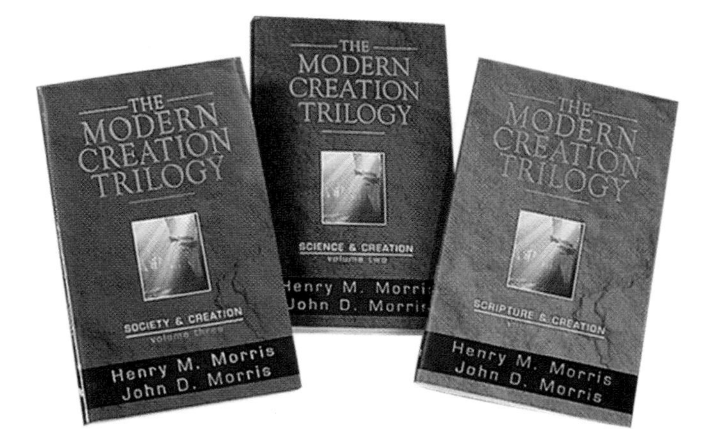

Produced by father and son, Drs. Henry and John Morris, this is the definitive work on the study of origins from a creationist perspective. This three-volume set looks at the creation/evolution issue from three main aspects: Scripture, science, and society. A masterpiece. Includes CD-ROM.

Vol. 1 — Scripture & Creation • 232 pages
Vol. 2 — Science & Creation • 343 pages
Vol. 3 — Society & Creation • 208 pages

ISBN: 978-0-89051-216-6 • paperback • Gift-boxed set • $34.99

Scopes: Creation on Trial

R.M. Cornelius & John Morris

What are the true facts and the real issues surrounding this "Trial of the Century"? The media has altered the truth once again. Find out what really happened and why there have been alterations to the facts in this explosive little book.

ISBN: 978-0-89051-257-9 • 48 pages • paperback • $3.99

TRAVELS IN CANOE COUNTRY

TRAVELS IN CANOE COUNTRY

Text by Paul Gruchow

Photographs by Gerald Brimacombe

Introduction by Patricia Hampl

A BULFINCH PRESS BOOK
LITTLE, BROWN AND COMPANY
BOSTON • TORONTO • LONDON

First Edition
A portion of *Compline* was previously published in *Modern Maturity.*

LIBRARY OF CONGRESS CATALOGING-IN-PUBLICATION DATA

Gruchow, Paul.
Travels in Canoe Country/text by Paul Gruchow: photographs by
Gerald Brimacombe: introduction by Patricia Hampl.
p. cm.
ISBN 0-8212-1893-X
1. Canoes and canoeing—Minnesota—Boundary Waters Canoe Area.
2. Outdoor life—Minnesota Boundary Waters Canoe Area. 3. Boundary
Waters Canoe Area (Minn.)—Description and travel. I. Brimacombe,
Gerald. II. Title.
GV776.M62B684 1992
797.1'22'09776—dc20 92-4542

Bulfinch Press is an imprint and trademark of Little, Brown and Company (Inc.)
Published simultaneously in Canada by Little, Brown & Company (Canada) Limited

PRINTED IN HONG KONG

Acknowledgements

I am deeply grateful to Gary Deason,
whose several readings of the text in draft have made it a far better work
than I could have managed by my own hand alone.

—P.G.

The totality of my photographic efforts for this book
probably would not have been realized had it not been for the memorable
and personal introductions into this unique wilderness
by Sigurd Olson and Miron Heinselman.

—G.B.

CONTENTS

Introduction by Patricia Hampl • 8

Lauds: A Psalm of Praise. Wilderness travel as an artistic act • 12

Matins: Daybreak. The songs of birds • 22

Prime: 6 A.M. Morning mists • 38

Tierce: 9 A.M. Water, the canoe, rock paintings • 52

Interstices: The Economy of the Canoe Country • 76

Sext: Noon. Rock, the swim, the dragonfly • 92

Nones: 3 P.M. Wind, portage trails, the storm • 106

Vespers: Evening. Calm waters, sunset rituals • 114

Compline: The Last Hour of the Day. Loons, wolves, night sounds, sleep • 132

Resource Guide • 142

INTRODUCTION

THE INSTINCT TO BEND THE KNEE, TO BOW THE head—there's no escaping it. The urge for reverence beats along the pulse of the most casual contemporary agnostic. So what's a techno-person to do? Pantheism may be the only religion left, Nature the only God the contemporary head will bow to. Nice irony for us moderns, though the joke's on us: that ancient "primitive" adoration of nature has grabbed us again, just as we go into the orbit of the next century, the next millennium, strapped to our FAX machines, our PCs and car phones, trailing clouds of video light from our VCRs and micro-chips, the beams of laser printers and fiber-optic voice messaging units fanning haloes around us.

We may call this new faith Environmentalism, betraying our doctrinal weakness for Science. But it's that old Druid madness, crazy for the trees, for the plants and roots, the springs and standing water of the wildwood. We trust them. We don't trust much else. Besides, we really are modern: we are connoisseurs of guilt, that twentieth-century besetting sin, and we know in our bones that we've done wrong to the planet. We know that the lakes and trees, even the plain dirt beneath our feet, have a strong brief written against us.

And it's beginning to dawn on us that this isn't Mother Nature crying out against us, after all; it's Brother Nature, Sister Nature. We belong to a complex fellowship in which we are expected to be responsible members, not reckless kids junking up the theme park, counting on Mom to pick up after us. We are becoming chastened, finally able to esteem not only the world's beauty but its vulnerability. We begin to see this beauty and vulnerability as part of the same inseparable glory which calls forth what glory has always demanded: reverence.

It should come as no surprise—but it does—that we are Romantics still, almost two centuries after Keats wrote in a letter that he was "certain of nothing but of the holiness of the Heart's affections and the truth of Imagination—What the imagination seizes as Beauty must be truth."

We are certain of hardly as much. The wilderness, seized by our modern imagination as Beauty, evokes not only "truth" but a measure of terror. We are afraid not so much *of* Nature, as the ancients were: we are afraid for it.

All the more reason to seek out the "wilderness experience," as we self-consciously call our treks into the woods. We must become acquainted with the terror in order to know the beauty at its core. That is, we must become acquainted with ourselves. For we're the scary ones, frightening the daylights out of creation with our toxic ways.

Division is the first act of creation: darkness separated into light, night detached from day, winter from summer, and so on down the endless distinctions and divorces that cause the world to exist. Creation is a rip in an opaque and seamless cosmic fabric we will never see. It's not God we take on faith, but the unbroken pre-creation darkness we can only imagine.

If the core of creation is separation, cell dividing from cell in a frenzy of molecular farewells—no wonder we're so weirdly attuned to alienation. It's our ancestry. And no wonder that we ache for the Romantic experience of nature, that primeval one-ness before individual existence. Or rather, we seek the Romantic experience *in* nature. For we want to get *in* there, to reach the intimate source of our divided selves. That is, to reach our creativity.

I've only travelled the Boundary Waters once, years ago, just for a long weekend. I went with two friends, one a veteran of many canoe trips, the other a wilderness-idiot like me. We were two lakes beyond the first portage when we realized that someone (no names, please) had left the mosquito repellent behind at the first carrying place. It was like losing all of Western Civilization. That was Friday morning. The hideous weekend loomed ahead, a pestilence-ridden dark age.

So: even in paradise, pettiness persists. But what astonishes me, and has for years whenever I think of the trip, is that *everything* remains of that weekend. I can see the beaded drops on the blond canoe paddle as I lift it out of the water and pause a beat before dipping it in again. I see the patience of my friend, showing me how to grip the paddle. I see the marsh marigolds and wild iris we passed on a Saturday portage. I see my pleasure in the harmless ownership that naming is: *marsh marigold, wild iris,* I wrote in my notebook by the campfire that night. The midnight loon with his insane laugh is there, too. I see the aluminum coffee pot with its tidy triangular spout. It sat drunkenly on the fire grate because its bottom was warped. The coffee was burned and was inexplicably delicious because of that.

It's all there. Frame after frame. I wasn't aware I was taking these pictures, and all the others stuffed into the album of that weekend. But what else is a mind wholly given over to attentiveness but a camera, snapping, snapping? In themselves, I suppose my interior Boundary Waters snapshots aren't worth trotting out. Yet in their rudimentary way, they partake of that defining instinct in creation. I recognized in them an intuition for awe, for wonder: an instinct for reverence.

The Middle Ages, that era rich in reverence, understood well the divisions implicit in creation. The medieval day was divided not only into hours but into prayers, giving meaning

—artistic form, we would say—to shapeless time. The medieval *Book of Hours* was a glory of language and illumination, the very text entwined with ivy and roses, as if the book itself were a bower of bliss. *The Book of Hours* is one of the profound exemplars of what a book is meant to be—a meeting place between creation and the solitary reader who holds it in hand.

Paul Gruchow has given us not only a compelling account of a canoe trip in a treasured Minnesota landscape, told in his precise, attentive prose. He has written a contemporary *Book of Hours,* illuminated by the dreamy photographs of Gerald Brimacombe. The medieval *Hours* was understood to be not simply a book, but something more—not a guide really, but a companion for the reader treading the secular world, hunting for the sacred.

That's what we have here: a wilderness companion, a book of hours for the wary late-twentieth-century pilgrim trying to reverence the glory of our divided world.

—Patricia Hampl

A Psalm of Praise.
Wilderness travel as an artistic act

BEING ON THE MOVE, SEEING WHAT YOU HAVE never seen before, not knowing where you will rest your head when night falls, receiving what comes as it comes, expecting everything and nothing: this is the allure of the canoe country. Every stroke of the paddle or step along the trail with a canoe on your shoulders or a pack on your back literally enlarges your world.

You travel under your own power and with the aid of ancient and elegantly simple tools — the canoe, the paddle, a pair of boots. Someone was traveling this way ten thousand years ago, and someone may be doing the same ten thousand years from now. In a world where change seems the only constant, where the past is increasingly suspect and the future ever more doubtful, it is exhilarating to be in touch with something that "binds together all humanity — the dead to the living and the living to the unborn."

The words are Joseph Conrad's, defining the work of the artist. Every earnest journey into the heart of the canoe country is, on the same terms, potentially a work of art, accessible to all.

The thinker, Conrad says, makes an appeal from ideas, and the scientist from facts. But "the artist appeals to that part of our being which is not dependent upon wisdom: to that in

us which is a gift and not an acquisition—and, therefore, more permanently enduring. He speaks to our capacity for delight and wonder, to the sense of mystery surrounding our lives; to our sense of pity, and beauty, and pain; to the latent feeling of fellowship with all creation —and to the subtle but invincible conviction of solidarity that knits together the loneliness of innumerable hearts, to the solidarity in dreams, in joy, in sorrow, in aspirations, in illusions, in hope, in fear, which binds men to each other, which binds together all humanity —the dead to the living and the living to the unborn."

A wilderness journey makes just this appeal. It speaks:

To that part of our being which is not dependent upon wisdom: Not to what we have learned from books, but to whatever depends upon experience with the physical world: knowing how to read a footprint in the mud, how to steer a canoe into the wind, how to make a fire in the rain, what sort of weather the clouds and the wind foretell, where to look for a moose, which of the mushrooms in the forest are edible, whether the sound in the night is sinister or benign, which bird sings overhead, what flower blooms in the marsh.

To that which is a gift and not an acquisition: For nothing one encounters along the way can be possessed beyond the span of a single lifetime, or turned to any monetary advantage that is not destructive, or preserved unchanged for so much as twenty-four hours. Nothing here—not the mists that rise in the morning, nor the wind that blows at midday, nor the curtain of colors that falls in the evening, nor the slap of a beaver's tail in the night—can be commandeered, or caused to happen, or forbidden.

To our capacity for delight and wonder: The water tumbling from one lake into the next, the laughter of loons, the howling of wolves, the waft of cool air upon a sweaty brow, the silence in cedar swamps, the majesty of tall pines, the soaring of eagles, the sudden shimmering of lights in the northern sky at midnight: all these, freely given, daily remind us

along the way of the grace abounding in the world.

To the sense of mystery surrounding our lives: The forest floor strewn with bones announces death; the string of bejeweled butterfly eggs laid out upon a leaf, the one mystery as large as God, life itself; and the beating of our own hearts, suddenly audible in the stillness of a moonless wilderness night, the thinness of the thread that binds the one to the other.

To our sense of pity, and beauty, and pain: Such old-fashioned words; pity—friendly sympathy, the desire to deliver mercy—being the most disreputable of the lot: "The gilded sheath of pity conceals the dagger of envy," Nietzsche, Conrad's contemporary, said, expressing the more modern view; and we have, perhaps, forgotten the connection between

beauty and pain—the words *awful* and *awesome* come from the same root—until we have all day long battled a fierce wind blowing out of the west and, at last, with aching muscles, have made camp in some sheltered cove, discovering then the bliss that descends with the silence after the last light.

To the latent feeling of fellowship with all creation: the sudden conviction, arriving in quiet moments, that the pine dancing in the breeze, and the otter cavorting in the lake, and the loon laughing in the unseen distance are not aliens after all, but neighbors, distant, yet potentially knowable, like the stranger who rides the same bus as you every morning: Latent because it is, for most of us, a feeling poorly exercised. It comes alive, the Zen master Dogen reminds us, not because of what we ourselves experience, but because of all that is experienced in our presence. "To carry yourself forward and experience myriad things," he said, "is delusion. But myriad things coming forth and experiencing *themselves* is awakening."

The journey is indistinct from the traveler. As it is the instrument of awakening, so the traveler is aroused; what stirs is the inner voice of the artist.

Daybreak. The songs of birds

I WAKEN IN CANOE COUNTRY. IT IS BEGINNING to be light. Birds sing in the forest undergrowth and in the canopy overhead. I stir in my sleeping bag, indulging the luxury of being half-awake but under no compunction to rise, just as I did a long time ago.

A pine cone thuds onto the roof of the tent. Then another. Soon they are plummeting like hailstones. There is no wind, and the cones are too numerous to be falling of their own accord. I am wide awake now. The first light of dawn has penetrated the netting of my tent door. What can be creating this ruckus? Above me, I hear the shrill, angry chattering of a squirrel. I suddenly understand: I, squatting on claimed territory, am admonished, belligerently, to pick up my things and get out.

Chastened, I think of rising. Another bombardment of pine cones hits. But I am still cosseted in my dreams. Shifting positions in my sleeping bag, feeling warm and groggy, I close my eyes, trying to resuscitate the dream I have already half-forgotten.

Since I was a child, I have rarely known mornings like this. "Rise and stomp," my mother would call every dawn with aggressive cheerfulness, "there's daylight in the swamp." (I did not know, nor, I think, did she, that this was a lumberjack's call.) I would refuse to respond, although usually I was already half-awake. From the beginning, I rebelled against authority.

But more than cantankerous independence kept me from obeying. Often I was summoned in the middle of one of those captivating dream stories that linger in the half-conscious blush of awakening. I didn't want to get up until I had finished the story.

People who stayed in bed after sunrise would never amount to anything, I was told, would never get on in life. I was a child. What would I have wanted to amount to? What was there to get on with?

Dreams in themselves were suspect in our household. We were fundamentalist Christians with a keen appreciation of self-discipline, and dreams were something one couldn't control. They were, like lust, envy, and pride, sins of unbridled passion—passion was always,

in the world of my youth, unbridled, and anything unbridled meant trouble. I was, worst of all, a profligate daydreamer. Daydreaming was doubly sinful, the union of unbridled passion and idleness. I dreamed, as usual, of grandeur, although of an odd and contradictory sort. Sometimes I envisioned becoming a wild man and sometimes a spellbinding orator, speaking before batteries of microphones to crowds of transfixed millions. When other Minnesota boys my age were fantasizing about Harmon Killebrew, I idolized Billy Graham and Bomba the Jungle Boy.

I seem to have survived my dreams. I haven't overcome the impulse to preach, but I have lost the delusion that it is of any use, and I have taken more or less satisfactorily to domestication: I don't pee on the carpets, and I use a knife and fork at the dinner table. I sleep too soundly, these days, to remember my nocturnal dreams, and it is, I suppose, a sign of middle age, or of resignation, that I seldom daydream of glory anymore. I imagine that if a lightning bolt were on the way, it would have struck by now.

In a sense, though, I have made dreaming the work of my life. Writing—any art—happens in a peculiar state of mind, more subconscious than deliberate, that the handbooks on the subject are always hard-put, and a bit embarrassed, to describe: a kind of trance, it is often said, but really an induced and alert dreaming. When I stayed abed those childhood mornings working out the endings of my dreams, I was rehearsing the work of the storyteller. It has never seemed like real work to me, but we live in a time when labor is expected to be drudgerous and unpleasant, the fifty weeks of servitude that we spend to buy two we hope will be happy.

Accustomed as I am to days of professional reverie, I nevertheless find the vividness of my dream life fully revived only when I have gone into a wilderness for a time. One reason, I suppose, is that I sleep then like a child. Because there is not much to do in the woods after the

sun has gone down, and because I am pleasantly weary after a day of paddling or hiking, I revert to the bedtimes of childhood, sleeping longer and at least some of the time less deeply, positioned to be conscious of my dreams. In the morning, I awaken not to the clanging of an alarm, but slowly, naturally. The benefaction of unfettered hours dawns. I am free again to savor to the finish what my dream-mind has begun.

And I accept, when I am in the woods, the idea that I do not completely command my life. To venture into a wilderness is to submit to the authority of nature. This may also seem a regression — adults command, children submit — but it is actually a progression toward a higher maturity, one that realizes the conceit of the enduring human dream of dominion.

Letting go of this dream, even temporarily, unstops the wilder and more creative dreams that we have not had access to since the last time — as children, perhaps — when we expected life to be an endless unfolding of surprises. It is only when we are prepared to be astonished and confounded that we are able to dream productively.

Every artist knows how futile the work of the imagination is until it has been freed to find its own way. The artist who tries to manufacture inspiration is frustrated at every turn, and the work that results is heavy and dull. But the one who tags along after the dream-line, attentive and open of heart, sometimes finds in the astonishing territory toward which it leads some treasure worthy of the embrace of memory.

Henry David Thoreau advocated the tonic of sauntering, another form of dreamy submission, the leisurely, meandering gait of the free of heart, who set out upon the road open to every possibility and closed to none. The word *saunter,* Thoreau suggests, in one of his most inspired bits of punning, derives from the pilgrims of the Middle Ages who cast aside everything to wander in search of the *Sainte Terre,* and came thereby to be known as *Sainte-Terrers*: Holy-Landers. "We should go forth on the shortest walk, perchance," Thoreau says, "in the

spirit of undying adventure, never to return,—prepared to send back our embalmed hearts only as relics to our desolate kingdom."

On my way into this wilderness, I tarried for a night along its southeastern boundary, Lake Superior's North Shore, where craggy cliffs meet an oceanic expanse of chill, deep, ice-blue water, a coastline worthy of the Pacific or the Atlantic. After dinner, restless and excited about the journey to come, I sauntered along the pebbled beach and out onto a spit of rock, seeking nothing in particular but to idle away an hour.

I admired the fist-sized blue and gray and sometimes black beach stones, rounded and smooth from centuries of churning in the now gentle, now thunderous, ever relentless waves. They seemed fallen and solidified pieces of sky, so much the same color were they as the blues and grays in the distance, where earth and heaven met vaguely, shimmeringly over the

lake. I looked into pools of water caught in shallow basins in the polished granite above the beach, arched like a surfacing whale, hoping in vain to encounter some creature staring back at me. I admired the tiny cushion plants blooming in the crevices of rock and the asters making a lavender splash on the leeward side of the spit, where, diverted by it, a river ran its last thousand yards parallel to the shore before finding an opportunity and slipping silently into the Superior. A man and his dog fished just above the bar of the outlet for steelhead trout. The trout seemed not to be biting. The fisherman alternately tended his line and his dog, for whom he now and then tossed a whitened stick of driftwood, which the dog bounded into the current of the river and fetched back, dreaming of what glory? The man, perhaps, fished as Thoreau's neighbors did, "much more in the Walden Pond of their own natures, and baited their hooks with darkness." Overhead, gulls wheeled, crying in the salty voices of the sea that these waters would at last reach in some future century.

The sun setting over the thousand-foot ridge behind me infused the sky with a salmon colored light which echoed in the granite's rosy crystals of quartz. I zipped my jacket against the evening breeze and turned back toward the car. Along the way, I became aware of a slight motion at the periphery of my vision. Pausing to take account of it, I found myself staring into the eyes of two baby mink, their dark coats fuzzy with the fine hair of infancy, their big eyes wide, their heads cocked and ears raised in curiosity, but with bodies tensed and legs crouched to flee. In a moment, they lost nerve and scampered and tumbled away.

I followed at a discrete distance. Naively, they led me to their den in a tumble of boulders at a place where ice had worked a crack in the spit and pried it apart. A pair of shrubby willows had taken root there and screened the place from the public parking lot just across the narrow river. The kits vanished into an opening among the boulders, but they could not stay hidden for long. Soon they peered out of crevices, all eyes, and, when they saw that I saw them, ducked

to safety again. We played peek-a-boo.

For a few minutes I enjoyed the game as much as they, and then I grew uneasy with the fear that my presence might compromise them. I turned and circled to the top of the spit to take my leave. But I desired one last glimpse of them. When I looked down, I saw not the babies, but the mother.

Her hair was sleek and dripping, and she was half-carrying, half-dragging a lake trout toward the den. The fish was half again as long as she and thicker in the body. I could not imagine how she might have caught it. Mink are fierce and swift, but trout are equally keen-eyed and wary. Perhaps the trout was carrion found along the shore or had been released by the fisherman downriver and had been seized while it was still disoriented or disabled. It, at any rate, was quite dead, and the mink was so occupied in hauling it home that it did not notice me. I watched until it retreated into the shadow of the willows.

By then dusk had fallen. The air had the graininess of some black and white photographs, and the lake looked more like a pool of light than like a body of water, a dreamy and transfigured landscape in which floated apparitions of mink and fish, of rock and flower, of birth and death, of day and night, of water and sky. Across the lake the Evening Star appeared, a stab of light in the taut stillness.

Not only with our feet and at our leisure, but also in our dreams, and in the works of our days, we can be saunterers, crusaders in search of whatever may be holy. We know how to undertake this work; it comes to us out of our bones when, wandering an evening away, we suddenly see that all is wild, or when, lying half-awake, as I have been this dreamy morning, we glimpse the wildness in our own hearts.

The squirrel in the tree above me scolds again, and hurls another battery of pine cones down upon my roof. Very well, I mutter, I submit, I submit. I rise, dress, and saunter forth.

6 A.M. *Morning mists*

I CRAWL FROM MY TENT AND STAND WIDE-EYED in the sharp, clean-smelling morning air. Fog shrouds the lake. The island across the way seems to be floating in it. I light my stove and boil a pot of coffee. A chipmunk warily advances to investigate the intrusion. I lean against a rock, drinking in the stillness with the coffee. Suddenly, I feel invisible.

There is the disabling invisibility of being out of place, either in society or in physical space, of not counting, of serving no apparent purpose, of seeming to be without choices. It is the invisibility of powerlessness. But that is not the sort of invisibility I feel this morning. I do not feel unnoticed, but only inconspicuous.

We impose another self-crippling invisibility upon the world by our habitual inattentiveness, our somnolence. "Only that day dawns to which we are awake," Thoreau says. And, "To be awake is to be alive. I have never yet met a man who was quite awake. How could I have looked him in the face?" He thought the best hour of the day was this one, the first after rising, when we are least asleep and, therefore, most alive.

The special aliveness of the dawning hour is nowhere more evident than when you are alone in some wild place, distant from the distractions of the workaday morning—the tinkling newspaper, the chattering radio, the scramble to get children dressed and fed and off to

school, to collect yourself for work—when there is time and silence enough to sit, as I do now, on a boulder at the edge of the water, listening to the morning songs of the birds, to the scurry of critters in the dry litter of the forest, to the splashings of the traffic entering and leaving the lake.

Every day has its seasons as surely as every year; there is the springtime of morning, the summer of midday, the autumn of evening, the winter of night; and there is the same repeated pattern of wakefulness and slumber in each—a fresh and even violent energy in spring, drowsiness after noon, rejuvenation toward autumnal evening, and finally full-bodied sleep. We are perhaps more nearly crepuscular—denizens of the dawn and the dusk—than we suppose. An astonishing portion of our lives, at any rate, is spent in outright sleep—two dozen years of an average life—and we pass another year and a half of our waking lives with our eyes closed simply because we have blinked them some four hundred million times. How many of our remaining years might we as well have been asleep for all that we failed to notice when we had our eyes nominally open?

As if our natural inclinations toward drowsiness were not sufficient to the day, we have also managed to obscure the world by our feats of engineering. You can, to take one example, traverse the interstate highway system at high speed from coast to coast, through valleys, across plains, over mountains and hills, day merging into night and night into day again, and never encounter an arresting scene, or come into contact with a local culture, or have a conversation that does not hinge upon a commercial transaction, utterly isolated from the land and its people.

The system is a marvel, one of the great public works, heroic in scale, artfully functional, efficient. Perhaps we ought to be proud of it, but what impresses me every time I travel upon it is how extravagantly reductionist it is, how successfully it shrinks to human scale, and to drowsy monotony, even something so vast and various as a continent.

Why climb a mountain when you can achieve a vista just as fine, and more thrilling viscerally, from the observation deck of the nearest skyscraper? Why run a rapids when you can experience the same rush of adrenaline effortlessly and in complete safety at any amusement park? What does any natural bridge offer that the Brooklyn Bridge or the Golden Gate doesn't? Why go to the forest when you can see its marvels a hundred times more vividly on a PBS nature program?

In "The Body and the Earth," the agrarian philosopher Wendell Berry observes that our well-being depends upon the accurate perception that we are small within the scale of the universe. This is something that we have understood—universally, it would seem—until very recently. To know the measure of our smallness is to appreciate our fundamental dependency upon wildness, upon the central alchemy of sun and water and soil that we can neither create, nor replicate, nor dominate. This appreciation saves us, Berry says: from pride, because it teaches us that we can never be gods; and from the despair of destructiveness, because, not tempted to try to be gods, we are also spared the possibility of becoming fiends. We submit ourselves, when we have understood our real place in the universe, to the conditions of our own wildness, which limit our actions and affirm our dependencies.

In acceding to what is vastly larger than ourselves, we are not diminished, but exalted. We assume then our rightful place in the magnificent whole of nature, indistinguishable from it. Grace is the manifestation of a favor from a superior force. The favor we receive in this transaction is life—the possibility, that is, of seeing—and the superior force by which we are endowed with it is the all-seeing Creation: the great wildness at the heart of the universe. We are heirs of the grace of wildness.

To deny this grace, to turn away from the Creation toward our own creations, inevitably

diminishes us, as Berry remarks, "because, say what we will, once we build beyond a human scale, once we conceive ourselves as Titans or as gods, we are lost in magnitude; we cannot control or limit what we do. . . . If we have built towering cities, we have raised even higher the cloud of megadeath. If people are as grass before God, they are as nothing before their machines."

Another consequence of living in such a world is the helpless, often foolish, way in which we bow to expertise at every turn, discounting the possibilities — the reality, even — of our own experience. I was driving in a Minnesota blizzard one day, stupidly determined to keep a speaking date. My car was buffeted by a fierce northwesterly wind. my hands tightly clasped the steering wheel, my eyes strained to make out the road, the nerves in my fingertips were on edge, alert to the possibility of a fatal skid into an oncoming truck. In the midst of all this, I risked disaster to turn on the radio. Then I realized why I had done it. I depended upon the radio to certify the reality of the storm that I already knew in every cell of my body.

Years ago, a companion and I were standing in London directly in the shadow of the Tower of Big Ben, perhaps the best-known clock in the English-speaking world. We had spent the morning doing the tourist rounds, and it seemed as if it ought to be lunchtime. A Londoner approached just as we were considering that possibility. My friend hailed him. "Excuse me, sir," she said, "do you have the time?"

She immediately regretted the words, but it was too late.

The Londoner fixed her in a withering gaze. "You've got to be kidding," he said tartly, and passed on by.

We are so accustomed to receiving the world on outside authority that the possibility of extracting real information from it on our own escapes us. We may live in a time when information is exploding, but the question is whether the explosion is of any use to us. In the

practice of our everyday lives, at any rate, we become less competent and more dependent every day. We work for big organizations in which our own roles are always supporting and seldom instrumental; we dwell in big cities, remote from any relationship with the earth that is not passively consumptive; we live encumbered by our conveniences, the workings of which we do not understand, and which we cannot fix when they fail. Once during an extended power outage a friend, who had no heat and no way of cooking, confessed that she couldn't even clean her teeth, since the only instrument she owned for this purpose was electrically powered.

I drain the last drop of coffee from my aluminum cup and return to the stove for a refill. I carry it back down to the lakeshore and sit on a boulder. The sun has almost cleared the tops of the trees. Its first direct rays penetrate the shroud of morning mist overhanging the lake. The island that seemed to be floating in midair has come down to earth again. The mist slowly vaporizes in the heat of the morning sun, palpable now upon the backs of my hands.

In a minute, I will stow my few belongings—they will fit into a single pack with a volume of three thousand cubic inches—and carry them down to the edge of the water. I will right my canoe and launch it, position the pack so that the canoe will track properly, take my paddle, climb aboard, and set out alone, under my own power, bound for a place in the universe that is entirely new to me.

I am not under the delusion that I will set out as a simple child of nature. The canoe I paddle is easy to portage—it weighs only thirty-two pounds—because its core is made of Kevlar. The fibers in my sleeping bag are of Holofil. The jacket that will keep me warm and dry should it rain is made of Gore-Tex. The food in my pack is lightweight and compact because it has been freeze dried. I am tied, even here, by the technologically marvelous strings of human invention.

But I am also, in many ways, set free by this journey, by necessity awakened to the world at hand, and so made more alive to it. If I should become lost, nobody will show me the way home. If a storm should arise, the technological sophistication of my canoe will not save me; by my own wits I will tack against the breaking waves and make my way safely to solid ground. If I should stumble and fall, cracking my ribs against a boulder, there will be nobody to bind up my wounds. No meterologist will forecast the weather; I must read it myself. The thin walls of my tent may keep me dry, but they will shield me from no danger. If I grow bored, no one will entertain me. When I am despondent, I will need to find my own cheer. It is I who will haul the water, and chop the wood, and catch and clean and fry the fish, and make the bed that I will lie down upon when evening comes.

I am freed from my customary slumber because I have made myself vulnerable, and because in my vulnerability I am cast upon my competence, and because, appreciating the limits of my competence, I open my senses. I hear more, see more, taste more, smell more, feel more. The world comes to me like a shock of icy water this foggy wilderness morning. My pores gasp, and the world enters them. I am filled with the world, indistinguishable from it. I feel invisible.

I launch my canoe, enter it, put down my paddle, pull against the water, and slide forward into the unknown.

TIERCE

9 A.M. *Water, the canoe, rock paintings*

I GREW UP IN TALLGRASS PRAIRIE COUNTRY. There the sky predominates, the soils are deep and black, the few stones heaved up by the frost are destined to become fencepost ornaments (or were in the days when there were still fences), and the surface waters run in languid, silty streams, or collect in shallow, fetid marshes rimmed with cattails. It is, to most eyes, a forbidding landscape, ugly, boring, and faintly sinister, like all unbounded places. But because I knew it long before I considered any other, I still feel most at home there. Many landscapes, I suppose, are more beautiful than mine, but beauty is not everything in a landscape, any more than it is in a face. So it took me nearly forty years to venture into the Boundary Waters Canoe Area, although I am a Minnesotan by birth and conviction and a traveler in wild places by vocation and compulsion.

The BWCA, as it is locally known, was the first national forest to be set aside as wilderness. It remains the largest roadless area east of the Rocky Mountains in the continental United States. Extending from Minnesota into Quetico Provincial Park in Ontario, Canada, this island of wildness encompasses five million acres along the Canadian Shield, where lies exposed some of the Earth's primal bedrock. It is a land of dense forests and thick bogs, of rocky ridges and deep, clear lakes, home to moose and black bears, timber wolves and loons, pine martins and flying squirrels, lynx and beavers. Its lakes number in the thousands, closely

spaced and interconnected, a great lacework sheet of moving water.

Although readily accessible by canoe, it is not easily navigable. When I venture into it alone, I carry my compass on a string around my neck. I need to consult it often, given my disastrously faulty sense of direction, and I fear losing it. Without the compass, I would be a danger to myself, commitable to some institutions. I assumed that this was an individual failing until I read Calvin Rustrum, a fine, now neglected canoe country writer. "Even most Indians and white woodsmen, who seem to have an uncanny ability to find their way in their own region," he writes in *North American Canoe Country*, "often fare badly in complex water areas, once they are beyond their own particular, familiar territory. . . . Considerable research has gone into the study of man's sense of direction, and the results have been quite conclusive: He has no *innate* sense of direction."

There are few signs and trail markers in the canoe country to point the way, a policy I wish were followed in all of the nation's wilderness preserves. The possibility of getting lost is among those that define the wilderness experience. Everyone who has spent much time in wilderness has been lost at least once, although few have admitted it, just as few confess the fear, loneliness, and misery that are equally inherent in the experience. Being in wilderness is never deliriously, ceaselessly epiphanic. Perhaps more people who feel inadequate to the test would be encouraged to try the wild if we who advocate it were more honest about our own blunders and tremblings.

At the same time, most guidebook writers, with one eye, perhaps, on the liability lawyers, solemnly sermonize against going into a wilderness alone, quite correctly pointing out all the horrible misfortunes that might befall you if you do, but never admitting the incomparable

A prairie person covets horizons, long views, openness. The closed and canopied spaces of dense forests feel, in contrast, confining and vaguely sinister. The peculiar terror of prairies is that there is no place to hide; in forests it is that so much is concealed.

The prairie world abounds in light. During much of the day it is direct and mercilessly harsh; there is an awful frankness about it, hard to accept, but, in the end, bracing. A person accustomed to such light finds the shadowy world of the forest at first subduing, then funereal, and only after long acquaintance peaceful.

Neither forest nor prairie, actually, much suits the human eye. We began in the trees, but it was on the savannas that we first came into our own as a species. Our lawns and gardens, our cemeteries, our college campuses, our city parks, our golf courses: those places where we recreate nature in idealized form are built on the model, carried by our ancestors from Africa to Europe and from Europe to North America, of the savanna: widely spaced trees, underplanted with short grasses and flowering plants, interspersed with gentle streams or quiet pools of water: places with both long views and discrete edges, where there is both strong light and shade, where land and water converge.

From the perspective of the paddler, the canoe country, although forested, recapitulates the pattern of the savanna: it is a landscape of open spaces bounded by edges that offer hiding places. One landscape feature of nearly universal appeal is the path that curves or moves through a series of constrictions, affording always the prospect of a fresh view just around the bend or beyond the next obstruction. This, too, is an attribute of savannas, and a feature of every satisfying garden. The best gardens organize these changes in prospect to coincide with contrasting patterns of light and shade.

The canoe country is, in this respect, classically compelling. Every lake makes a bright opening in the shadowy forest. The lakes, formed by glacial striations or fault lines, may

stretch for miles, narrow and wider in the middle than at either end. Many of them, from the seat of a canoe, appear to curve gently, so that when you launch out upon one, the portage that lies at the far end remains long obscured. When you reach it, you find a narrow trail, a shaded opening in the forest, which usually climbs a ridge, or a succession of them, and descends again to another sunlit sliver of transluscent water.

So you are led on, as down a garden path, from light to shade and back again into the light; from open place to narrows or bend, and back into the open; from the clamor of darkness toward the silence of light; from the ambiguity of shadow toward the purity of light; obsessed to discover what lies ahead, just out of sight. One mystery unfolds into the next. The journey is, in the American tradition, the transcendental one, from meanness toward the sublime, from sound toward silence, above all toward the silence of the soul, which is a kind of light, a luminescence, mirrored in the eye, in the sky, in the stillness of waters.

There is a rhythm in the pattern of paddles and portages as hypnotic, once your body is attuned to it, as the beating of drums. Both paddling and portaging are, in themselves, matters of rhythm, the former a rhythm of the upper body, the latter a rhythm of the feet, both of ancient origin, the rhythms of the drumbeats of the long-ago savannas. They are wonderfully complementary. After a few days of breaking in, it is possible to sustain either without great strain from dawn until dusk. You have achieved, when this happens, a kind of bodily fluency, an incarnation of grace.

The canoe itself is such an incarnation, one of the inspired human designs, elegant, efficient, simple, adaptable, perfectly fitted to its purpose. It is sleek enough to slip through the water, even when it bears heavy loads; stable in turbulence; capable of tracking a straight line in a wind, but maneuverable through a rapids; light enough to be carried, but tough enough to withstand collisions and scrapes; stealthy in an environment where silence rules and

every sound carries enormous distances; and it can be built—although it seldom is anymore—from materials abundantly at hand locally. It is a tool supremely suited to its place, a work of indigenous genius.

I set out this morning intent upon making my passage from one lake to the next by way of a narrow, slow-moving river. The route will carry me to a widening of it where there are rock paintings, one minor site among scores of them in this country. I want to see the paintings because, obscure though the intentions now are of the people who created them, who are also unknown, I hope that they might tell me something about what it means to be indigenous.

To be inherent to the place: this is a feeling that, despite our long habitation here, we

Americans have yet fully to experience. Our presence on this continent still seems somehow tentative, our roots still underdeveloped, our claim to ownership still fraught with moral doubt. "Our day of dependence, our long apprenticeship to the learning of other lands, draws to a close. The millions that around us are rushing into life, cannot always be fed on the sere remains of foreign harvests," Ralph Waldo Emerson boldly declared in 1837, electrifying his Harvard audience. But more than a century and a half since, we still perceive that ours remains a Western rather than an American culture, and when we speak of *native* Americans, it is not the founders of our republic or their descendants to whom we refer, but an older race of discoverers, who probably followed the ice south from Siberia. "We may have colonized

this continent," the geneticist Wes Jackson says, "but we have not yet discovered it."

My own voyage of discovery carries me this morning across the shallows of the lake over bottom boulders that look so near in the refracted light of the crystalline waters and so mysteriously alive in the ripples of my wake that I think they might at any moment rise up and seize me. If anything can claim to possess this place surely it is they, who have lain here for centuries, receptive to the great turnings of the seasons, in times of ice and thaw, of pollen and ash. I wish for them the power of speech, that they might tell me what I am in search of, for I do not know whether it is myself I seek, or the land, or the connection between them, or if, in fact, there is any difference.

At the narrows of the lake I cross over a little arch of land and put in at the river, which, in this shadowy morning light, looks like a dark artery, or vein, running deep in the dense body of a forest so tropically profuse that it seems impervious, foreign, organismic, a place where the trees cannot be seen for the forest. I stifle my breath, so raucous it seems in the surrounding stillness, and paddle my way dreamily upriver, turning the blade at the end of each stroke and pulling it forward underwater so as not to violate the reverential air.

Around one bend I pass a huge beaver lodge; around the next, a reedy marsh in which a bull moose, magnificently racked, feeds without interruption, as if I were merely a bit of flotsam; and around the next, a pileated woodpecker, which takes precipitously to the air, its scarlet crest glowing in a shaft of sunlight, crying what sounds a curse. The cry echoes back, and the forest falls silent again.

Faintly at first, like a whisper of wind, I hear the sound of running water. As I approach it, its language becomes more distinct, the babble of many voices in an unfamiliar language. And then I am upon it, the water slipping over stones like liquid silk, its voice now a low murmur, the sound of an astonished crowd.

I portage around the falls, a distance of a few rods, and when I arrive at its upper end and am about to take to the river again, I see a flash of yellow in the shallows beside the canoe. A clump of irises blooms there. I know from their goldenness, the indigenous irises being blue, that they, like me, have traveled far to reach this place. They are fleur-de-lis, specimens of which were carried by traders on the Silk Route from Asia to Europe, becoming there the ensign of the kings of France, and from Europe to North America by French fur traders, who thought them a touch of home — the sort of confusion that perhaps all vagabond humans share. Once when I was a newspaper editor, I sent a young journalist to interview the poet John Berryman on the occasion of some new prize, and when she asked him about his roots, a

phrase then in currency, he exploded. "Roots!" he bellowed. "What do you think I am, some goddamn *plant*?"

Thoreau, reading Gray's *Manual of Botany*, was inspired to think how nearly like plants we in fact are, if we are healthy, especially in the matter of roots. "The mind is not well balanced and firmly planted, like the oak," he wrote in his journal, "which has not as much root as branch, whose roots like those of the white pine are slight and near the surface. One half of the mind's development must still be root,—in the embryonic state, in the womb of nature, more unborn than at first. For each successive new idea or bud, a new rootlet in the earth. The growing man penetrates yet deeper by his roots into the womb of things. The infant is comparatively near the surface, just covered from the light; but the man sends down a tap-root to the center of things."

This is not, by and large, the country of oaks. Here the shallow-rooted white pines reign, or used to before the days of the lumbermen, and in any case, given the shallowness of the soil and the impenetrability of the bedrock that lies just beneath it, deep taproots are not generally an option. I see, however, how firmly the balsam that lies uprooted just upriver has embraced that rock, raising a massive chunk of it as it fell, even though it had not been grounded in the darkest regions of the Earth.

And I see how successfully, how gracefully these Asiatic irises have taken hold here at an ancient crossroads of the global village, not one of the highways traveled by the birds or the winds, but a lane opened by the wanderlust of enterprising humans. If the fleur-de-lis are not by now indigenous here, if they will always be, as the botanists say, alien, still they look securely at home.

They remind me that although we think of this place now as wilderness, as a refuge where nature might make a last defense against the ravages of culture, and although it is a for-

bidding place in which to make a living, nevertheless it has been occupied by humans for at least eight or nine thousand years. It is likely that the portage I have just crossed was already in more or less continuous use before the first artifact of my own civilization was struck. The ancient crossings may sometimes now be obscured, Sigurd Olson, the bard laureate of this country, has written in *The Singing Wilderness*, but "they are always there, and when you pack your outfit across them you are part of a great company that has passed before. . . . The way of a canoe is the way of the wilderness and of a freedom almost forgotten. It is an antidote to insecurity, the open doorway to waterways of ages past and a way of life with profound and abiding satisfactions. When a man is part of his canoe, he is part of all that canoes have ever known."

I paddle again upriver until I round another bend and come upon the widening of it that I have sought. Along one bank, an ice-polished face of granite rises, perhaps three hundred yards long and fifty feet high. When I draw near to it, I see that it slopes toward me and find myself enshrouded in its perpetual shadow. The rock is dark, stained, and rifled with cracks, but unsullied by lichens, and when I draw very close, I can see a long line of markings, just above the level of my eyes, the color of old blood, but faded, some beyond recognition.

I paddle to the head of the cliff and drift past the paintings, turn and do it again, and again. A few of the markings are immediately recognizable: A canoe, a moose, a human figure, a thunderbird. Others, including the most prominent figure here, which looks to me like the backside of a mission-style rocking chair, are utterly mysterious. The markings were, it is thought, applied with pigments made from animal grease, or the eggs of gulls, or the roe of fish, and tinctures of iron-bearing oxides, probably, judging from their durability, by people who lived here within the last two-thousand years. One or two of them, in a rudimentary way, are even readable. The thunderbird, for example, was a supernatural creature living high in the heavens which bellowed and flashed its presence by flapping its wings to make thunder and by blinking its eyes to produce lightning.

Beyond these few facts little is known. It is not clear why they were made; or why they were made *where* they were made; or what, in general, they signify; or to whom they were addressed. This much seems clear: that they were messages; and this much more can be conjectured: that not all of the messages were addressed to humans, that some of them, at least, were meant to be—perhaps still are—communications with the gods, who were once thought to dwell in this land, and perhaps still do.

These people, whoever they were, were not indigenous. They also came from somewhere else—they may even have come from the home-place of the fleur-de-lis—and followed the glaciers of the last Ice Age northward as they melted, and settled here, and came to know the place spiritually as much as physically. When the Europeans arrived, these forecomers were the natives, and so they remain. It may be that this is what it means to be native to a place: to know it intimately enough so that one can say where lives its spirit, or spirits.

"Whatever their interpretation," Sigurd Olson writes of the painted rocks in *Listening Point*, "they marked the period during which Stone Age man emerged from the dark abyss of his past into the world of mind and soul." Olson was not indigenous to this place either, but he stayed long enough, once he had arrived, to notice, to take account of—to discover—and so at last to learn to sing its poetry. Let us also agree that this was sufficient to have made him native.

The Economy of the Canoe Country

THE BUSIEST ROUTE INTO THE HEART OF Quetico Provincial Park, the part of this wilderness north of the United States border with Canada, begins on Moose Lake and is made by way of Prairie Portage, where there is now a Canadian customs office. It was once a resting place of the voyageurs. Motorized boats are allowed that far, although from the boat landing on Moose Lake northward, the country is all now unsettled and preserved as wilderness. In recent years, many — perhaps a majority — of the canoeists crossing the border by this route have taken advantage of tow services to be sped into the heart of the wilderness. The canoeist who paddles the whole way — to do so adds only half a day to the journey, coming and going — is assaulted at the peak of the summer season by a relentless parade of power boats, burdened to the gunwales with canoes and supplies, their engines revved to full speed, their whine shattering the silence of what is nominally a wilderness preserve, their fat wakes washing steadily against what might otherwise be peaceful shores.

To travel in this way is the wilderness equivalent of journeying overland by jet aircraft rather than meandering the back roads from one city to another. It is to cast away all the rich ceremony of arrival in the wilderness and of departure from it, which is, after all, central to the possibility that a journey will be refreshing: the sense of having come a long way, of contrast

between what is familiar and what has been newly experienced. Such sensations, to be fully realized, need to be savored, to unfold slowly, in all of their detail. It is the difference between fast food gulped down on the run and a meal lovingly prepared and lingered over with friends. When I am being tossed in the wake of one of these ferries, I am angry that my own efforts to approach the wilderness reverently have been so rudely violated. Later, I am sorry for all that those who have sped past have sacrificed of the real journey for a few hours and a few miles of convenience.

No engine yet devised can speed the workings of the spirit. If you have hurried to get into the wilderness physically, still you will not be there mentally or emotionally. You will still need to decompress; to set aside the cares and preoccupations of the world you have just left; to slow yourself down to canoe time; to release yourself from the dictates of the clock and to submit to the ancient cycles of sunrise and sunset; to allow your sensory organs to open wide again—the overstimulation of the industrial world of our everyday lives causes our bodies, in sympathy for themselves, to damper down. Hurtling into the wilderness under engine power saves no time at all if it is the experience of the wilderness you are after; it may, in fact, waste time.

Perhaps human beings in every age have labored under some characteristic insensibility. The distinguishing handicap of our own age is our weakness for false economies. We love every kind of efficiency, so long as it is spendthrift. Our agricultural economy is the paradigm. We have, over the past half century, driven all but a handful of our farmers from the land, at an enormous expense of soil, water, fuel, and biological diversity. At the same time, we have accepted the unemployment and underemployment of millions of our citizens as reasonable and normal. If this is efficient—as is widely claimed—then the logical question—which Wendell Berry has raised—is, What are people *for*?

By the same token, if the wilderness needs to be approached at mechanized speed, with

every possible convenience of home in tow, then what is *wilderness* for? Why not simply stay at home? I have encountered people who carried alarm clocks into the wilderness!

We have the benefit of, but have never mastered, the instruction of Thoreau. If he has walked to the next town while his neighbor has taken the train, Thoreau asks, which of them has saved time? The cost of a train ticket is a day's labor, he says, but it takes him only a day to walk there, so he will already have arrived before his neighbor has set out, having earned, along the way, all the benefits of a day of walking in the countryside. Which of us, he asks, has practiced the greater economy?

As it happens, the economics of the canoe country compute in exactly the same way. It

costs half a day's wages to be ferried to the Quetico border. I can paddle there just as quickly. In doing so, I will have earned not only the pleasures of the journey, which were my objective in going, but also the benefits of half a day's preparation for the experience of being in the wilderness, which I will have needed in any case, and I get to keep the half-day's wages besides. But we have lost our capacity for rational economics; the ferry boats do a brisk business.

We have lost our economic bearings largely because we have come to a narrow and debilitating sense of what it means to be efficient. "Performing or functioning in the best possible manner with the least waste of time and effort," my dictionary says. Time and effort are measures of labor; we now understand efficiency to be chiefly a matter of saving labor. This makes sense only in an industrial economy, and then only if the worth of what we do can be quantified in dollars and cents.

But not every economy worth nurturing is industrial. The economy of nature is, by industrial standards, hopelessly profligate. Industrialism values uniformity, reliability, predictability. Manufacturing the greatest number of things in the least amount of time with the least possible investment of human energy depends upon the greatest possible degree of conformity.

The great British biologist J.B.S. Haldane, asked for his conception of God, in whom he did not believe, is said to have replied, "He is inordinately fond of beetles." If an industrialist had been in charge of designing nature, he would never have imagined anything so preposterous as beetles. There are perhaps a million and a half species of them on Earth — some 350,000 of them have already been named—as compared with about five thousand species of mammals, in what we presume to be the Age of Mammals. It was by counting the variety of beetles to be found in the crowns of a certain species of tree in the Panamanian rainforest—some twelve-hundred species were collected from nineteen trees over a period of three years—that we were suddenly obliged, as recently as 1982, to revise upward by a factor of fifteen our

estimation of the number of species currently alive on the planet.

The beetles have in common a moderate size and, as compared with the other insects, a seemingly modest adaptation in form: a pair of anterior wings that function not for flight but as protective covers for the posterior wings. Had an industrialist been put in charge of designing a natural world efficient by contemporary standards, he would not have thought this variation on the idea of the insect desirable in the first place, but supposing he had, he certainly would not have regarded a million and a half variations on the variation as necessary or useful. In the industrial sense of efficiency, fewer kinds of beetles—if there needed to be beetles at all—could surely have been made to suffice. Indeed, even in an ecological sense, it is not at all clear that so many kinds of beetles serve any vital purpose. And then to devise them in every color of the rainbow! To endow them with fecundity as a strategy for surviving extravagant mortality! To expend so much design attention on something with such a short life span! (It is true, of course, that beetles have survived pretty much in their present form for a hundred million years, and that they probably have a better chance of enduring environmental holocaust than most other creatures, but the industrialist's eye is not on the long run.)

Before the current century, the emphasis of meaning in the word "efficiency" was not on productivity, but on adequacy. The compact edition of the Oxford English Dictionary, reflecting its age, defines efficiency as "fitness or power to accomplish, or success in accomplishing, the purpose intended; adequate power, effectiveness, efficacy." By this definition, a canoe is an entirely efficient craft for the exploration of the Quetico-Superior country, even though it is slower and requires more physical labor than a motor boat: it is adequately powerful, it is effective, and it is, especially, efficacious: it is, that is, an appropriate means to the end, assuming that one travels into Quetico-Superior country to encounter the country itself, and to measure oneself against it. In either case, both speed and artificial power are disadvantages; they are, by the classical definition, in fact, inefficiencies.

Profit—the end product of efficiency—has undergone a similar evolution in meaning. When efficiency meant an adequate power appropriately applied to a desirable end, profit referred to anything useful. Both a loaf of bread and a day of leisure could once have been said, with exactly the same meaning, to be profitable. Now, when we think of efficiency as a savings of time and effort, we define profit as a pecuniary gain. The effect of this shift in meanings is to divorce the idea of profit from the attribute of usefulness, which is its essential quality.

This divorce has narrowed and cheapened our sense of work: it counts as profitless every labor undertaken for some cause other than economic gain; but more importantly, it has cheapened our sense of ourselves: if we count as profitable even work that is of no use, and if we count as loss every labor undertaken solely out of love—if we deny ourselves the possibilities of life as an unfolding of gifts—then we cheat ourselves out of every kind of luxury.

Instead of approaching a journey as if each part of it had some unexpected gift to offer, as if it were an experience to be savored, to be allowed to unfold in its own way and in its own time, we count minutes and labors as if they were pennies to be pinched, saving an hour here and an exertion there, and find, when we have arrived, that we have never left home at all.

The efficiencies of the canoe country are all of the prodigal kind, and none of the profits are pecuniary. If we would experience it, we must learn again to wager in an older and wiser economy.

SEXT

Noon. Rock, *the swim, the dragonfly*

It is noon, and I have sought respite on a knoll of granite, in which the etchings of the glaciers of ten thousand years ago are still vivid, out of considerations as various and complex, as amalgamated, as the materials in the rock. I have been paddling since early morning. The muscles in my arms are weary; my legs, which I have alternately stretched and tucked under the seat of my canoe, are cramped; and I am hungry. I have passed through early mists down the winding Kawishiwi River, have glided so stealthily past a bull moose feeding on water plants in a marsh that I did not disturb its breakfast, have examined the residences of beavers, have admired the bloom of irises, have savored the melody of a white crowned sparrow, have made the acquaintance of a loon so near that I could peer into the startling scarlet of its eye, have threaded a bewildering maze of islands and ventured across open water in the dazzling glare of the high morning sun: I stop out of consideration for all that has transpired, that I might lock it in memory. I stop because it is the middle of the day: out of consideration for habit. I stop because I have traveled for a long time on the thin skin of lakes and rivers, an alien place: out of consideration for my standing as a creature of the earth. I stop because when this small island appeared on the horizon, it beckoned to me: to honor my curiosity.

As I approach the island, I see that it is a walled fortress, presenting only a narrow,

pebbled slit upon which to land. I coast toward it and backpaddle until, parallel to the beach, I have drifted smoothly to shore. This manuever pleases me, as does the proper use of any tool. I step onto the beach, remove my pack, and lift the canoe from the water. For a moment I am disoriented; my inner ears need to adjust to the sudden equilibirium of solid ground. Overhead, herring gulls cry, as they do in ports everywhere. I feel as much the mariner as Captain Ahab.

Now that I am ashore, I can sense, as I could not while I was still paddling, the elixir of tiredness in my body, a pacific contentment, in part induced by pheromones released during exertion, the natural drugs, also set loose when we laugh, that make physical labor so addictive, so satisfying.

I climb with my pack to the top of the island and find there a shaded, grassy opening in a clump of birches. The shade feels cool and soothing. I realize that my skin has been burning in the intense light reflected from the water. My skin is gritty with the salts of dried sweat. When I lift my eyelids, they feel like fine sandpaper.

I sit on the grass—so luxuriant a patch of it is rare in this country—and eat my lunch of dried fruit and nuts, cheese and sausage, and a bar of chocolate, washing it down with long draughts of water drawn from the lake, soft as rain. The island seems the more remote because my repast is undisturbed by the opportunists — the chipmunks and gray jays — that hang around more frequented campsites.

The lines of communication here about food free for the scavenging are sometimes stupendously effective. One night, when I had filleted a bass for supper, I took its remains down to the lakeshore and laid them on a rock for the gulls, though I had not seen one all day. Within minutes, the place was as rowdy as a rock concert. Half a dozen herring gulls had converged out of nowhere and had begun to fight and scream, in their surpassingly dis-

agreeable way, over the few scraps of fish. At first, the smallest of them had possession of the prize piece — the head — too large to swallow, which it nevertheless valiantly defended against the shrieks and dive-bombings of its larger fellows, until the assaults became merciless, and it dropped the head and retreated, ignoring the lesser but ingestible scraps of fish floating nearby. The same fracas repeated itself half a dozen times. Finally one of the biggest gulls managed to lift into the air with the head of the bass clamped in its bill and flapped off to the next lake, hotly pursued by its taunting, but weaker, mates.

I could not imagine how the gulls had found my few scraps so swiftly, except that they had obviously been biding their time somewhere nearby in the hope of just such an opportunity. It left me a bit unnerved that they had. All the rest of the evening, I felt uncomfortably conspicuous, keenly aware that although I was, so far as I knew, the solitary human in the neighborhood, I was a long way from being alone. I tried to avoid imagining how many pairs of eyes and ears were tracking my every move.

After the meal, I clamber back down to the cove where I landed my canoe, strip, and plunge into the lake, so deep a few feet out that it looks almost green. Although I expect its coldness, it arrives, as it does every time, with a shock. My heart leaps, skips a beat, and I gasp. I thrash about, noisy as a moose, duck my head a few times to rinse the grime from my hair, and turn up on my back. Because I spent my boyhood far from any swimming hole, my technique has never advanced much beyond the dog-paddle. I retain a landlubber's fear of water. I have learned enough about it to believe that if I don't fight it—if, my women friends say, I give up the male delusion of being in control—I will float, but I have learned little enough so that every time I try, I think myself the beneficiary of a small miracle. The sun is bright and the season advanced; there is a thin zone of tolerably warm water near the lake's surface. I float in it as long as I dare, take one last headlong dive, reveling in the balming coolness of the lake against

my sunburned face, and crawl up the algae-slickened boulders to shore. A bath towel is one of the encumbrances I forego on these trips; I shake myself and sit in the sunlight, like an animal, to dry.

While I am basking in the pleasure of the two baths, the one in the water, and the one in the sun, feeling as unfettered in my nakedness as a dog off the leash, the corner of my eye catches a miniscule commotion. The ice of centuries has wedged a crack in the ledge of granite that I am sitting on. When I look closely, I see along its edge a creature as green as a fresh pea —at first I mistake it for a luna moth—emerging from the ferocious-looking carapace of a water insect.

The carapace is the nymphal form of one of the *Macromiidae,* an order of dragonflies. It is an inch and a half long, has very long legs, which grip the stone tightly, like the fingers of a baby, and a squat, chitinous abdomen, a bit larger than my thumbnail, barbed at the edges of the plates, that resembles the shell of a turtle. Its oval head is preposterously small for its body and disproportionately apportioned to a pair of dark eyes. Between them, there are two antennae, and, between the antennae, a prominent horn with a nasty hook. The nymph is a dark gray-brown, the dreary color of the silts at the bottom of the lake, where it has spent its sedentary life for the past year or two, preying promiscuously on practically everything that has passed—other nymphs, mosquito larvae, water bugs, even small fish—by means of a long,

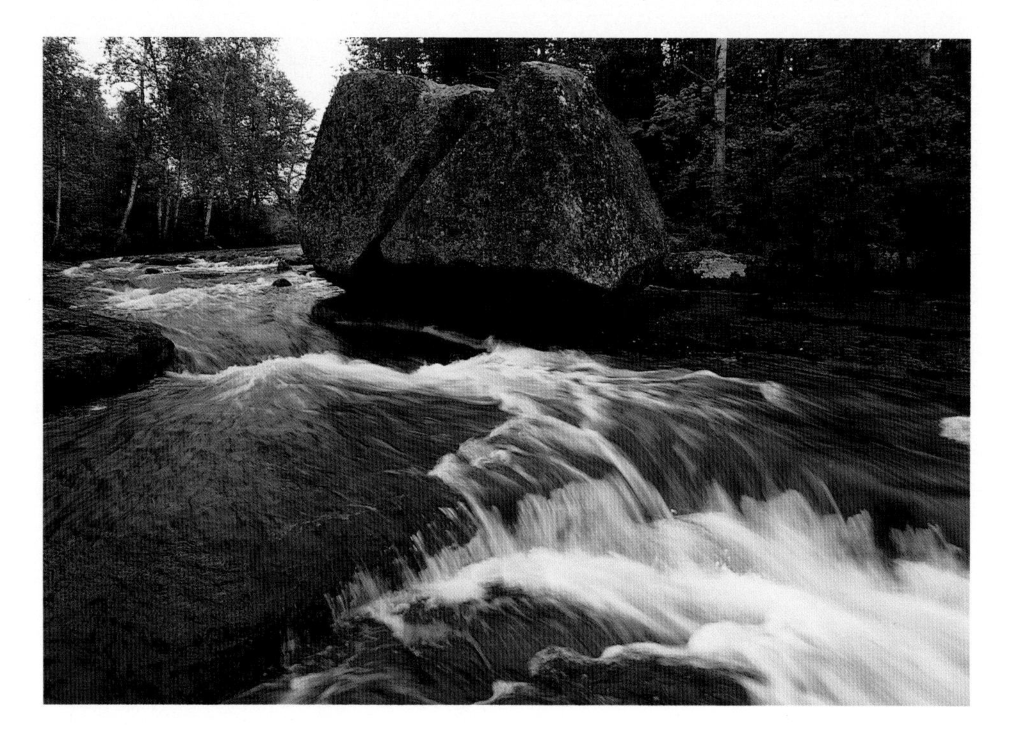

double-hinged exterior lip, tucked under the thorax when it is not in use, so big as partially to obscure the creature's face. This lip is equipped with a pair of sharp, moveable hooks. The prey approaches. The dragonfly nymph skewers it on the thorns of its suddenly ejaculated tongue, able then to snack on it at its leisure, employing for the purpose a powerful pair of mandibles. It breathes through its ass.

As I watch, the fierce, ugly creature's body splits down its back at the mid-dorsal line and from it, in incredibly slow motion, emerges an enormous adult dragonfly. First the thorax appears, then the head with eyes so huge they nearly meet at center brow, then the six long legs, which grope for footing on the rock, and finally the long abdomen, soft and crumpled as a freshly washed swatch of cotton. The whole creature is five or six inches long, dwarfing the skin of its nymphal self. It is as ridiculous as a crowd of clowns emerging from a toy car.

The limp creature dangles impassively for a moment, and then draws in a big gulp of air, leaving behind forever the gills of its water existence, committing itself to a new life on the wing. Its abdomen suddenly stiffens, and, with a faint shivering, its double wings begin to unfurl and straighten. They look soft, wet, and silken. Blood has begun to course through the dragonfly's veins. The creature is perpendicular to the rock, its forward pair of legs hooked over the top of the boulder, its head aiming toward the Milky Way.

For more than an hour, the creature hangs there, moisture falling a drop at a time from its abdomen, while its wings harden and become translucent and the green of its exoskeleton dulls and becomes etched with a delicate tracery of brown lines, like porcelain cracking with age. I watch it anxiously, knowing that this is its most perilous hour. Immobile, it is ripe for the voracious eyes of any bird, and even something so capricious as a sudden strong breeze might rumple a wing and cripple it for life.

Since it first pulled its abdomen from its nymphal skin, the dragonfly has not moved.

Now in a single graceful and seemingly effortless motion it lifts from the rock and takes to the air, which it will scarcely leave until it is finally felled by the first hard freeze of autumn; its long subaqueous respite has passed; it has been born again into a brief moment of exuberant beauty. The transformation is as astonishing, Edwin Way Teale wrote, "as though a trout should suddenly shed its skin and become a robin."

The carapace of the nymph from which the dragonfly emerged still clings to the rock. I reach for it. It has the rock in a death-grip and must be gently pried loose. In my hand, it seems to weigh less than a feather. Were it any less substantial, it would not exist.

I rise and head up the knoll to gather my things. It is time to push on. I suddenly notice the discarded skins of dragonfly nymphs everywhere. I have, it seems, tarried in a paradise of metamorphosis. As I take to the water again, I feel a new man myself.

3 P.M. *Wind, portage trails, the storm*

IT IS THE FIFTH HOUR OF THE DAY, THREE P.M. A stiff wind is blowing, as it often does at this hour. I am headed into it, as, it seems, I eternally am. I shift my pack toward the bow and move forward myself, onto my knees, to counter the force of the wind, which would otherwise swing me back in the direction from which I have just come.

Once years ago I was marooned for hours in a wind like this. I had set out alone, inexperienced, in a clumsy canoe, intent on catching a mess of crappies around the leeward point of a large island. I was staying on the mainland opposite it. A storm was brewing, and my stringer soon was full. I pulled it in and headed home. But when I rounded the bend toward the cabin, the wind spun me around and sent me back toward the fishing grounds. I tried again, with the same result. I positioned myself in as many ways as I could imagine, but every time I tried to cross the channel from the island to the mainland, my canoe pirouetted.

Although I didn't want to paddle the whole way around the island, there seemed no alternative. When I had arrived at the channel from the opposite side of the island, however, I faced the same problem. I could get to within sight of the cabin, but no matter what I did, I could not hold the canoe in the wind. Around and around I spun, tossing in the waves like a bobber. I cursed. I redoubled my efforts at paddling. I went at the barrier of the wind like a

chicken trying to break a fence, over and over, stupidly, blindly, until I was a gibbering mess. In the end, I had to wait out the wind in the shelter of the island. For a long time afterward, I couldn't imagine what anybody saw in canoeing.

Now I expect the wind and welcome it. It is a regularity of the day, like the mists of morning and the mirrored waters of evening, one of the pulses at the heart of the land by which I know it to be well. When I fall to my knees before the wind and dig in hard with the blade of my paddle, I know that before another lake or two has passed, it will be time to put ashore and make a camp for the night.

In becalmed waters, the canoe seems hardly to move. Now, when I struggle just to hold position against the wind in the tricky air currents off the points of the lake, I feel airborne. Our perceptions of nature, I think, are often contrary and misleading in this way, accustomed as we are to falsely imagining ourselves as at the center of things.

I like the moist wind in my face. I like the tiny wake that rises as the canoe cuts through the waves. I like the gentle rocking of the boat. I like the feel of my muscles straining to maintain a forward momentum. I like the way the drops of water falling out of the curls of the combers glisten in the sunlight. I like the sound of wind and water in my ears.

When the wind blows, the whole landscape seems in motion, throbbing with energy. It seems possible that it might, at any moment, explode into something even grander. This watery world is never more exuberantly alive than when it roils in the wind.

Overhead the clouds pass like great ships, stately and powerful. They are dark with rain. They gather and stream forward until they blot out the sun. The light, which has been harsh and white, turns a soft, incandescent yellow. I race for the portage ahead.

I carry the canoe up a forested ridge, brushing against ferns and brackens, stumbling over rocks in the premature twilight. At the other end of the portage, a tiny lake perches on a glacial shelf rimmed with birches. Water lilies, yellow with blossom, float in its rippled shallows, their pads curling in the wind. I double back for the pack. A stream tumbles from the smaller lake into the bigger one, cutting inexorably away at the rock straining to contain it. Here, even the rock is on the move.

There is a sudden stillness, then a gust of wind moaning in the limbs of the trees, then stillness again, and, as I arrive back at the place where I have stashed the canoe, the first patter of raindrops. They are huge and heavy. I see them collide with the surface of the lake, bounce, and fall back again into the saucers they have made. The surface of the lake is covered with a pattern of tiny, concentric rings, as if it were a pot about to boil.

I put my rain jacket on, tuck my pack beneath the overturned canoe, and take shelter in a clump of cedars. The rain quickens, falls nearly in sheets. Its din is deafening. The water beads and runs in tiny rivers down my sleeves. I feel my wrists moistening and the water running down my face and neck. When I can no longer see through the lenses of my glasses, I remove them and tuck them into a pocket. The world becomes a vague blur of wet, writhing blues and greens and grays such as Monet, in the end, saw in his garden.

In twenty minutes, the sky brightens. A minute later, the sun falls, like a spotlight, on the lake dimpled with raindrops. A minute or two after, the rain stops altogether. Overhead, there is blue sky, but in the forest the water continues to drip.

I retrieve my glasses, remove my rain coat, right the canoe and launch it, load the pack, get in myself, and set out across the lake. I am no longer on my knees. The trunks of the birches look as white as snow, the shining rocks as red as blood, and every green leaf glistens like jade. I am in motion again, skimming double-time across the water, inhaling the sweet smell of ozone, intoxicated by the newness of everything.

VESPERS

Evening. Calm waters, sunset rituals

At the height of the summer season in canoe country, it is advisable to begin looking for a place to camp by early afternoon. The best places are quickly taken, and camping is allowed only at designated sites. These are usually situated above the sloping slabs of granite or gneiss that the glaciers cut long ago. They provide convenient landing places for canoes; make natural openings in the forests that, elsewhere, overshadow the edges of the lakes, unless the shores are lined with cliffs; and offer comfortable prospects upon which to idle, after the evening meal is finished, with a cup of coffee and—if you are a traditionalist—a cigar or pipe, watching the sun fall.

Assisting the sun on its daily journey over the western horizon is one of the necessary labors of any journey into a wilderness. The work requires close attention. If you are with a companion, the conversation must be hushed and never too urgent. It will not do to argue or joke the sun away. Patience is a virtue diligently to be practiced at all times, but especially at evening; the sun will not be hurried. It is reticent about crossing the horizon. When it reaches that threshhold, it takes the pause that every dramatist knows well, the brief sigh of silence, before it makes its exit and the curtain falls. Then, especially, one must not break the mood with unseemly chatter or busyness of any kind.

The hours immediately preceding the departure of the sun are the ones, in the wilderness

day, of domesticity. A certain ritual attends them. The canoe, once landed, must be unloaded and the canoe itself carried to safe ground and overturned, in case a wind should rise or rain should fall in the night.

Then one's camp shoes must be located and exchanged for one's canoeing shoes, which will have grown damp and cold during the day's travels. I carry a pair of high-topped L.L. Bean canvas shoes with rubber soles, once tan, but now weathered to a comely gray, like favorite pieces of patio furniture. They are duplicates of my canoe shoes, but dry. A pair of dry and familiar shoes, which carry somewhere in their scuffed, stained, and softened threads the memory of all the campsites past, are the essential first step in making of a stopping place a home, however temporary. When they have been donned and securely tied, and one's toes have found their proper places among the subtle indentations of the soles, the wet shoes and socks must be laid out to dry.

Next, the site for the tent—although it will be obvious, having already been chosen by a thousand previous occupants—must be carefully scrutinized, with an eye toward the exact square of maximum levelness, taking into account the direction in which runoff waters might flow in the event of a storm, and how the doorway of the tent must be placed to take advantage of the first rays of the morning sun. No matter how many times the spot has been previously prepared, one must remove, if only ritually, a stray pebble or two, a bit of twig, and a pine cone, lest one's slumbers be offended by too casual an approach to the pitching of the tent. Then the ground cloth must be laid, and repositioned, and the tent unfolded upon it, and staked, and raised.

Every wilderness traveler develops a fondness for a reliable tent. It becomes, with frequent use, an island of security, a counterbalance to the sometimes overwhelming instability of travel. Mine is a two-person Eureka Timberline. I bought it many years ago, before I became a solo traveler in wild places, on a whim. It was on sale, and I had the vague notion that I might use it sometime. It was, it turned out, not a whim, but an inspiration: lightweight, easy to pitch without assistance, absolutely dependable. And it was an inducement. Once I owned it, I felt obligated, as a practicing Lutheran, to use it.

My tent has traveled with me thousands of miles since in every kind of terrain and weather. I have been lonely in it, tired and depressed, exhilarated, terrified, contented. I have repaired to it when I was lost, and when I was delighted to have found my way. I have sometimes known, when I retired to it, what my journeyings were about, and sometimes I have been confused and perplexed. Now, whenever I crawl into it, I have the sense of being accompanied. I am reminded of all the places we have been together, all the nights and moods and circumstances we have shared. It seems to me that it, like my camp shoes, in some mystical way carries the memory of those times within its fibers. Portable though it may be, it is, for me, a kind of home.

Where I grew up, in the countryside of western Minnesota, people had home-places. The home-place was where your grandparents lived, perhaps where they had been born, where one of your own parents had been raised, where your father still worked the land. It was the epicenter of familial life, recognized as such not only by you, but also by your friends and neighbors. If you said to a friend, "We're having a picnic Sunday night at the home-place," your friend knew where to go, even though you yourself didn't live there anymore. The home-place was the settling place, the one your forbearers had come to from the old country; the place where, for better or worse, they had concluded to try their fortunes; or it was the final stop in the family's wanderings, the place where luck, or money, or resolve had run out, where one made a last stand.

I was born in the baby boom of the late 1940's, in the year that 2,4-D, the first miracle chemical of industrial agriculture, was introduced. Although farm children had already for generations been forsaking the farm for the brighter opportunities of cities, and although a million farm families were driven by economic forces from the land during my elementary school years, still it was hoped that I, like those of my lineage, would settle down, make my life where I had been born, and someday take over management of the home-place. The idea had its attractions, and I might have been persuaded by them—although I doubt happily—if it had not become obvious by my teens that I was hopelessly ungifted mechanically, and not very adept, either, at concentrating on the details of the farm work at hand.

My mind wandered even when my feet couldn't. I was always catching the drag in the

fence at the end of the field and pulling it down, or running out of gas at the wrong end of the farm, or cultivating out the corn rather than the weeds, or letting the grain wagon spill over. My father, in the end, acknowledged that I had better think of something else to do with my life, but he could not accept the idea in his heart. On the day when I left for college, he made it a point not to be around to say goodbye.

I have come to terms with my father's disappointment. I'm quite certain I would have starved if I had tried to be a farmer. Still, I often wonder what I left behind when I set out for Minneapolis on that September day so many years ago, my worldly possessions in a cardboard box and a hand-me-down suitcase, throbbing with excitement, but my sense of where I belonged yet in limbo. I think that what I left behind was not farming; not, certainly, the community of which it was a part, about which I then had much less positive feelings than I do now; not family, for my family, like most modern ones, quickly scattered to distant cities; not even the place itself, for place is, as Robert Farrar Capon says, not a location, but a session; what matters most about it is not where you are but who, or what, you are with; it becomes real only in the engagement between the two. What I had left behind was the home-place.

I have lived and visited since in many places. Some of them I have lingered in, or visited frequently, long enough or often enough for familiarity. They are places, even, that I have come to depend upon, that give my life shape and dimension, in the sense, at least, that they are in some way measures of myself. When I return to a book I have often read, or to a piece of music long familiar, or to the liturgies I have recited almost since I was an infant, or when I visit an old friend after a long absence, I find in the stirrings of my heart, in the memories that are provoked, in the dreams that follow, a gauge of the ways in which I have changed, or stayed the same.

"My, how big you've gotten!" the out-of-town aunts would invariably exclaim when we gathered for a baptism or graduation, a wedding or funeral. I was always, in the way of children, exasperated at their stupidity. What did they think, that I was going to remain forever two? I knew that I had been accepted as an adult when they started to say, "Well, you haven't changed a bit!" "It would turn your hair blue to know the ways," I would think. And then I was suddenly old enough to be flattered, and before long I found myself saying the same things to the children of friends.

When we were pre-schoolers, my sister and I often wandered down the lane to the neighbors on the next farm, a kindly and elderly couple who talked to us seriously and kept a bowl of caramels, and had a refrigerator, a device as exotic to us as a Martian spaceship, in which there was ice cream. They liked us and we adored them. Then I moved to Minneapolis, and to other places, and my parents died, and for a long time I put them and the home-place out of mind.

One night I was invited back there to tell about a book I had written. With some misgivings, I went. Irene, the woman on the next farm, had died, I learned. Indeed, she had been buried that very afternoon. But Jake came to the talk, a gift that touched and shamed me. How selfish and neglectful I have been, I thought. I hugged him fondly, recognizing too late that he had been one of my fathers; we talked; we posed for pictures. Suddenly, while my eyes were still dazzled from the glare of the flash bulbs, I realized that when I had been running down the lane to pound on Jake's refrigerator door, a behavior that always produced a laugh and a bowl of ice cream, he had been not an old man at all, but somebody my age!

Some surprise always lurks in the familiar, some bit of history one can appreciate only with the passing of time and by comparison with the particulars of a thing intimately known — a person, or community, or place. The surprise of the familiar is a deeper and truer discovery than the surprise of the exotic or strange because it is the kind of surprise that enlarges our sense of connectedness, rather than that of our separateness.

This distinction is frequently lost in the endless preoccupation we now have with matters of self-esteem. Esteem comes from the knowledge of belonging, not from the fractures of difference. Our deepest longing is to have a place—in the family, in the community, in the culture, in the world. This is why adolescence is such a torment. It is the time of life when our need to understand ourselves as individuals necessarily overwhelms our sense of ourselves as ordinary. We are obliged, for that time, to concentrate on the things that distinguish us from the crowd. We find ourselves, in consequence, isolated, alienated, humiliatingly conspicuous. Some cultures, but not ours, have sympathized with the wretchedness of this work by offering their youngsters, at the end of this trial by separation, a ritual way of re-establishing connections, especially the most fundamental one, the connection with nature.

This, as I understand it, is what the vision quests of the Plains Indians were about. A native child was sent alone to a sacred place for three or four days to await, in silence and in fasting, a vision from the spirit world of nature. The vision came not from inside, but from without. It came in the form of a bear, or a crow, or a snake—in the form of some other *creature*—from whom one took one's name, in whom one found the spirit of one's life-work, and with whom one was allied for the rest of one's days. The vision named you as an individual—it gave you claim of special standing in the community of the tribe—but it also, and more importantly, affirmed you as a member in good standing of the community at large, the community of nature. It was a way of marrying into the world.

When one has a home-place and takes the idea of it seriously, when one feels bound to it and responsible to it for a lifetime, then one has, in the same way, undertaken the adult work of living both as an individual with unique qualities *and* as a citizen of the commonwealth of a place, with all of the connections that implies: to other individuals, to the whole community of the place, to the work of the place, and to the land itself; and it is this sense of being joined

to something good and whole that gives one the confidence, the esteem, necessary to persevere. The conviction is possible then that one does not stand alone. And out of that conviction emerges also the prospect of an endless unfolding of surprises, surprises that reveal the intricacy, and diversity, and invincibility of our ties to all of creation.

Now my tent has become a kind of home-place, an anchor to return to in the evenings wherever I wander, a link with all of the sessions I have held in wild places, and a reminder of my human limits: "Even nomads live within boundaries," Gary Snyder says.

After the tent has been pitched, water must be gathered and filtered or boiled. I filter mine, preferring its taste to that of boiled water, which seems to me to go flat, like old beer, in the purifying heat. It is the one camp duty that seems to me a chore, perhaps because it is necessary at all. Even fifty years ago, I might have dispensed with it, but by now our world is generally contaminated, including all of its waters.

There are signs at the entrances to the canoe country these days warning you against eating too many fish. The fish carry in their flesh concentrations of mercury and other toxic metals that have drifed in the atmosphere from distant industrial sites and precipitated in the rainfall. One once went, like Thoreau, to the wilderness to be freed and purified. Freedoms and purifications of the soul are still to be found there, but the body cannot now escape the transgressions of our industrial labors.

After the water has been rendered drinkable, there will be, if one's travels have ended at a merciful hour, time to sit against a boulder or the trunk of a tree, writing in a journal perhaps, or reading a book (although I find that I lose my appetite for books in the wilderness), or surveying the scene, or daydreaming: time to play in the mind, which is frisky after a day of physical labor. There will be time for a jigger of brandy, raw in the throat and warm in the belly.

Then a fire must be laid, or the stove (which I always use) must be lit and a supper prepared. Canoeing affords mealtime luxuries not possible to backpackers, but I have become so accustomed to trail food over the years that I now prefer it: a bowl of steaming soup; a dish of noodles or rice and a simple sauce; a salad, when the right materials are at hand, gathered from near the campsite, marsh marigold leaves, perhaps, with fiddleheads or mushrooms; maybe some bannock, studded with berries if they are ripe; sometimes a package of freeze-dried ice cream, one of the benefits of technology that I enthusiastically endorse. Afterwards, something hot to drink, usually chocolate, but on occasion a cup of Tang or lemonade. Extravagant meals are unnecessary in the wilderness. The humblest fare, when you have been active out of doors all day, invariably tastes like a feast. Food never seems closer to sacrament than then.

When I turn off the stove after the water for drinks has come to a boil, I am freshly reminded of the stark silence of the wilderness. The tiny flame hissing beneath the pot makes a noise that would scarcely be audible in any other setting; here it seems, when it has been suddenly extinguished, as if it had been emitting a mighty roar.

The dishes must be washed and packed away with the foodstuffs in a sack, and the sack must be hung from a line secured between two trees downwind of the camp so that the bears can't get at it. This brings the domestic labors of the day to a close. The performance of these chores lies at the heart of the wilderness experience: the work gives us common standing with the rest of life. The squirrel gathering pine cones for the winter midden, the mother bear browsing berries with its cub on the ridgetop, the father osprey flying back to the nest with a bass skewered in its talons, may be wild, may be in many particulars incomprehensible to us, but they also, like us, are bound to their daily chores. It is in our mutual roles as domestics that our lives most clearly converge.

By then, whatever wind has been blowing will have died, and the surface of the lake will have become like glass. This is the time for a last turn in the canoe, gliding slowly, noiselessly across the smooth waters, drifting atop the mirror image of forest and sky while the mayflies hatch, and the fish surface to feed upon them, and the families of ducks take a social swim, and the sweet coolness of evening rises in the air.

As you return to camp at the edge of dusk, water and sky have taken on a pink and mauve glow. You beach the canoe. You change into a long-sleeved shirt and long pants: now the mosquitoes, even if they have been absent all day long, appear suddenly in energetic masses. They drone an ostinato to bring down the sun. With the mosquitoes come the dragonflies. They dart up and down the shoreline, their legs folded into baskets to gather the mosquitoes, skimming the surface of the water and swooping skyward again like kites, their wings clacking. Now and then, if one watches closely, one can also see the shadowy form of a bat winging at high speed out toward the lake, intent on sharing in the bounty. The mosquitoes never stay for long. By the time the trees on the opposite shore have turned from green to black, they will have gone again into hiding. It is as if they are as compelled as we to attend to the fall of the night.

The blue in the dome of the sky deepens to the color of cobalt. The line of trees across the water loses not only its color but also its shape. The distinction between earth and heaven blurs, then disappears. The first star appears, then another, and another.

I sit on a rock at the edge of the water in the gathering darkness, staring into the depths of the lake and thinking of something Thoreau said, when he was perhaps in a similar mood, about Walden Pond: "A lake," he said, "is the landscape's most beautiful and expressive feature. It is earth's eye; looking into which the beholder measures the depth of his own nature."

Down the lake a solitary loon cries. The sound is low and mournful. It is sometimes mistaken for the howl of a wolf. I think that the cry might have come from my own heart. When it

echoes back across the water, it also echoes inside me, and the reverberations do not die away. I shiver, and button my wool shirt, and pull a jacket over it, but I think it is not the sudden coldness alone that stirs within me.

In a few months I will be as old as my father was when he died. I can see him now, looking up at me out of the depths of the lake. He is smiling. He always wanted to be in a place like this, but he never found the time or the means to get here. I see that it did not matter, that he is here now, and always was.

Forty-five years was the span of his life. Thoreau was the same age when he died. This rock has been here for two billion years. Somewhere, loons have been crying for a hundred million years. There were already loons when this shore I sit upon was still buried within the heart of a great mountain. Long before the Rocky Mountains, there were loons. Somewhere a wolf is prowling. I can feel it in my bones. I can feel the vibrations in this stone. Thirty million years ago there were wolves. In an hour, I will hear one howling. Before the ice came, it was already howling. Nine thousand years ago, this lake was here. Eight thousand years ago, on a night very like this one, perhaps, an ancestor of mine sat upon this boulder, or on one nearby. A loon was crying, and its cry echoed across these waters, and the echo reverberated in my kin's heart, and it reverberates still.

Tonight, I have a session with myself. I look into the eye of the earth, and I find there myriad things coming forth and expressing themselves: flowers, poets, fathers, lakes, mountains, wolves, loons, boulders of granite, both inside my body and out of it. I have found, after all, the thing I was looking for, the home-place. It is here, I see, everywhere and inside me, where it always was.

I rise, go up the hill, and build a fire against the chill and the darkness. It crackles and spits. Idly I stir a stick in the coals until it glows, and wave it, writing a neon dance in the night.

I stare absent-mindedly into the blue and orange flames, hypnotized by them in the ancient way, feeling myself letting go of my body. My eyelids begin to droop, neither with weariness, nor with sleepiness, but with peace.

When the fire has burned itself down, I bank the coals and turn in. At first the sleeping bag feels clammy and chill, but it warms quickly. It is good to be confined within the bag after so much movement, good to be in the embrace again of solid ground after so much water. I turn once or twice or three times, discover the way my body fits best against the contours of the ground, and close my eyes, hoping that I might awaken in the night to hear gentle rain against the fly of the tent or the lapping of water against rock. Then I might fall asleep a second time, a proper lullaby in my ears, bringing gentle dreams.

COMPLINE

The Last Hour of the Day.
Loons, wolves, night sounds, sleep

SOMETIMES ON A CLOUDY NIGHT THE CANOE country turns as dark as the bottom of the sea. It is impossible then to see your hand in front of your face. You lie in this utter darkness, feeling the hardness of the earth in your hip bones and shoulder blades. You have never been more aware of being entirely alone.

Across the lake, a wolf howls. It is not so much a howl as a wail, a long lament, not languorous but full-toned and intense. The wolf has a tenor voice. It carries operatically across the lake, dies away, echoes back upon itself.

OooooooooooooooooooOOOOooo.

You do not stir, but your skin tingles. Some wild part of you desires to rise up and give answer. But from far away comes a better reply, three high trumpet-like notes on an ascending scale.

Ah! Ah! Ah!

On lakes near and far, the loons, hearing the primordial cry, voice their own response, a tumultuous laughter, ecstatic, echoing across all the hard surfaces of this land of rock and water.

A long silence, and then the wail again. And the same answer. And the same ecstatic laughter, deep throated and joyous. You have never heard music to equal it. It croons you into a dreamy half-sleep.

Later—you do not know how much later, time seeming to have vanished in the darkness of the night—you are abruptly awakened by a loud noise. It sounds about ten feet from your ear, made by some living creature, a snort or grunt or perhaps a sneeze. You bolt upright in your sleeping bag, your heart pounding, your mouth gone dry, trying not to breathe audibly, listening through the pores of your skin. You hear only an eerie silence. You reach for your flashlight, train its beam across the little clearing in the forest where you are camped. Nothing glitters back at you; only the dull gray radiance of bark and matted needles and mosses reflects in the light-thirsty night.

You switch off the flashlight. It seems darker now than ever. You lie down again, but you do not sleep. Every particle of you awaits some further sign from the mysterious companion who has come to share the night with you. You hear every snapping twig, every rustling leaf, every lap of water.

You finally drift into the sleep that will hold you until morning. When you have descended into dreams, when your body functions according to its preconscious will, as it has operated through all the millenia of humankind, when you have abandoned yourself fearlessly, automatically, to whatever the night and the forest might bring: then you come as near to wildness, to a life in nature, as any human can.

"The civil wilderness of sleep," Robert Herrick called it. You cannot know, when you enter it, whether you will ever return. It was like that for my father. One evening he slept, and after that the mornings, for him, ceased to rise, although many times since, high in the sky and in watery depths, I am quite sure that I have caught glimpses of him. He seems to be awake

still, more awake, perhaps, than ever. "There is more day to dawn," Thoreau said. "The sun is but a morning star."

Somewhere a squirrel flies, and somewhere the moon glows, and you sleep. Somewhere a beaver swims, and somewhere a fisher hunts, and you sleep. Somewhere a night breeze stirs. Somewhere an owl rides upon it, and you sleep. Your face has fallen, and somewhere the stars have risen. Your face has fallen into innocence. For this little while, at least, you can do no harm. You look it; you look young and harmless, as if you might never again be streetwise and carelessly knowing. "Praise ignorance," Wendell Berry's Mad Farmer advises, "for what man has not encountered he has not destroyed."

Somewhere the stars have risen, all hundred million of them in this galaxy, one of a hundred million galaxies. Somewhere there among them you sleep, and dream. You dream of Robert Frost demanding of the fairest star in sight that it speak. And, although loftily reticent, it does say something in the end; it asks of you a certain height.

Somewhere the vegetable mold is becoming humus. Somewhere your own heart is beating. Somewhere the sun is shining. Somewhere your mind is dreaming, and your body is inside your dream, and you sleep. Somewhere mists are rising and birds are stirring, and still you sleep.

Everywhere everything is changing. Everything is in a state of becoming. When the day dawns, it will be be a new day. When the day dawns, there will be a new you. Your hair is lengthening, your brain is slaking cells, your body is being cleansed and refurbished. You sleep and you cease to be and you start becoming. You look as innocent as a baby, and you sleep like one, as well you might. You *are* momentarily innocent, risen in the ethereal air of sleep to a suitable height. You are only being. You are only becoming. You *look* becoming.

You waken. It is light. Birds chirp in the forest undergrowth and in its canopy. You crawl from your tent and stand in the sharp, clean-smelling morning air. Fog shrouds the lake. The

island across the way seems to be floating in it. You light your stove and boil a pot of coffee. A chipmunk warily advances to investigate the intrusion. You find a rock to lean against, drinking in the stillness with the coffee. You feel, suddenly, invisible.

You have vanished into the forest, taken a proper place in it. You stand there belonging, anointed with the heavenly, the homely, grace of wildness.

RESOURCE GUIDE

THE STANDARD CANOE GUIDE is *Boundary Waters Canoe Area* by Robert Beymer. It comes in two volumes, one for the eastern unit of the preserve, and one for the western, and is published by Wilderness Press. Beymer has also written *Superior National Forest,* a guide to the often less crowded wilderness areas south of the preserve. It is published by The Mountaineers. William N. Rom, M.D., offers an introduction to the northern canoe country across the North American continent. It is called *Canoe Country Wilderness,* published by Voyageur Press. Anglers will want to consult *A Boundary Waters Fishing Guide* by Michael Furtima (NorthWord Press). Visitors to the region might want to consider side trips to two nearby national parks, Voyageurs National Park, and Isle Royale National Park. The standard guides are by Jim DuFresne, and they are published by The Mountaineers. Two good introductions to the natural history of the region are *Northwoods Wildlife: A Watcher's Guide to Habitats* by Janine M. Benyus (NorthWord Press) and *The North Woods: Sierra Club Naturalist's Guide* by Glenda Daniel and Jerry Sullivan (Sierra Club Books). Readers interested in exploring the literature of the region would do well to begin with the books of Sigurd Olson, particularly *Listening Point* and *The Singing Wilderness,* both published by Knopf; and *Canoe County* and *Snowshoe Country* by Florence Page Jacques, published by Minnesota Historical Society Press. All four books are illustrated with the wonderful woodblock prints of Francis Lee Jacques.

BWCA CANOE OUTFITTERS
WESTERN BWCA

ARROWHEAD OUTFITTERS
Star Rt. 1, Box 3299 (Fernberg Trail)
Ely, MN 55731
218-365-5614 or 800-245-5614

BELAND'S WILDERNESS CANOE TRIPS
Box 808, Ely, MN 55731
218-365-6244 or 800-777-4431

BOB ANDERSON'S CANOE OUTFITTERS
7255 Crane Lake Rd. EM,
Crane Lake, MN 55725
218-993-2287 or 800-777-7186

BOUNDARY WATERS CANOE OUTFITTERS
Box 447, 1323 E. Sheridan St.,
Ely, MN 55731
218-365-3201 or 800-544-7736

CANADIAN BORDER CANOE TRIP OUTFITTERS
Box 117M, Moose Lake, Ely, MN 55731
218-365-5847 or 800-247-7530

CANADIAN WATERS
111 E. Sheridan St. MS, Ely, MN 55731
218-365-3202 or 800-255-2922

CANOE COUNTRY OUTFITTERS
Box 30-EM, 629 E. Sheridan St.,
Ely, MN 55731
218-365-4046 or 800-752-2306

CLIFF WOLD'S CANOE TRIP OUTFITTING CO.
1731 E. Sheridan St., Ely, MN 55731
218-365-3267

DUANE'S OUTFITTERS
Hwy 21, Babbitt, MN 55706
218-827-2710 or 800-777-8524

ELY CANOE LIVERY OUTFITTERS
Box 247, 410 E. Sheridan St.,
Ely, MN 55731
218-365-6287 or
319-393-0078 (off-season)

JACK & TONI'S FALL LAKE WILDERNESS CANOE TRIPS
Box 780-EM 92, Ely, MN 55731
218-365-3788 or 800-777-8594

JOHN HERRICK'S MOOSE BAY CO.
Box 697, Ely, MN 55731
218-365-6285

JOHNSON'S WILDERNESS CANOE TRIPS
Box 658, 1001 E. Sheridan St.,
Ely, MN 55731
218-365-3559 or 218-365-3171
(call collect)

KAWISHIWI LODGE AND OUTFITTERS
Box 480 Lake One, Ely, MN 55731
218-365-5487 (May 1-Sept. 30)
or 218-365-3259 (Oct. 1-Apr. 30)

NORTH COUNTRY CANOE OUTFITTERS
Star Rt 1, Box 3000,
White Iron Lake, Ely, MN 55731
218-365-5581 or 800-552-5581

NORTHWIND CANOE OUTFITTERS
Box 690, Fernberg Rd., Ely, MN 55731
218-365-5489

OLSON'S BORDERLAND LODGE AND OUTFITTERS
Box 92, Crane Lake, MN 55725
218-993-2233

OUTDOOR ADVENTURE CANOE OUTFITTERS
Box 576, White Iron Lake,
Ely, MN 55731
218-365-3466 or 800-777-8574

TIMBER TRAIL OUTFITTERS
HC 1, Box 3111, Ely, MN 55731
218-365-4879 or 800-777-7348

TOM & WOODS' MOOSE LAKE WILDERNESS CANOE TRIPS
Box 358, Ely, MN 55731
218-365-5837 or 800-322-5837

VOYAGEUR NORTH OUTFITTERS, INC.
1829 E. Sheridan St., A92,
Ely, MN 55731
218-365-3251 or 800-848-5530

WILDERNESS ADVENTURES, INC.
943 E. Sheridan St., Ely, MN 55731
218-365-3416 or 800-843-2922

WILDERNESS OUTFITTERS
One E. Camp St., Exp. 92 MN,
Ely, MN 55731
218-365-3211 or 800-777-8572

EASTERN BWCA

BEAR TRACK OUTFITTING CO.
Box 937 Ex., Hwy 61,
Grand Marais, MN 55604
218-387-1162

CLEARWATER CANOE OUTFITTERS & LODGE
355-0 Gunflint Trail,
Grand Marais, MN 55604
218-388-2254 or 800-527-0554

GUNFLINT NORTHWOODS OUTFITTERS
750 Gunflint Trail,
Grand Marais, MN 55604
218-388-2296 or 800-328-3325

HUNGRY JACK CANOE OUTFITTERS
434 Gunflint Trail,
Grand Marais, MN 55604
218-388-2275 or 800-648-2922

NOR'WESTER LODGE & CANOE OUTFITTERS
Box 550, Gunflint Trail,
Grand Marais, MN 55604
218-388-2252 or 800-992-4386

ROCKWOOD OUTFITTERS
HC 64, Box 625, Gunflint Trail,
Grand Marais, MN 55604
218-388-2242 or 800-942-BWCA

SAWBILL CANOE OUTFITTERS
Box 2127TR, Sawbill Trail,
Tofte, MN 55615
218-387-1360

SAWTOOTH OUTFITTERS
Highway 61, Box 2214, Tofte, MN 55615
218-663-7643

SEAGULL LAKE CANOE OUTFITTERS
Seagull Lake, Gunflint Trail,
Grand Marais, MN 55604
218-388-2216 or 800-346-2205

SUPERIOR NORTH CANOE OUTFITTERS
HC 64, Box 965, Gunflint Trail,
Grand Marais, MN 55604
218-388-4416 or 800-852-2008

TOP OF THE TRAIL CANOE OUTFITTERS
Saganaga Lake, Box 1001,
Gunflint Trail,
Grand Marais, MN 55604
800-869-0883

TUSCARORA CANOE OUTFITTERS
870 Gunflint Trail,
Grand Marais, MN 55604
218-388-2221 or 800-544-3843
(for reservations)

VOYAGEUR CANOE OUTFITTERS
HC 64, Box 990,
Grand Marais, MN 55604
218-388-2224 or 800-777-7215

WAY OF THE WILDERNESS
947 Gunflint Trail,
Grand Marais, MN 55604
218-388-2212 or 800-346-6625

MINNESOTA DEPARTMENT OF TOURISM